MW00773410

SOUNDTRACK TO A MO.

Soundtrack to a Movement

African American Islam, Jazz,
and Black Internationalism

Richard Brent Turner

NEW YORK UNIVERSITY PRESS
New York

NEW YORK UNIVERSITY PRESS
New York
www.nyupress.org

References to Internet websites (URLs) were accurate at the time of writing. Neither the author nor New York University Press is responsible for URLs that may have expired or changed since the manuscript was prepared.

Library of Congress Cataloging-in-Publication Data
Names: Turner, Richard Brent, author.
Title: Soundtrack to a movement : African American Islam, jazz, and black internationalism /
Richard Brent Turner.
Description: New York : New York University Press, [2021] |
Includes bibliographical references and index.
Identifiers: LCCN 2020034473 (print) | LCCN 2020034474 (ebook) |
ISBN 9781479871032 (cloth) | ISBN 9781479806768 (paperback) |
ISBN 9781479849697 (ebook other) | ISBN 9781479800360 (ebook)
Subjects: LCSH: Jazz—Social aspects—United States—History—20th century. |
Jazz—Religious aspects—Islam—History—20th century. | African American Muslims. |
African Americans—Religion. | Internationalism—History—20th century.
Classification: LCC ML3918.J39 T87 2021 (print) | LCC ML3918.J39 (ebook) |
DDC 781.65089/6073—dc23
LC record available at https://lccn.loc.gov/2020034473
LC ebook record available at https://lccn.loc.gov/2020034474

New York University Press books are printed on acid-free paper, and their binding materials are chosen for strength and durability. We strive to use environmentally responsible suppliers and materials to the greatest extent possible in publishing our books.

Manufactured in the United States of America

10 9 8 7 6 5 4 3 2 1
Also available as an ebook

To the memory of John Coltrane and his music

CONTENTS

Introduction

Jazz Brothers in Rhythm and Spirit

On March 8, 1965, two weeks after Malcolm X's assassination, tenor saxophonist Archie Shepp recorded "Malcolm, Malcolm Semper Malcolm," a tribute to his hero's revolutionary political consciousness. It was later included on the album *Fire Music*.[1] Shepp, who played with John Coltrane on several albums, identified a continuity between Coltrane's music and Malcolm's speeches:

> I equate Coltrane's music very strongly with Malcolm's language . . . they were just about contemporaries. . . . And I believe essentially what Malcolm said is what John played. If Trane had been a speaker, he might have spoken somewhat like Malcolm. If Malcolm had been a saxophone player, he might have played somewhat like Trane.[2]

Unlike Malcolm X, the Pan-Africanist leader and spokesman for the Nation of Islam, noted jazz saxophonist and composer John Coltrane did not identify himself as a black revolutionary. But Archie Shepp was not the only one to note the parallels between Coltrane's music and Malcolm's politics. As trumpeter Miles Davis pointed out,

> Trane's music . . . during the last two or three years of his life represented for many Blacks, the fire and passion and rage and rebellion and love they felt, especially among the young Black intellectuals and revolutionaries of that time. . . . He was their torchbearer in jazz.[3]

Malcolm X and John Coltrane were two of the leading stars in what might be called the golden age of African American Islam and jazz. This book explores the historical connections between jazz, African American Islam, and black internationalism from the 1940s to the 1970s.

It shows that from about the late 1940s through about the 1970s, Islam rose in prominence among African Americans for reasons that were related to the embrace of the religion among jazz musicians. The rise of black Islam is most often framed in relation to the Nation of Islam, and often we hear about how prison experiences, like that of Malcolm X, were influential in spreading Islam among African American communities. That was certainly a part of the story. But this book sets out to show that the golden age of jazz music was instrumental in shaping black encounters with Islam, and that not only the Nation of Islam but other strands of Islam were involved in this influential interplay between religion and black culture.

This book argues that the values that Islam and jazz shared were key to the growth of African American Islamic communities, and that it was jazz musicians who led the way in shaping encounters with Islam as they developed a black Atlantic "cool" that shaped both religion and jazz styles as well as black masculinity and femininity. As we will see, jazz musicians even used their participation in America's Cold War diplomacy cultural programs to foster connections between jazz, Islam, and black internationalism in both the United States and the Third World. Through their efforts, Islam became a prominent theme in US State Department jazz tours beginning in the Cold War and continuing up to the civil rights and Black Power movements in the 1960s. An understanding of shared black global connections in the golden age of African American Islam and jazz reveals how much jazz musicians contributed to the development of a new diasporic Afro-American identity in the 1960s. African American Islam and jazz shared parallel goals and values of black affirmation, freedom, and self-determination. Black followers of Islam and jazz musicians expressed these values by rejecting systemic racism, constructing black notions of masculinity, and developing a sense of African American religious internationalism. The term "black internationalism" in this book refers to a global black consciousness and interconnected resistance movements that led African Americans to think universally about their struggles for freedom. As the middle of the twentieth century approached, they began to see themselves in a larger global context, as part of the worldwide liberation struggles of blacks in the African diaspora and Africa, and also sometimes in solidarity with the oppositional struggles of people of color who were not black.

During this period, blacks in the United States exemplified the growing trend of religious internationalism and developed a new sense of self, in which they embraced spiritual and musical experimentation and constructed religious and racial identities, musical styles, and political protest movements against the background of rising black internationalism. This resulted in the contemporaneous development of a global diasporic consciousness connecting people of African descent. In Boston, New York, and Philadelphia, black jazz artists experimented with new musical forms, religious identities, and ideas about freedom that appealed to their fans, who were largely northern blacks, southern migrants, and Caribbean immigrants. These musicians' solidarity with the Muslim religion was one of the ways they expressed the jazz world's relationship to black internationalism.

While World War II was being fought in Europe, Asia, and the Pacific, the leaders of modern jazz and the black Islamic movements transformed the musical and religious identities of black communities in the northern cities of the United States. This era of migration, urban religion, and musical creativity also witnessed a change in black masculinities (i.e., the gendered constructions and representations of the black male body and experience), expressed in the programs of Marcus Garvey's Universal Negro Improvement Association, the Nation of Islam, the Ahmadiyya Muslim Community, Sunni Islam, and the black Atlantic cool that provided performative structure and aesthetic shape to both black religion and jazz styles. Black musicians infused jazz with cool during their performances in clubs, dance halls, and jam sessions as well as performances for Muslim communities. They also interfaced with the programs of Muslim communities to consider their own conversion to Islam and to influence others in the 1940s and the post–World War II era. Black Atlantic cool emerged among these self-determining musicians as an alternative musical and spiritual vision characterized by an embodied, transcendent, and purifying African diasporic mode of style, performance, self-composure, social balance, and resistance that shaped the construction of black identities in religion and music.

This book traces the history, experiences, and identities of diverse African American Islamic groups from the 1940s to the 1970s, including some whose practices and theology did not conform to the traditional beliefs of Sunni Islam. Black Muslims dazzled the United States with their new communities in the urban North, communities that encountered the successive presentations of Islam during the Great Migration by religious leaders including Noble Drew Ali, W. D. Fard Muhammad, Elijah Muhammad, Mufti Muhammad Sadiq, Sheikh Daoud Ahmed Faisal, Wali Akram, Muhammad Ezaldeen, Sheik Nasir Ahmad, and Talib Dawud. This book reveals how new constructions of blackness and religion in the Nation of Islam interacted with the differing versions of Islam shaped by the transnational Ahmadiyya Muslim Community and the Sunni communities in the United States, and how the debates among the proponents of Islam in black America influenced the religious and musical landscape of jazz. Ahmadiyya Muslim missionaries were exemplars of transnationalism: they circulated their religious message widely across a number of countries, ranging from India and Pakistan to England, Ghana, and the United States, and their mission to blacks transformed the meaning of conversion among African American jazz musicians. Communities like these relied on global networks created by international migrants whose spiritual and political identities were shaped by their travel and by their religious connections to both their countries of origin and their communities in their host countries.

John Coltrane was at the forefront of those black American musicians who infused jazz with Islamic themes and with musical and religious forms from regions spanning Africa and Asia,[4] and Malcolm X led a movement to connect black American liberation to religion and politics in the Third World. Coltrane admired Malcolm's internationalist political and religious perspectives and attended his speeches in New York City. His conception of jazz was deeply influenced by Islam, and he considered converting to the religion when he was living in Philadelphia. In his early years, Malcolm was a lindy hopper star in Boston and New York. He loved jazz and was involved with Muslim communities during the rise of African American Islam, interactions that influenced his own youthful musical and religious expression. John Coltrane and Malcolm X were jazz brothers in rhythm and spirit. They lived during the era of global black liberation that spanned the period from World War II to the very beginning of the Black Power movement. During this period, hundreds of jazz artists experimented with Islam, Christianity, new forms of jazz, and other black Atlantic connections that linked Africa, the Americas, and the Muslim world, searching initially for personal transformation and freedom and ultimately circulating their claims for African American religious internationalism in national and global contexts. Coltrane and his musical colleagues played an important role in what music historian Ashley Kahn has called the "golden age of jazz," which lasted from the late 1950s to the 1970s, "when more jazz players than ever before (or since) were alive, representing every era of the tradition."[5] Paralleling the golden age of jazz was a golden age of African American Islam, which lasted from the 1940s to the 1970s, an era when many prominent black Muslim leaders and their communities presented the religion in all its dynamic diversity to the United States. As a result of their efforts, Islam emerged during the 1940s and 1950s as the iconic religion of African American religious internationalism.

Malcolm and Muslim musicians including Yusef Lateef, Art Blakey, Kenny Clarke, and Max Roach were the link between these two golden ages. Their stories reveal the intersecting goals and values of Islam and jazz and offer a wide lens on this era, in which musicians and their fans explored black Atlantic performance styles and began to understand spirited connections between swing, bebop, hard bop, free jazz, Christianity, Islam, and new representations of black masculinities. This book explores parallels between the social, political, and cultural foundations of both jazz and African American Islam within the broad historical context of the Great Migration, the Marcus Garvey movement, and the impact of Afro-Caribbean communities in the big cities of the 1940s and 1950s.

The story of black Boston, a community in which musicians took the lead in exploring the interactions between Garveyism, black Christianity, the Ahmadiyya Muslim Community, the Nation of Islam, Sunni Islam, and modern jazz, is central to this inquiry into the origins of the golden age of African American Islam. The theme of African American religious internationalism also has a compelling history in New York City, as exemplified by the soul-searching performances of black musicians including Dizzy Gillespie, Duke Ellington, Ahmed Abdul-Malik, Max Roach, Abbey Lincoln, Art Blakey, Pharoah Sanders, Ahmad Jamal, Sahib Shihab, and Etta James. This book, then, explores a history of this internationalist era, offering a picture in which jazz frames and reshapes diasporic blackness, black American interactions with Islam, and black Atlantic religious consciousness.

In the golden age of African American Islam and jazz, performances of music, dance, and religious forms inspired and celebrated a new African American religious internationalism, which was expressed in the black Atlantic cultural innovations of jazz musicians. In the urban-based African American Muslim communities that flourished in the twentieth century, African American religious internationalism circulated visions of freedom, identity, black Atlantic cool style, artistic creativity, self-determination, and conversion.[6] Cultural historian Paul Gilroy, in *The Black Atlantic: Modernity and Double Consciousness*, reveals how jazz musicians' "boundary-breaking"[7] performances of modern jazz and embrace of African American Islam exemplify the musical and political spirit of African American religious internationalism in the black Atlantic world:

> Examining the place of music in the black Atlantic world means surveying the self-understanding articulated by the musicians who have made it, the symbolic use to which their music is put by other black artists and writers, and social relations which have produced and reproduced the unique expressive culture in which music comprises a central and even foundational element. . . . Apart from the music and the musicians themselves, we must also take account of the work of those within the expressive culture of the black Atlantic who have tried to use its music as an aesthetic, political, or philosophical marker.[8]

Malcolm X, the Nation of Islam leader and Pan-African convert to Sunni Islam, grew up in Boston, and during his teenage years, the city's vibrant jazz culture deeply influenced his identity. Even as a young man, he strove to expand his family's Pan-African consciousness beyond Marcus Garvey's UNIA, with its focus between World Wars I and II on black internationalism, to incorporate black musical identity, black Christianity, and black Islam. Pan-Africanism can be described as a modern black consciousness promoting the global unification, freedom, and empowerment of people of African descent. Its goals are the decolonization and liberation of Africa through means as seemingly diverse as the recrafting of African culture and identity in the African diaspora and the emigration of diasporic peoples back to Africa. These ideals, African American religious internationalism, and the performative practices of jazz experimentation and improvisation shaped Malcolm's conversion to the Nation of Islam while he was in prison in his twenties as well as his interactions with religion and politics after his release.

John Coltrane, the great jazz saxophonist, had a spiritual awakening in Philadelphia in 1957 while he was married to his first wife, Juanita Naima Austin, a Muslim. He also shared cultural and political affinities with influential Muslim jazz musicians of the 1950s and 1960s, including McCoy Tyner, Art Blakey, Yusef Lateef, Sahib Shihab, Ahmed Abdul-Malik, Idrees Sulieman, Kenny Clarke, Lynn Hope, Kenny Dorham, and Rashied Ali.[9] Islam was largely responsible for shaping his musical and religious identity and his expressions of black independence, self-determination, and freedom. Coltrane's spiritual awakening inspired his second wife, pianist Alice Coltrane, saxophonist Pharoah Sanders, and other jazz musicians to synthesize musical and religious forms from a variety of black Atlantic sources including Christian nations, West and North Africa, and the African diaspora in their performances as well as in their religious lives. Coltrane's iconic performances and albums (especially *A Love Supreme*) and his spiritual quest in the 1960s fostered awareness of the enduring connections between music, religion, and freedom in the United States, the global African diaspora, and Africa—connections that paralleled Malcolm X's internationalist perspectives on black liberation in the last year of his life. Coltrane's jazz, then, provided "a soundtrack to a movement,"[10] a musical iteration of an international-ist Afro-American identity encompassing race, religion, and politics that Malcolm described as unity between black Americans, the Third World, and Africans in a struggle for freedom "by whatever means necessary."[11]

Another musician whose career reveals the mutual influences of Islam and jazz was jazz and rhythm and blues singer Etta James. James was drawn to the jazz brotherhood that Malcolm and Coltrane exempli-fied, and she immersed herself in African American Islam. As a young woman in Atlanta in the 1960s, she converted to the Nation of Islam and changed her name to Jamesetta X. In 1960, while she was living in the Theresa Hotel in Harlem, James came under the sway of Malcolm X. The young boxer Cassius Clay—later known as Muhammad Ali—was one of her fans when she performed in New York City, and she tried unsuc-cessfully to convert him to the Nation of Islam when he was eighteen years old. James eventually left the Nation of Islam and embraced the

Ahmadiyya Muslim Community, but her musical career continued to be influenced by black Islam.[12]

Tenor saxophonist Yusef Lateef was a close friend of John Coltrane and his first wife, Juanita Naima Austin. In 1948 Lateef became a devout Muslim and converted to the Ahmadiyya Muslim Community because, he explained, "it taught all of the virtues, of being kind and respectful to your parents and others, to have feeling and compassion for the poor. . . . When almighty God turns a person's heart toward Islam (peace) there is no other choice for the person."[13] Yusef Lateef's Islamic faith had a clear influence on his music. On albums such as *Eastern Sounds*, for instance, he incorporated Arab and Asian musical sounds into his jazz compositions.

This book explores the historical relationship of jazz not only to Islam, but also to global black religious consciousness more broadly. The stories of the jazz musicians in this book exemplify a larger history of American musicians, fans, dancers, religious folk, and political activists who practiced African American religious internationalism, which encouraged black people in diaspora to think of themselves as more in concert with Africans and the "darker races of the world" than with Europeans and white Americans. They used these ideas to construct powerful strategies against racial oppression in the United States. For many musicians, then, jazz provided a springboard for global perspectives about blackness, self-determination, social justice and resistance, and liberation.

This era also witnessed the dynamic connections between Muslim jazz artists' spiritual journeys and the way their iconic performances of jazz, their belief in Islam, and their projection of black internationalism intersected with one another to recreate rhythms, sounds, rituals, and memories evoking the legacy of Africa, the global African diaspora, and the black liberation movement in the United States. Only a few musicians, including Yusef Lateef, Ahmed Abdul-Malik, John Coltrane, and Pharoah Sanders, achieved this ambitious goal of connecting the dots between their religious discipline and musical performance practice. The performances of these Muslim jazz artists exemplified and circulated Atlantic world visions of Africa, diaspora, and blackness, showing the creative resistance strategies of black Americans that were nurtured by the extraordinary urban jazz and Muslim communities that thrived in American cities from the 1940s to the 1970s.[14] Their performances also resonate with performance studies scholar Joseph Roach's reflections about the provocative relationship between memory, performance, and the recreation of the genocidal and diasporic histories of the black Atlantic world in *Cities of the Dead* and African American studies scholar Mark Anthony Neal's reflections about black masculinity and popular culture in *Looking for Leroy*.[15]

The Great Migration, immigration from the Caribbean and West Africa, and the global travel of jazz musicians fueled dynamic interactions between Islam, jazz, and African American religious internationalism in the black communities of cosmopolitan cities including Boston, New York, and Philadelphia, where both Malcolm X and John Coltrane lived. A focus on African American religious internationalism allows us to map the thematic links of jazz and Islam to Black Power, civil rights, black nationalism, Pan-Africanism, and anticolonial movements in Africa, the Middle East, and the Americas. African American religious internationalism also prompts an investigation of constructions of diaspora, which recall some of Paul Gilroy's "Black Atlantic" reflections about race, enslavement, and modernity in Caribbean, British, and black American contexts, and the way these themes find expression in subversive musical sounds and identities.[16]

This book is motivated by several essential research questions: What is the historical relationship of jazz to Islam and African American religious internationalism in the lives of black jazz musicians? How does the identification of important jazz figures with African American religious internationalism and black masculinities and femininities in Boston, New York, and Philadelphia help us to document the golden age of African American Islam and jazz? How are their performances of music and religion connected to the internationalist black Christian and black Islamic "communities of resistance" and to intercultural perspectives about Africa, the African diaspora, and African American freedom?[17] What are the identity claims and controversies surrounding Islamic jazz musicians' black Atlantic religious and musical legacies in the late 1960s and early 1970s?

As research in the humanities and the social sciences suggests, the life stories, performances, and political legacies of important jazz musicians are central to our understanding of the black Atlantic roots of

African American Islam and jazz in the 1960s. In *John Coltrane and the Jazz Revolution of the 1960s*, Frank Kofsky studies Afro-Asian influences and black nationalism in avant-garde jazz, exploring the political connections between Coltrane and Malcolm X from a Marxist perspective. Kofsky understands that jazz musicians "perceived a fundamental reality about this country . . . that you could only know if you were black and had worked your way up through the tangled, fetid jungle of jazz clubs, dance halls, bars, narcotics, alcohol, gangsters, and so on."[18]

This book fills an important gap in the scholarship on the mutual influences of Islam and jazz in the history of popular music and African American religion. No one has systematically utilized the religious studies scholarship on urban religions and the new research on black masculinities to analyze the religious and musical significance of Islamic jazz musicians in the African diaspora. This book unites three traditions and situates the stories of Muslim musicians and their fans in the context of work in African American religious studies, black masculinity studies, and African diaspora jazz studies. All of these perspectives underline the ways the lives and work of black musicians articulated the complex connections between jazz, American religion, and the African diaspora.

The book includes four chapters and a conclusion. Chapter 1 examines how important stylistic changes in jazz's sounds and musical practices, which influenced the reception of swing and bebop, helped to shape the construction of African American religious internationalism in black Christianity and Islam. It explores how the interplay between jazz and African American Islamic identities played out in Boston and New York in the 1940s. Chapter 1 presents the journey of Malcolm Little—later Malcolm X—as a swing jazz dancer and a practitioner of black religious internationalism and Garveyism in Boston and New York City during World War II as a case study of the larger themes of social justice and African American representations of masculinities that jazz and Islam shared. The chapter traces the origin of Malcolm's jazz practices and constructions of masculinity to black Atlantic cool, the influences of Duke Ellington, Billie Holiday, and Dizzy Gillespie, and the specific historical, economic, sociological, and demographic factors in the Roxbury community of Boston, where Afro-Caribbean immigrants and black southern migrants experimented with Christian and Islamic influences in jazz, ultimately shaping African American religious internationalism in the 1940s. Chapter 1 also discusses Malcolm's early interactions with African American Christianity and the way they influenced his first encounters with Islam, which took place when he studied the religion with Malcolm "Shorty" Jarvis and an Indian missionary and musician from the Ahmadiyya Muslim Community in Roxbury.

Chapter 2 traces the development of the Nation of Islam and its first appearance in American prisons, where themes of black masculinity, Asiatic identity, racial separatism, and restoration of the black body took root. It examines Malcolm X's and Shorty Jarvis's identification with the Nation of Islam in Massachusetts prisons in the 1940s and 1950s and shows how African American Islam and jazz became synthesized in the minds of black youth during this period. The chapter then goes on to explore bebop jazz, which encouraged new performances of black masculinities and religious and musical configurations outside the earlier musical world of swing. Bebop also offered a creative space where new visions of African American religious internationalism flourished due to its heady mix of spiritual philosophy, musical practices, and experimentation. Finally, chapter 2 explores the interplay between musical and religious traditions at Boston's Nation of Islam Temple, which Malcolm X established along with black jazz musicians and budding civil rights activists in 1954.

Chapter 3 looks at the forces of transnationalism, black internationalism, masculinity, freedom, and social justice that encouraged black bebop musicians to convert to the Ahmadiyya Muslim Community in the 1940s and 1950s, forces that expanded the Ahmadis' popularity in the jazz community during this period. It examines the transnational Islamic mission of the Ahmadiyya community in Boston, Chicago, and Detroit, the spiritual awakening of jazz artists such as Ahmed Abdul-Malik, Dakota Staton, Talib Dawud, and Yusef Lateef, Kenny Clarke's migration to Paris, the Muslim musicians in Dizzy Gillespie's band, the missionary work of the drummer Art Blakey in New York City, his sojourn in West Africa, and the Jazz Messengers and hard bop.

Chapter 4 examines the shared goals and values of jazz and Islam through the wider lens of Sunni Islam, the Nation of Islam, the Ahmadiyya Muslim Community, and the soulful and militant aesthetic of hard bop and free jazz in the late 1950s and 1960s. This was a period in which black internationalists saw a contemporaneous emergence of black American and African freedom struggles and diasporic consciousness in religious and political movements across the modern black Atlantic world. The chapter argues that the conversion of jazz musicians to Islam was central to the ascendancy of the religion in the internationalist era of the 1960s. It tells the story of the jazz musicians who used their participation in America's Cold War diplomacy cultural programs to foster connections between jazz, black internationalism, and the transnational reception of African American culture in the Islamic world and Africa. The US State Department jazz tours began during the Cold War in 1956 and continued during the era of anticolonialism, African independence, and civil rights in the 1960s. The African American artists dispatched on these tours, including Duke Ellington, Dizzy Gillespie, Louis Armstrong, and Randy Weston, played their music in Muslim countries in the Middle East, Asia, and Africa, and their performances and political insights celebrated transnational musical collaborations with Third World musicians and the freedom struggles raging across diverse countries in the Islamic and African diasporas. Chapter 4, then, takes us to Philadelphia, where African American musicians like saxophonist John Coltrane, drummer Rashied Ali, and pianist McCoy Tyner forged vibrant links between Islam, jazz, and rhythm and blues in the late 1950s and 1960s. Coltrane's spiritual awakening in 1957 and his new religious identity made him an exemplar not only of black Atlantic musical and religious practices, but also of the emerging Islamic spirit that was coming to infuse Philadelphia as it had New York City and Boston.

Chapter 4 also looks at the religious and musical performances of John Coltrane, Max Roach, Etta James, Malcolm X, and several other jazz musicians, performances that exemplify the culmination of African American religious internationalism and shifting black masculine and black feminine identities in the 1960s. This chapter traces the Islamic roots of Max Roach's *We Insist! Freedom Now Suite*, Etta James's spiritual awakening in the Nation of Islam, and Coltrane's artistic and spiritual quest in hard bop, free jazz, and the Black Arts movement in New York City. It also describes how Malcolm X's and John Coltrane's quintessential meditations on Islam, jazz, and African American religious internationalism across space, time, and soundscapes resonated with the spirit of Afro-American freedom and identity during the civil rights and Black Power era, a period that saw similar black Atlantic liberation and identity formation movements in Asia, Africa, and the Americas. African American religious internationalism was a pivotal spiritual and political philosophy for Malcolm and Coltrane in 1964, an iconic year when their parallel religious and artistic paths intersected profoundly in a way that would ultimately shape the golden age of African American Islam and jazz. For in this year, John Coltrane composed his most spiritually oriented album, *A Love Supreme*, and Malcolm X performed the hajj in Mecca, became a Sunni Muslim, and articulated his jazz story and his journey to Sunni Islam in *The Autobiography of Malcolm X*.

The conclusion completes our exploration of African American Islam and jazz by analyzing the black Atlantic visions of Islamic jazz artists and their musical and religious legacies among jazz musicians including Alice Coltrane and Pharoah Sanders during the post-Coltrane era in the late 1960s and early 1970s. It calls our attention to the generation of hip hop artists who embraced Islam in the late 1970s and early 1980s. Islam and jazz exemplified the rhythm, spirit, and political and musical mood of urban black America in the golden age of African American Islam and jazz and beyond.

Malcolm X, John Coltrane, Max Roach, Yusef Lateef, Art Blakey, Lynn Hope, and several others committed their lives to exploring black Atlantic religious and musical forms. In doing so, they spoke eloquently to diverse communities throughout the African and Islamic diasporas in ways that allow us to understand their political and cultural connections to one another and to black revolutions in the United States and the Third World. Their religious practices and musical performances expressed the vitality of a new Afro-American racial identity in the 1960s and 1970s and continue to provide insight into the black international experience in African American Islam and jazz in the twenty-first century. In short, Muslim jazz artists' search for new ways to express black affirmation, self-determination, freedom, black masculinities, and African American religious internationalism, as well as their opposition to systemic racism, exemplify the parallel goals and values of jazz and African American Islam and speak profoundly and universally about the loftier possibilities of the creative imagination and the power of the human spirit.

1

Islamic and Christian Influences in Jazz

Boston and New York during World War II

Boston is a New England city known for its colonial and Revolution-ary War history, world-class universities, and ethnic neighborhoods. It is also a metropolis central to the black Atlantic story, whose neigh-borhoods witnessed transformative interactions between jazz and African American religious traditions in the 1940s. New York is a big northeastern city noted for its skyscrapers, its political and religious creativity, its nightlife, and its black and brown people who danced to swing jazz and shaped the emergence of bebop in the World War II era. During this period, black people in the United States expressed a growing sense of African American religious internationalism: they embraced spiritual and musical experimentation and constructed reli-gious and racial identities, musical styles, and protest movements in a world where blacks were increasingly aware of the important role they played on a global stage.

Chapter 1 unfolds the story of black Islamic and black Christian in-fluences on World War II jazz, influences that originated in Boston at the beginning of what I hope to show was to become a golden age in which African American Islam and jazz shared parallel goals and values of racial affirmation, freedom, and self-determination. Increasingly dur-ing this period, jazz musicians and fans explored a diverse spectrum of Islamic ideas that were flowing into the United States, offering American blacks new, liberating options that appealed to them, ideas that influ-enced their music and made a significant impact on black artistic cre-ativity and politics more generally as well. Boston's Pan-African and jazz communities were important sites of cultural creativity for thousands of blacks from the North, South, and Caribbean, who reshaped religious, musical, and political forms drawn from Christianity, Islam, and the African diaspora into a modern black Atlantic culture in a major expression of African American religious internationalism. These complex fusions of music, religion, style, and spirituality impressed blacks in the jazz community and influenced their musical identities, their practices of Christianity, their global vision of blackness, and ultimately their participation in Islam. We will also see how the African American jazz artists who performed in Boston and New York created a new soundtrack of black identities that celebrated performance forms from swing and black Christian religious traditions and then explored bebop and its links to new transnational religious traditions such as Islam.

A significant part of this story focuses on the role played by the black masculinities—the gendered constructions and representations of the black male body and experience—that were exemplified in various jazz musicians' and fans' interactions with the Universal Negro Improvement Association (UNIA), the Ahmadiyya Muslim Community, the Nation of Islam, and Sunni Islam. Black masculinities are also evident in the expressions of black Atlantic cool that gave performative structure and aesthetic shape to both jazz styles and Islam during World War II and the postwar era.

The chapter ends with a biographical section that links the young Malcolm Little's story to the chapter's main themes. His interactions with Boston's and New York's daily life, diverse peoples, black institutions, and distinctive sounds, rhythms, and cultures shaped his black Atlantic perspective, allowing him to move beyond the traditions of Marcus Garvey's Universal Negro Improvement Association that he inherited from childhood and to begin to think that blacks in diaspora could find a more appropriate spiritual home in urban-based Islamic movements than in Christianity. It was also during his Boston years that Malcolm Little first experienced the jazz world and, inspired by his interactions with the Ahmadiyya, an Indian Muslim community, began to explore the mutual values of black affirmation, freedom, and self-determination associated with Islam and jazz.

First, however, we must document the extraordinary rise of Boston's black Atlantic community in the 1940s, when thousands of southern migrants and Caribbean immigrants brought a new vitality to the cultural, economic, and political life of the city. Understanding the global identities of Boston's black community when Malcolm arrived there in 1940 is essential for understanding the links between jazz and experimentation with Islamic influences among black musicians as well as Malcolm's own dynamic involvement with jazz, Christianity, and Islam during World War II. At the same time, Boston's black community helped define the 1940s as the beginning of the golden age of African American Islam by defining the spirit of the black metropolis in terms of jazz's cultural and political creativity, which included the black Atlantic cool style of African American religious internationalism.

Caribbean Immigrants, Southern and Midwestern Migrants: Religion and Politics in Black Atlantic Boston

The decade between 1940 and 1950 was a dynamic period of growth in Boston when the Great Migration of blacks from the South and Midwest and black immigrants from the Caribbean increased the city's African-descended population from 23,679 to 40,157 people and from 3 to 5 percent of Boston's total population. By 1940, white institutional racism in Boston had forced the relocation of the black community from Beacon Hill (its historic location in the eighteenth and nineteenth centuries) to densely populated immigrant and migrant enclaves in the South End (around Massachusetts Avenue, Tremont Street, Columbus Avenue, and Shawmut Avenue), and to Roxbury, below the Dudley station commercial area on Washington Street. At the same time, a small number of working-class and middle-class blacks were buying large homes in Roxbury around Humboldt Avenue and Walnut Avenue (on "the hill"), and on the side streets around Blue Hill Avenue and Warren Street.[1] Although Roxbury was still a Jewish, Irish, and Italian community and only 14 percent of its residents were black, a dynamic black Atlantic community there was beginning to reimagine important connections between politics, religion, and music in 1940.[2]

In this crucial period, when some blacks strove to expand their Pan-African consciousness beyond Garvey's UNIA (which had focused between World Wars I and II on black internationalism) to incorporate new political ideas emerging among swing jazz and bebop musicians and recent converts to Islam, Roxbury was one of the most important black neighborhoods in the Northeast, with an Afro-Caribbean population deeply rooted in powerful expressions of Pan-Africanism. Immigrants from Jamaica, Barbados, and Montserrat made up almost 12 percent of Boston's black community, and for these Afro-Caribbean immigrants, Boston was one of their most sought-after destination cities in the United States after Miami and New York.[3] According to former Massachusetts state representative Mel King, who grew up in an Afro-Caribbean family in the South End, many of these blacks had survived British colonialism, maintained transnational networks, and did not plan to become American citizens or make Boston their permanent home; rather, they planned to return to the West Indies to retire.[4] These Caribbean blacks, he pointed out, were accustomed to the Pan-Africanism of Marcus Garvey's Universal Negro Improvement Association.[5] Pan-Africanism, exemplified by the UNIA, is a modern black consciousness promoting the global unification, freedom, and empowerment of people of African descent and the decolonization and liberation of Africa through political, economic, and cultural organizations and programs that might glorify and study African history, recraft African culture and identity in the African diaspora, and encourage emigration to Africa. As we will see, no political movement in this era expressed the ideals of African American religious internationalism expressed in jazz and the quest for new black identities that led to the golden age of African American Islam more creatively than the UNIA. The UNIA was part of a Pan-African historical continuum that evolved to include black American Muslim groups such as the Ahmadiyya, the Nation of Islam, and the Islamic Mission of America.

Roxbury had an important branch of the UNIA on Tremont Street. Founded in 1919, this branch was very active in the first half of the twentieth century, and its members organized vibrant Pan-African activities to express Marcus Garvey's powerful black Atlantic message of race pride and self-improvement to the black community: "Up you mighty race, you can accomplish what you will. . . . Africa for Africans at home and abroad."[6] Among the influential Boston Garveyites was the famous Roxbury community activist and artist Elma Lewis. Lewis was founder of the Elma Lewis School of Fine Arts (1950) and the National Center of Afro-American Artists (1968) in Roxbury, and her center hosted jazz musicians like Duke Ellington. She was inspired by Garvey's black Atlantic political and cultural vision of blackness, freedom, and self-determination and explained that she "was raised to be a Pan-African. . . . We all belonged all our lives to the Universal Negro Improvement Association. Mother was a Black Cross nurse. . . . [Father] belonged to the African Legion. My brothers sold *The Negro World*. . . . I was a Girl Guide."[7]

Blacks in Boston lived in the midst of Garveyites such as the Lewis family, who expressed "a sense of belonging to a colonial union" and connected black Americans to global freedom struggles beyond the United States.[8] This black Atlantic ethos, which was a decisive influence on African American musical and religious consciousness, was circulated in street parades, public lectures on black internationalist issues, the balls and parties of Caribbean associations, the UNIA newspaper the *Negro World* (a weekly publication distributed in the United States as well as in the global African diaspora and translated into several languages), and the *Boston Chronicle* (a weekly newspaper established in 1915 by Jamaican immigrants in Boston).[9]

The *Chronicle* became Boston's most important black newspaper in the 1930s, known for its reporting on local black American protest and colonial conditions in the Caribbean and Africa. Its international black focus provided a model for the *Muhammad Speaks* newspaper that the Nation of Islam was to establish in the late 1950s, with its rich reporting on African American religious internationalism. The *Chronicle* was sold in the black community, and it described itself in its Pan-African motto as a "fearless and uncompromising advocate of justice, rights, and opportunities."[10] The newspaper's presentations of black Atlantic global issues such as colonialism, apartheid, racist violence, and segregation, which also involved African American and African communities of resistance, had a strong impact on the transnational consciousness of black migrants, because in Boston these West Indians and northern and southern blacks lived in the same neighborhoods. Moreover, the Jamaican and Barbadian population of Boston made an important imprint on black Atlantic identities there in the 1940s and 1950s, when Afro-Caribbean immigrants expressed four interrelated forms of identity in the black community: "their island identity; a pan-west Indian identity; a British identity; and . . . a black American identity."[11]

The diverse African diaspora communities that blacks encountered in Boston also included immigrants from Bermuda, British Virgin Islands, Panama, Guyana, and Trinidad. As we will see, the politics, the black Atlantic practices of African American religious internationalism, and the musical styles of Caribbean blacks had an impact on the spread of African American Islam among black communities in the 1940s and 1950s, just as it did on the performance of swing and bebop jazz. These Caribbean immigrant communities are central to the story of the black Atlantic community in Boston, the development of jazz and Islamic communities, and the linkages between global identities, diasporas, and migrations that were shaped by the UNIA.

Thousands of Cape Verdeans who spoke an Afro-Portuguese language and called themselves "Portugee" migrated to the South End and Roxbury from New Bedford, Massachusetts; Providence, Rhode Island; and the Cape Verde Islands in Africa. They were sometimes clannish, aloof, and divided by skin color into their own light and dark-skinned enclaves. Some of the Cape Verdeans had reddish hair and complexions that resembled black Americans.[12]

The black Atlantic ethnic diversity in the South End and Roxbury was remarkable for a community of its size in this era. It had a significantly smaller population of southern migrants than New York City, Newark, or Philadelphia during the Great Migration (1915–1970), when several million black southerners moved to major northern, midwestern, and West Coast industrial cities to escape poverty, sharecropping, and lynching in the South and to seek new economic opportunities. However, southern migrants in Boston, who were primarily from Virginia and North Carolina but also from South Carolina, Georgia, and Louisiana, had the greatest impact on the links between jazz and Islam. Black southerners were the most politically important and economically successful segment of Boston's black Atlantic community, and also its largest group, constituting more than 50 percent of the city's black population. Black southerners began to outnumber Boston-born blacks in 1870, and their numbers continued to grow substantially during the years of the Great Migration.[13]

New and groundbreaking work on the Great Migration by Isabel Wilkerson and Stewart E. Tolnay shows that in cities such as Boston, southern migrants had more jobs, less unemployment, less poverty, and better incomes than blacks born in the North.[14] Moreover, Stephan Thernstrom's analysis of racial demographics in Boston demonstrates that blacks in 1940 generally had the same level of education, 8.3 years, as the typical white citizen of the city and that by 1950, their education levels had surpassed those of the Irish, French Canadian, and Italian immigrants to the metropolis.[15] Yet, because of institutional racism, black men in Boston in 1950 earned "only 0.179 of the white median income."[16]

In spite of the systemic obstacles to racial equality in Boston, the black southern migrants' ethos of homeownership and business ownership was impressive in the South End and Roxbury. Southern migrants owned all but two of the thirty black businesses that served the everyday needs of black Bostonians in the 1940s. Barber shops, beauty shops, Bennett Cooperative Grocer, B. J. Benn Grocery, Jesse Good's Grocery, Roberson Real Estate, E. Z. Roundtree Real Estate, Arrington Hairdressing Salon and Beauty School, Chisolm's Funeral Chapel, Estelle's Restaurant, and Slade's Barbeque were just a few of the businesses that black southerners owned in Boston.[17] As Adelaide Cromwell's analysis of the black upper class in Boston shows, black southerners and West Indians were leaders in every occupational area of the black community except teaching. In 1940 they constituted the vast majority of Boston's twenty-six black doctors, seventeen black dentists, twenty-nine black religious leaders, seventy-four black music teachers, and the few black lawyers and social workers in the city.[18] Indeed, an urban style of blackness and masculinity was reshaped by their presentations of black Atlantic religious and musical identities, and their ethos of homeownership and business ownership impacted the economic programs of the Nation of Islam in Boston in the 1950s and 1960s. We will see later, in chapter 2, how Boston's black business community influenced the religious identities of Nation of Islam members, spurring them to establish their first temple in Roxbury, which served the city's many jazz musicians, World War II veterans, and entrepreneurs.

Black churches in Roxbury and the South End expressed a vibrant mix of African American religious internationalism and southern, northern, and Caribbean interpretations of black Atlantic coolness. Art historian Robert Farris Thompson defines black Atlantic cool as a spiritual consciousness and performance strategy of expressive culture, aesthetic vision, and artistic self-presentation originating in West and Central African concepts of ancestral wisdom and emphasizing the power and beauty of music, dance, and rhythmic balance:

The primary metaphorical extension of this term . . . seems to be control, having the value of composure in the individual context, social stability in the context of the group. These concepts are often linked to the sacred usage of . . . powers which purify men and women by return to freshness, to immaculate concentration of mind, to the artistic shaping of matter and societal happening. . . . Put another way, coolness has to do with transcendental balance.[19]

Many of the black musicians who came to exemplify the mutual influences of Islam and jazz were initially drawn to Boston's black churches as a way to experience the balance and composure associated with black Atlantic coolness. The city's black neighborhoods were brimming with an impressive variety of large, historic black churches, where blacks who had arrived during the Great Migration worshiped alongside immigrants from the Caribbean and beyond. Ultimately, however, many jazz musicians did not experience in Roxbury's churches sufficient support for the values promoted by Garveyism like black self-determination, freedom, and affirmation, or for black protest against systemic racism. As a result, they eventually abandoned Christianity. But before they did, they were able to experience the black churches where many black Muslims began their religious lives in the period between 1940 and 1970.

Black jazz musicians were well aware of the prominent Black Baptist churches in Boston: Ebenezer Baptist Church on West Springfield Street in Roxbury, established by African American migrants from Virginia in 1871; Twelfth Baptist Church on Warren Street in Roxbury, founded on Beacon Hill in 1840 as an anti-slavery church and a black Atlantic refuge for fugitive slaves; People's Baptist Church on Camden Street, begun as a congregation in the African Meeting House on Beacon Hill in 1805 and revitalized by migrants from Virginia, North Carolina, and Georgia in the 1930s and 1940s; Townsend Street Baptist Church in Roxbury; and Concord Baptist Church on Tremont Street in the South End.[20]

The Baptist impact on music and coolness was especially strong in this era. The National Baptist Convention, the largest black religious denomination in the United States, was known for the performance spaces it provided within its churches. Indeed, it was in Pilgrim and Ebenezer Baptist churches in Chicago that Thomas Dorsey and Mahalia Jackson launched gospel music in the 1930s. Gospel music is a black Atlantic fusion of the rural blues of black southerners and the modern emotional worship music of working-class southern migrants in the urban North. Dorsey, a former blues pianist who came from Georgia and who worked with Ma Rainey, established the "modern gospel era" in 1932 with his hit song "Take My Hand, Precious Lord."[21] Walter F. Pitts, in *Old Ship of Zion: The Afro-Baptist Ritual in the African Diaspora*, traces the cool emotionalism of the Black Baptist ritual frames, the improvised use of the body, the shouting (sacred dancing to the Holy Spirit), hand clapping, and ecstatic rhythms and singing of gospel blues, to reimagined black Atlantic sources derived from the West and Central African sacred rituals of trance and transcendental balance. Sylviane A. Diouf traces the roots of the blues' melancholy sounds (from which gospel blues was derived) to the African-Islamic style of reciting the Qur'an among enslaved West African Muslims in the South.[22] The rhythms, sounds, and improvisation techniques of the Black Baptist churches had a great impact on jazz and rhythm and blues performance practices, and also on jazz musicians' knowledge of black musical styles and dance forms, which they reshaped as they constructed their jazz-based musical identities in Boston.

Black gospel music and charismatic preaching were also central to the religious life of the African Methodist churches in Boston. These churches were rooted in historic black Atlantic congregations that began on Beacon Hill before the Civil War and followed the movement of blacks to new religious spaces in the South End and Roxbury in the twentieth century. Black migrants from North Carolina and Virginia played key roles in the Columbus Avenue AME (African Methodist Episcopal) Zion Church and the Union United Methodist Church in the South End. Charles Street AME Church on the corner of Warren Street and Elm Hill Avenue was dominated by African American southern migrants and had a reputation for drawing so-called elite blacks with good working-class and middle-class jobs.[23]

In these neighborhoods, jazz musicians saw striking churches that West Indian Garveyites attended with southern and northern blacks. St. Cyprian's Episcopal Church was across Tremont Street from the Boston UNIA branch in the 1940s. Built with money provided by blacks, it was the most important Afro-Caribbean church in the city, with more than one thousand registered members, including Louis Walcott (Louis Far-

rakhan), the future Nation of Islam minister of Temple No. 11 in Roxbury, who was baptized at St. Cyprian's as a baby. Black Episcopalians
also attended St. John's Church on Tremont Street and St. James Church
on Washington Street in Roxbury. An African Orthodox Church on
Washington Street in Roxbury represented the official black Atlantic religious denomination of the UNIA.[24] Fitz Herbert Payne, a Barbadian
immigrant who owned a home on Perrin Street, was the founder in 1930
of United Emmanuel Holiness Church on Windsor Street in Roxbury,
where he served as bishop.[25]

One hundred fifteen black Catholics (most of them Jamaican) were
members of St. Augustine-St. Martin Church on Lenox Street in the
South End.[26] Roman Catholicism, with its numerous parishes and parochial schools in Roxbury's Irish enclaves, was making headway in converting blacks during World War II. By 1940, according to one estimate,
one-tenth of Boston's black community was Catholic, and Bishop Cush-
ing was developing plans to establish Boston's first black Catholic parish,
St. Richard's Church on Walnut Avenue. The Sisters of the Blessed Sacra-
ment, founded by Katherine Drexel, with a ministry to black and American Indian Catholics, opened their convent in the South End in 1914 and
eventually moved to Roxbury, to follow the migration of African Americans and West Indians in Boston.[27] Roxbury's Catholic churches were
populated by Irish and Italian parishioners, but also attracted northern
blacks, southern blacks from Louisiana and Maryland, Jamaicans, Cape
Verdeans, and Spanish-speaking Catholics from Puerto Rico and Cuba.

Roxbury's diverse iterations of black Christianity reflected the breadth
of religious internationalism across African American, Afro-Caribbean,
and Afro-Latino cultures. But we should not ignore how the religious
enclaves of Roxbury's white immigrant communities also shaped black
ideas about racial inequality, classism, urban religious diversity, and African American religious internationalism in jazz. George Lipsitz defines
US cities as new and dynamic sites for cultural interactions between
white and black migrants during World War II. Roxbury in the 1940s
was populated not only by thousands of Irish Catholics, but also by one
of the largest Jewish communities in New England. The Jewish community in Roxbury was the starting point for ninety thousand Jewish
residents (with roots in Germany and Eastern Europe) whose Hebrew
schools, synagogues, cafeterias, and butcher shops dominated the urban

landscape of Blue Hill Avenue, a major street that began in Roxbury and encompassed Dorchester and Mattapan. The sweet aroma of breads, pastries, and cakes prepared daily at the Jewish Kasanoff's Bakery on Blue Hill Avenue (across the street from St. John's Catholic Church) permeated the morning air in the upper Roxbury neighborhood. A short walk from Kasanoff's Bakery brought Roxbury residents to Hebrew Teacher's College, the Crawford Street synagogue, and Mishkan Tefila, on Seaver Street, "the oldest Conservative synagogue in New England."[28]

The Jewish jazz critic Nat Hentoff was a student at Boston Latin School, a jazz fan, and a resident of Roxbury in the 1940s. Although he interacted with black jazz artists such as Duke Ellington in Boston's jazz clubs, Hentoff's book *Boston Boy: Growing Up with Jazz and Other Rebellious Passions* includes reflections about the racial separatism that blacks experienced in white Roxbury in the World War II era: "My street, Howland Street, was not entirely Jewish. Toward the end of its four-block length were a number of black families. . . . But we never nodded or spoke to them, nor they to us. . . . They were colored."[29]

Black migrants and immigrants embraced values of self-determination and freedom by moving to the North, but their struggles against systemic racism continued in the northern cities. Although Roxbury was not a ghetto and was racially, ethnically, and religiously diverse during World War II, Boston was a metropolis of intense racial inequality and violence in the 1930s and 1940s. White people owned most of the properties in Roxbury. The majority of black Bostonians in the 1940s had manual labor jobs in the city's white communities. More than 50 percent of blacks were stuck in so-called "Negro jobs," struggling as janitors, porters, waiters, laborers, and servants.[30] People of African descent in the city had insufficient collective power in numbers to elect a black state representative until 1958.[31] Moreover, lunch counters and restaurants were segregated in Boston, and public and private behavior and practices supported racial inequality.[32]

The city's black Caribbean community led the way for militant protest that was inspired by the black internationalism of the UNIA. Boston's radical West Indian newspapers such as the *Chronicle* and the *Guardian* tapped black Atlantic anticolonial resistance strategies and challenged Boston's reputation as a beacon of liberty by reporting the frequent incidents of racist violence in the city. On July 8, 1934, the Boston police invaded the Roxbury home of a black man, J. Borden. Borden, who lived on Copeland Street, was shot and arrested on a minor charge. The black community tried unsuccessfully to organize a police brutality case on Borden's behalf, and a *Chronicle* reporter interviewed his lawyer.[33]

The *Chronicle* often published lists of racist attacks such as the following incidents in Boston:

> A group of white men chased, caught, and beat up two negro men. . . . Negro women kicked in the stomach on Tremont Street by white gangsters in broad daylight. No arrests. . . . Aged . . . infirm Negro beaten by white hoodlums. . . . Two Negroes have their skulls split by axe and nightstick when police went on a rampage. . . . Attack on . . . renowned tenor Roland Hayes in 1935, when his home in Brookline Village was vandalized by a group of White youths. . . . West Indian William B. Harrison . . . lived in the Humboldt Avenue middle-class area of Roxbury . . . in April 1947, a group of black-hating youths ambushed and beat him severely only a few blocks from his home.[34]

During the World War II era, black Bostonians desperately needed powerful civil rights leadership and activism to stem the tide of racist assaults. Yet neither the UNIA nor the black churches were able to provide it. For a while, militant Afro-Caribbean immigrants who were reporters for the *Chronicle* attempted to challenge institutional racism on behalf of US-born and West Indian blacks in Boston. Barbadian-born Victor Bynoe did his part, serving as a key figure in reviving black membership in the NAACP in Roxbury and the South End in the 1940s.

Despite these efforts, the militant transnational activism of black Jamaicans and Barbadians in the Marcus Garvey movement was no match for the systemic racism of police, courts, employers, politicians, businesses, educators, and realtors during World War II in Boston.[35] Bynoe, a prominent member of St. Cyprian's Church, pointed out, "You couldn't get people to talk about civil rights then. . . . We didn't get actively involved in politics until after World War II."[36] In sharp contrast to other northern cities with larger African American populations, Boston lacked civil rights leadership during this period.

Soon, hundreds of black youth in Boston and New York left Christianity behind. Modeling themselves on the jazz musicians who espoused values of black affirmation, freedom, and self-determination, they sought refuge in African American Islam. They had arrived in the urban centers of the Northeast looking for freedom, but instead found pervasive structural racism and de facto segregation that even the churches and black civic organizations could not mitigate. Islam and jazz, which together offered them a new black international identity, beckoned them down a new path.

The Zoot, Religious Identity, and Black Atlantic Cool: Jazz and Resistance to Racism

The story of Boston's jazz culture is part of a larger story of black youth who participated not just in the jazz world of 1940s Boston, but also in the overlapping spheres of Christianity, Islam, and black internationalism. Thousands of jazz artists and their fans experienced in jazz music and dance improvisational "rituals of performance," expressed in new clothing styles, new perspectives about black history, and new religious networks that embodied black Atlantic cool and forms of transcendent balance.[37] There were creative tensions between, on the one hand, the sacred spaces of African American Christianity, which viewed jazz as something outside the churches, and, on the other hand, the bars and clubs with their popular dance and musical performances; the result was that black youth constructed new identities—sometimes merely outside Christianity, but sometimes in opposition to it. For many blacks in the jazz world, their experimentation in jazz as black Christians influenced their black Atlantic religious consciousness in radical ways and led to their first encounters with Islam during World War II.

In the 1940s, Boston was one of America's major jazz cities, a reputation based on its black jazz community in the South End with clubs such as Roseland State Ballroom, Professional and Business Men's Club, and Wally's Paradise on Massachusetts Avenue; the Hi Hat Club, Tangerine Room, Golden Gate Café, and Old Club Savoy on Columbus Avenue; the Pioneer Social Club on Westfield Street; and Estelle's on Tremont Street.[38] Billie Holiday, Johnny Hodges, Jimmy Rushing, Cootie Williams, Sidney Bechet, Bunk Johnson, Duke Ellington, Lester Young, Ben Webster, Count Basie, Louis Armstrong, Billy Eckstine, Fletcher Henderson, Lionel Hampton, Ella Fitzgerald, Buddy Pearson, Cat Anderson, and Cab Calloway performed in these clubs.[39] Some black jazz fans imitated the style of these musicians by sporting conk hairstyles and zoot suits.

The zoot suit and the larger controversies surrounding its successive presentations in the black Atlantic world will help us understand how jazz and Islam helped to define the political and cultural mood in the nation's urban centers in the 1940s. Some black Americans, Mexican Americans, and Asian Americans had worn the zoot style—long drape jackets, baggy-pleated pants pegged at the ankle, and wide-brim hats with feathers—in Boston, Harlem, Los Angeles, and other cities in the 1930s, but it was Clyde Duncan, an African American restaurant worker in Gainesville, Georgia, who popularized the zoot suit among larger urban youth networks when his photographs appeared in *Men's Apparel Reporter* in 1941 and the *New York Times* in 1943, at the time of the Zoot Suit Riots, the effects of which we will explore in more detail below.[40]

Robin D. G. Kelley points out that the oppositional politics of the "hipster subculture" and the hustling and pimping life that the chemically processed "conk" hair and the zoot suit represented for working-class blacks and Latinos emerged powerfully in the World War II era.[41] It was a period that began with the Japanese bombing of Pearl Harbor in 1941, a year that also included A. Philip Randolph's threat of a March on Washington, a new wave of the Great Migration, and foreshadowed the Los Angeles Zoot Suit Riots. Kelley shows that jazz, exemplified by the expressive style of the zoot suit, played a significant role in the radicalization of many youth who experimented with both African American Islam and jazz. Jazz allowed members of dynamic youth cultures, existing on the periphery of city life, to construct style and community, to express new modes of black and brown affirmation, freedom, and self-determination, and to embrace identities that resisted the institutional racism of the dominant white culture, the unsophisticated customs of black migrants and immigrants from rural cultures, and the classism of the black middle class.[42]

The zoot suit subculture, then, is an important lens through which we can understand the evolving urban spirituality of jazz and Islam, iconic jazz performances in Boston and New York nightclubs, and participation in the emergent black Atlantic cool practices of jazz. Yes, zoot suits were worn by frequenters of jazz clubs, but even more importantly, they represented the resistance struggles of the disenfranchised young people who found them so attractive. All of these themes had strong political overtones involving young black Americans, Muslims, and Latinos in global struggles to reimagine identities that could express resistance to white supremacy and imperialism—identities embraced by the lindy hoppers and the beboppers. Travis A. Jackson sees improvisation in jazz performance as a "sacred ritual act" in which jazz musicians, dancers, and fans use music to engage in spiritually inspired expressions of the cool aesthetic and transcendence symbolized by the zoot suit.[43] As we will see later, this perception of clothing and style as aesthetic and ritual elements can be found not only in the world of jazz, but also in other black Atlantic musical traditions, in religious traditions like Islam, and in the spiritual and musical sampling practiced by African Americans who were experimenting with religious internationalism in this period as well.

Novelist Ralph Ellison explained the zoot suit's powerful connection to the larger black Atlantic communities: "Perhaps the zoot suit conceals clues to great potential power if only Negro leaders would solve this riddle."[44] Although he did not mention the zoot suit's profound religious meaning as a clue to the links between African American Islam and jazz, at the very least the cool expressive style of the zoot suiters influenced the cosmopolitan spirituality and the dissident protest strategies of jazz, and by doing so, inspired the radicalization of diasporic race rebels in black, Latino, and Islamic communities during World War II, especially after the zoot suit was outlawed by the Los Angeles City Council in 1942 as being in violation of the War Production Board's conservation guidelines on fabric. In some cases, the zoot suiters' affinity for radical experimentation with clothing, music, and dance styles paralleled their openness to experimentation with Christian and Islamic styles and practices in the cosmopolitan cities in which jazz thrived during World War II. Against this backdrop, music and religion interplayed as the zoot suiters became proficient in the arts of political disguise, resistance, and performance.

They created their own social space where they could experiment musically and politically with cultural and ethnic identities and express their spirituality and growing interest in Islam without a heavy religious

slant. But beyond the obvious appeal zoot suiters gained from their powerful sense of cool, George Lipsitz reads them as "icons of opposition
among aggrieved peoples."[45] For blacks, "the zoot suit was the garb that
fitted [their] rebellious mood."[46] Dressing in zoot suits and dancing in
swing jazz clubs allowed them to escape the drudgery of their exploitative working-class jobs, the dangers of police brutality, and the black
Christian ethos that promoted middle-class respectability.[47] Similarly,
Luis Alvarez sheds light on the cultures, youth relationships, identities,
and "body politics of dignity" that African American, Mexican American, and Asian American zoot suiters produced to resist the violent marginalization of nonwhite young people during World War II.[48]

The *New York Times* photograph of the zoot-suited Duncan was published in the summer of the Los Angeles Zoot Suit Riots, which culminated on June 7, 1943, when eight white sailors attacked a Mexican
American teenager, Victor Morales, during the Lionel Hampton Band
performance at the Orpheum Theater, broke his nose, cracked his ribs,
and destroyed his zoot suit. This attack was part of ten days of violence
in downtown Los Angeles and in the city's Mexican American and African American neighborhoods, during which white sailors, marines,
and soldiers beat up hundreds of primarily Mexican American, African
American, and Filipino zoot suiters and stripped them of their drape
clothing in the streets, movie theaters, nightclubs, and restaurants.[49]

Douglas Henry Daniels's research on the Zoot Suit Riots reveals how
the zoot suit exemplified the black cool influence on Latino popular
culture. For Mexican American, Filipino, and African American youth,
counterculture clothing "sometimes went beyond fashion and entertainment statements, embodying an intellectualized political position."[50]
Many brown and black Americans in US cities were attacked and ste-
reotyped as delinquents and criminals because they were bold and beautiful people of color, self-identified as hep cats, Pachucas, and Pachucos
who wore sharp zoot suits and performed the lindy hop in jazz clubs.
This discrimination fanned the flames of some of the more sophisticated
of these urban youth, leading them to create new urban communities
defined by jazz, black and Latino cool styles, and ultimately African
American religious internationalism and jazz.

Hundreds of African American and Mexican American youth coop-
erated and fought together during the Zoot Suit Riots to stop gangs of

white sailors as they tried to attack the black neighborhood on Central Avenue and 12th Street in Los Angeles on June 7, 1943.[51] Some Nisei youth (second-generation Japanese Americans born in the United States) also wore zoot suits in the Los Angeles community called "Little Tokyo" and in their gangs in the West Coast internment camps, after the US government forcibly removed 37,000 Los Angeles residents of Japanese descent from the city in 1942 to comply with President Roosevelt's Executive Order 9066, which imprisoned 120,000 Americans of Japanese descent during World War II.[52]

Mexican American zoot suiters called themselves Pachucos and Pachucas, spoke to one another in Caló (a vernacular language of Spanish and English slang), and were often victims of racist violence against black and brown people in California.[53] These youth were immersed in the jazz culture that had adopted the zoot suit as one of its symbols of resistance. Some of the Pachucos and Pachucas emphasized the Atlantic coolness of their jazz identities. Manuel Delgado, who was one of the nineteen tried and convicted Mexican American defendants in the 1942 Los Angeles Sleepy Lagoon murder case, called his zoot style "frantic as the Atlantic, . . . terrific as the Pacific," and connected his drawings of the zoot suiters in Pachuco youth culture to the artistic creativity of Rembrandt and Michelangelo. Later on, in the 1950s, some Mexican American youth like Delgado, youth immersed in the jazz culture that had adopted the zoot suit as one of its symbols, joined the Nation of Islam in Northern California.[54]

The 1943 Hollywood film *Stormy Weather*, which included performances by famous black jazz artists such as the Nicholas Brothers, Katherine Dunham, Bill "Bojangles" Robinson, Cab Calloway, Fats Waller, and Lena Horne, concluded with a scene in a USO nightclub where glamorous zoot-suited dancers performed for black soldiers, presenting some of the stars of jazz as powerful symbols of African American patriotism during World War II.[55] This movie, with its all-black cast, circulated throughout the black Atlantic world and shaped the expressive culture of thousands of working-class blacks, who contested the politics of white masculinity and middle-class respectability. They donned their zoot suits as a symbol of pleasure, leisure, and coolness as they danced in the ballrooms and bars of the urban ghettos, imitating the elegant lindy hop performances of their favorite African American celebrities.[56]

Later in New York, however, zoot suiter, jazz trumpeter, and bandleader Dizzy Gillespie highlighted his black Atlantic anti-war thinking and exhibited a cool strategy of concentration, performance, and improvisation during his interview with an Army psychiatrist in 1940. He was able to receive a 4-F classification because he stood "naked with my horn in a paper bag" and said, "In this stage of my life here in the United States . . . the white man's foot has been . . . buried up to his knee in my asshole! . . . You're telling me the German is the enemy. . . . I can never even remember having met a German. So, if you put me out there with a gun in my hand and tell me to shoot at the enemy, I'm liable to create a case of 'mistaken identity,' of who I might shoot."[57]

The oppositional politics of zoot suiters and jazz musicians like Gillespie emerged in reaction to racism and oppression and reflected the larger values of black affirmation, freedom, and self-determination that jazz and Islam shared. Although President Franklin Roosevelt signed Executive Order 8802 in 1941 and established the Fair Employment Practices Committee to prohibit racism in hiring practices in defense industry jobs, violent racism and white supremacy continued in the United States. This influenced the anti-war values of members of the Nation of Islam as well. For their part Elijah Muhammad and his son Emmanuel, of the Nation of Islam, engaged in militant resistance to the draft and even went so far as to express their solidarity with the Japanese cause. They were incarcerated for Selective Service violations from 1942 to 1946.[58]

The Lindy Hop, Resistance, and Religious Internationalism

Swing jazz dance, exemplified by the lindy hop, offered yet another way for blacks in Boston to express resistance to systemic racism—reshaping spiritual and musical forms drawn from Christianity and the African diaspora into a new expression of religious internationalism. Dancers and musicians used the complex rhythms of the lindy hop to experiment with black Christian influences and cool in jazz. The lindy hop's "syncopated two step, with the accent on the offbeat,"[59] along with its breakaway steps, created extraordinary opportunities for creative improvisation: to reimagine in a new urban context the mesmerizing cadences and call-and-response rituals of black preaching; the shouting (holy dancing) from Black Baptist, African Methodist Episcopal, and Pentecostal religions; and the rhythms of gospel blues from African American Christianity in Roxbury.

Duke Ellington's swing orchestra often played the music at Boston's Roseland Ballroom for the lindy hoppers, who generated electrifying communal energy on the dance floor. Their performances exemplified the black Atlantic cool style's emphasis on balance, concentration, spontaneity, initiative, change, and motion.[60] When "Duke kicked off showtime . . . the crowd clapped and shouted in time with the blasting band,"[61] while "the spotlight would be turning, pink, yellow, green, and blue, picking up the couples lindy-hopping as if they had gone mad."[62]

In his work *Race Music*, Guthrie P. Ramsey Jr. develops an understanding of jazz from "the private and communal realms of lived experience, . . . the cultural work performed by music in the processes of African American identity making, . . . and . . . the importance of dance and the centrality of the celebratory black body."[63] Ramsey's analysis of "community theaters," urban nightclubs, house parties, and religious venues as African American modernist spaces for dynamic engagement with "black consciousness," new musical practices and meanings, and the reimagining of black cultural memory from the North, South, and Caribbean in the 1940s helps us to understand jazz-inspired improvisational lindy hop performances in Roseland Ballroom as joyful and liberating expressions of the black body and black Atlantic cool.[64]

Indeed, the lindy hop often seems to combine musical and religious rituals, some of them drawn from black Christian musical traditions and some reflecting the influence of jazz—rituals that expressed a growing sense of religious internationalism among urban African Americans. As with the second line, a group of dancers who improvise behind the first procession of a jazz brass band during a religious or social occasion in the streets of black New Orleans, swing jazz dancers also created their own social space and became proficient in the arts of political disguise, resistance, and performance. Katrina Hazzard-Donald has noted the kinetic, aesthetic, and spiritual qualities of black American social dance that were reinvigorated in the black Atlantic cool style of the lindy hop performance: "Although the dancer[s] may be performing a frantic, fury of complex steps or figures, they never lose the asymmetrical juxtaposition of coolness, equilibrium, and control."[65]

John Storm Roberts noted that the connections between jazz's poly-rhythms and African diasporist forms of expression in black Atlantic musical traditions have a lot to do with the intimate and creative rapport between musicians, dancers, and audiences that we noted when describing performances in Boston's Roseland Ballroom, with their instrumental and dance call-and-response patterns among the lindy hoppers and Duke Ellington's Orchestra. The "African totality" of such performances would later be reimagined and exemplified in diverse black Atlantic contexts, such as the performances of West African dancers and Puerto Rican social dancers in New York City.[66]

Travis A. Jackson's research on "jazz performance as ritual" sheds additional light on the polycultural connections between swing, cosmopolitan spirituality, and black Atlantic cool that lindy hoppers tapped in to as a means of transcending their everyday struggles with systemic racism and experiencing a state of ecstasy, peace, and healing.[67] Jackson writes that the communal experiences of dancers and musicians participating in a mind-blowing performance of swing derived from black Christian influences that were sometimes "virtually indistinguishable" from the trance and Holy Spirit possession experiences in African American Baptist and Pentecostal church services.[68] "What was true" of the rhythmic and harmonic forms of improvisation in black churches was "equally true" in the Roseland Ballroom when musicians, dancers, and circles of spectators reshaped every aspect of jazz musical production, including "space, time, tune, form, other performers, and other participants," embracing a performance identity outside the realm of Christianity.[69] In such a setting, musical and dance performances had the potential to ascend to a transcendent level—the musicians, dancers, and audiences often described their experiences as "out of this world."[70] Jackson explicates this transcendent/mystical aspect of the lindy hop performance: "Every element of a performance seems to fit, and each individual appears to be making a contribution to what is occurring. Some of the feeling associated with possession or ecstasy led to an apparent nullification of time outside of the performance and of space outside the venue. . . . The musical event is said to be 'swinging,' 'burning,' 'on,' . . . that indicates positive motion, activity, and good feeling."[71]

Moreover, the key elements of ritual and religious experimentation in the lindy hoppers' jazz experience required that the music be performed in a sacred space of sorts (a nightclub such as Roseland Ballroom, a veritable temple of jazz). There was even a special dress requirement (a ceremonial robe—the zoot suit) for the most creative performers and audiences in the nightclubs and dance halls—the ritual spaces of jazz.[72] According to Jacqui Malone, "African American musicians, dancers, and singers all testify to the spiritual dimension of their art," which they experience when their creative and communal energies "converged to create a union that personifies what jazz is all about."[73] Hazzard-Donald shows us that African American social dance improvisation is done "to rebalance the universe" through performances defined by the "ability to cross-reference the sacred."[74] It involves reorienting the body and releasing the energy and soul power of the dancers in a communal context.

Their immersion in the music influenced the lindy hoppers to experiment with Christian influences in jazz and to reshape the rhythms and sounds of black Christianity through their dancing. It also allowed them to experience the resistance and the cosmopolitan spirituality of black Atlantic cool, with its emphasis on balance, control, composure, healing, purification, and African American religious internationalism. Musical and dance performances of black Atlantic cool circulated spiritual energy in jazz communities, allowing people to transcend tragedy and hardship through what Jackson calls "metaphoric encodings of deeply held values and strategies for survival" in black America.[75] As I have demonstrated, black Atlantic cool was an important influence in the jazz youth culture that the lindy hoppers experienced in Boston. Jazz's vision of resistance, improvisation, and cosmopolitan spirituality encouraged them to look at a variety of black religious cultures, to tap their urban rhythms and spiritual philosophies, and to learn "how to move easily between [these] cultures."[76] Eventually, their exploration of the rich musical and religious connections between jazz and black identities in Boston evolved to include Islam.

Duke Ellington, African American Religious Internationalism, and the Cool Aesthetic

The dynamic youth identity that the lindy hoppers forged in the golden age of African American Islam and jazz can also be traced to the creative power that Duke Ellington brought to the religious imagination and the dance practices of swing. His interactions with black Atlantic cool, the zoot suiters, the conk style, and Afro-Caribbean and Latino cultures shaped the aesthetic experimentation, the soul searching, and the musical styles that eventually advanced Islam in the larger black jazz communities to which he belonged. Ellington (1899–1974), a prominent composer, pianist, and bandleader, played in Harlem's segregated Cotton Club from 1927 to the early 1930s, when he achieved international fame.[77] In this period of his career, live performances of his classic hits such as "Mood Indigo," "In a Sentimental Mood," and "Black and Tan Fantasy" were heard by thousands across the United States through CBS radio broadcasts.[78] For some of Ellington's listeners, the music's appeal was its exoticism. But Ellington himself articulated the significance of his music in a way that resonated with the spirituality of black Atlantic cool and the values of black affirmation, freedom, and self-determination that jazz and African American Islam shared. He wrote in 1931,

> The music of my race is something more than the "American idiom." It is the result of our transplantation to American soil, and was our reaction in plantation days to the tyranny we endured. What we could not say openly we expressed in music, and what we know as "jazz" is something more than just dance music. We dance it not as a mere diversion or social accomplishment. It expresses our personality, our souls react to the elemental but eternal rhythm. . . . In Harlem we have . . . our own city. . . . We have almost achieved our own civilization. The history of my people is one of great achievement over fearful odds.[79]

Ellington, then, saw jazz as an interpretive lens for understanding the mystical interactions between African American ancestral wisdom and larger black resistance struggles, and lindy hop dance performances and zoot suit traditions in Harlem and other northern cities as new presentations of sophisticated urban blackness. They were also powerful but subtle strategies for black dignity in the United States that influenced the emergence of African American Islam among black youth.

Ellington, who described himself as composing African as well as American music, led the way in incorporating African American, Caribbean, and Latino musicians and sounds that transcended the racial stereotypes of jazz into his orchestral music. Expressing his own vision of black internationalist sounds in 1947, he composed the *Liberian Suite* for the Liberian government to celebrate the independence and the centenary anniversary of the West African nation, established in 1847 by emancipated blacks who were enslaved in the United States.[80] Later on in the 1960s, Duke Ellington's jazz was also influenced by the Islamic world, when his orchestra performed in Senegal, Egypt, Jordan, Syria, Lebanon, Indonesia, Iraq, Turkey, Iran, India, and Pakistan and he won a Grammy Award for his album *The Far East Suite*, which was inspired by his experimentation with the musical sounds of the Middle East, Asia, and Africa.[81]

Although Duke Ellington's music created new visions of black culture that resonated with the Garveyites and the prospective Muslim converts in his midst, jazz artists and their African American fans certainly felt the pulse of American racism in places like the Cotton Club. Such clubs were controlled by hustling white gangsters and businessmen who exploited African American musicians to frame blackness in a primitive light. In the 1940s and 1950s, most of the black musicians whose vision of jazz was shaped by Islam, including Yusef Lateef and Ahmad Jamal, played in these clubs, and like Duke Ellington, they struggled with the way these venues influenced their spiritual goals and values as well as their music. Ellington was an intellectual and artistic leader of twentieth-century jazz, and he overcame the early stereotypes of African American music by rejecting systemic racism and expressing a sense of African American religious internationalism in his orchestra's new musical forms. Before John Coltrane, he was one of the jazz artists who most elegantly embraced Islamic and Christian influences in jazz and the style of black Atlantic cool.

Ellington was a multifaceted artist who used jazz clubs and ballrooms not only as spaces to entertain audiences with his musical performances, but also as community theaters for the cultural production of black history and spirituality. And although Ellington was a Protestant Christian, his musical soundtrack ultimately influenced the inclusion of Islamic elements in jazz that black youth identified with in the 1940s and 1950s, Islamic elements that also influenced the conversion of jazz musicians to the African American Muslim movements. Just as his star trombonist, Joe "Tricky Sam" Nanton, used the plunger mute to add wa-wa sounds and musical themes from his Afro-Caribbean heritage to the orchestra's performances,[82] so Ellington's analysis of the West Indian roots of his artistry allows us to trace the significant connections between Garvey-ism and African American Islam that circulated widely in the black musical world, and that some zoot suiters and lindy hoppers embraced in Boston:

> He [Nanton] was . . . playing a highly personalized form of his West Indian heritage. . . . Tricky and his people were deep in the West Indian legacy and the Marcus Garvey movement. . . . A whole strain of West Indian musicians came up who made contributions to . . . jazz . . . and they were virtually descended from the true African scene. It's the same now with the Muslim movement and a lot of West Indian people are involved in it. . . . Bop . . . is the Marcus Garvey extension.[83]

Ellington's lived experience in music, then, highlights the parallel goals and values of Islam and jazz that Christopher W. Chase explores in his essay "Prophetics in the Key of Allah": that numerous black performers in jazz converted to Islam or were deeply shaped by the religion, attracted by its emphasis on freedom, self-determination, and racial equality, and that many of the great musicians who did not become Muslims, "such as John Coltrane, nonetheless bear the stamp of Islam's influence."[84]

The valve trombonist Juan Tizol brought another important presentation of black Atlantic cool to Duke Ellington's Orchestra, one that stimulated the zoot suiters, the lindy hoppers, and other African Americans to think about the musical and spiritual interactions between blacks and Latinos during this period. Tizol was born in Puerto Rico, and Ellington hired him in 1929. He and Ellington composed their big hit "Caravan" in 1937, and the bandleader observed that "that Puerto Rican strain gave us a new dimension. . . . 'Caravan' was the launching pad and vehicle to flights of popularity on the national and world charts."[85] Tizol's compositions "Conga Brava," "Lovely Isle of Porto [sic] Rico," "Jubilesta," "Pyramid," and "Carnaval" brought Latino sounds, melodies, and rhythms into the orchestra's repertoire.

Duke Ellington's early incorporation of Puerto Rican sounds and themes into his jazz style transformed the music of Roxbury, black New York, and Spanish Harlem and helped shape new social and political interactions between blacks and Puerto Ricans in East Coast clubs and communities. Eventually, the Latino jazz connections that Ellington initiated among his musicians evolved into a jazz culture of Puerto Rican youth who experimented with Islam because of their "geographic and political proximity to African Americans" and their solidarity with the black liberation struggle and its freedom sounds.[86]

A powerful example of this solidarity between blacks and Puerto Ricans unfolds in the story of a World War II-era Latino conversion to African American Islam that evolved from the music and street life of New York City. Puerto Rican author Piri Thomas's autobiography *Down These Mean Streets* traces his teenage and young adult years in Spanish Harlem in the 1940s and his interactions with the music, masculinity, black affirmation, and cool style of his African American friends, which led to his conversion to the Nation of Islam in a New York state prison in the 1950s. Thomas's story draws on the black representations of masculinities that jazz and Islam shared, which inspired him to recraft his own racial identity. During his incarceration, Muhammad, an African American imam, taught him how to pray in Arabic, introduced him to the Qur'an and to Elijah Muhammad's religious movement, and gave him the new name Hussein Afmit Ben Hassen. Piri Thomas stopped practicing Islam after his release from prison and returned to Spanish Harlem in 1958.[87] However, African American Islam was important in his life as a symbol of justice, racial pride, manhood, transformation, and religious internationalism.

The intermingling of Latino and black musicians shaped jazz's black Atlantic cool styles in a variety of ways. By the early 1930s, the Savoy Ballroom was Harlem's "temple of . . . black swing," where African Americans danced the lindy hop in the 1940s. John Storm Roberts points out that the lindy hop incorporated Latino styles of expressive culture and that Puerto Rican musicians were part of a larger story of Latino and black dance and musical styles in jazz, which "existed separately, with largely separate audiences, yet intertwined, each feeding off and nourishing the other."[88] Latino musical and dance performances were also an important countercultural expression in the dynamic black Atlantic communities made up of Puerto Rican, Dominican, and Cuban immigrants in Boston and New York. Not only did these performances infuse jazz with Latino cool styles, but they also influenced the zoot suiters in other ways, emphasizing the significance of black-brown relations in African American Islam and jazz as they played out in the lives of black and Puerto Rican converts to Islam.

Duke Ellington understood the aesthetic and spiritual power of cool and expressed it in his musical performances, with their representations of life in the black cultures and sounds of northeastern cities. He forged his own variety of black Atlantic cool visions in his music, which inspired lindy hoppers and zoot suiters who eventually converted to Islam in Boston. Ellington contributed to a spirituality that affirmed new creative presentations of blackness among urban African American youth and their search for a global identity in jazz.

World War II Jazz and the Construction of Black Masculinities

Black male followers of Islam and jazz musicians in the World War II era expressed the period's larger themes of black liberation by constructing black notions of masculinity. Representations of masculinities in the golden age of African American Islam and jazz reflected the resistance struggles of disenfranchised young people who were searching for new styles of freedom and new religious and political identities that embraced blackness, opposed white supremacy, and eventually expressed the parallel goals and values of Islam and jazz. The radical agency that led the zoot suiters and the lindy hoppers to explore African American religious internationalism and ultimately to convert to Islam was shaped by their adoption of the styles of black masculinities that they identified in jazz. Jazz musicians often rejected the bourgeois black masculinity of the African American middle class and constructed a compelling and charismatic black cool strain of masculinity that served them well on the jazz stage. However, we will see below that despite their shared values of black liberation, musicians in the jazz world and in the Nation of Islam developed patriarchal structures of power exemplified by male dominance and the devaluation of women's leadership and experience.

It is not surprising that young marginalized African American and Latino men, who used the zoot suit as a countercultural challenge to the power of hegemonic white masculinity and as a "rite of passage into 'coolness'" that allowed them to use their bodies to show self-respect and confidence, would also objectify the women they interacted with in jazz.[89] Robin D. G. Kelley emphasizes that African American zoot suiters in Boston and New York rejected the racist denigration of black males by creating a black masculine ritual of calling one another "man," yet they emulated jazz musicians and hustlers who denigrated women as "property to be possessed, sported, used, and tossed out."[90]

The zoot suiters' gender politics were complex. They danced to music that celebrated the black woman as a "Sophisticated Lady" and promoted African American religious internationalism and experimentation with Islamic and Christian influences in jazz, yet their black masculinity was also influenced by World War II-era jazz musicians who used a familiar line to brag about living on the income of their women: "Romance without finance is a nuisance."[91] As Kelley understood so clearly, "resistance to wage labor for the hep cat frequently meant increased oppression and exploitation of women, particularly black women" who had jobs and money to spend on their men.[92] Yet the zoot suiters' black masculinity and relationships with women in the 1940s challenged the boundaries of race, class, gender, and skin color, especially in the preference for light-skinned and white women among some of the jazz musicians they admired like Duke Ellington and Cab Calloway.

Skin color played a role in the formation of black masculinities, the gender politics of jazz, African American religious internationalism, and the Nation of Islam. It is important to understand the meaning and significance of skin color in the black Atlantic world and in the links between African American Islam and jazz. Nina G. Jablonski points out that the African American preference for a lighter shade of black in the twentieth century can be traced to "the skin-color hierarchy that became entrenched and institutionalized" during the centuries of enslavement in the United States.[93] As late as the twentieth century, some black institutions engaged in colorism to promote light-skinned African Americans to positions of leadership. Walter White, African American president of the NAACP in the 1940s, looked like a white man.

W. E. B. Du Bois and Marcus Garvey engaged in public debates with one another that included vicious remarks about their skin color. Moreover, in the 1930s black newspapers and magazines bombarded African American women with advertisements for skin lighteners, such as Palmer's Skin Success creams. Jazz communities were so influenced by their preference for light skin color among blacks that Bessie Smith sang, "I'm as good as any woman in your town / I ain't no high yella, I'm a deep killer brown"—lyrics that expressed her counterculture narrative and decried discrimination against dark-skinned women in jazz and blues.[94] Indeed, colorism was also evident in African American Islamic religious communities, as many of the most important male leaders of the Nation of Islam from 1930 to 1980 were light-skinned men: W. D. Fard Muhammad, Elijah Muhammad, Malcolm X, Warith Deen Muhammad, and Louis Farrakhan (who was a calypso musician when he converted to the Nation of Islam).

Black men presented several variations of African American masculinity that contributed to the evolution of masculinities in jazz and the Nation of Islam. Their destructive practices of hustling and drug addiction (reactions to systemic racism and marginalization) reflected the patriarchy and aggression of black hypermasculinity, although it is important to emphasize that these same men nonetheless also engaged in "struggles for self-determination and Black redemption" in jazz.[95] Zain Abdullah emphasizes that African American Muslim men have practiced a variety of masculinities that intersect with one another in their lived experiences. His research celebrates the rise of masculinities that demonstrate complex forms of black uplift and agency—masculinities that emerged in spite of American heteronormative and racist practices that circulated violent and hypersexual representations of the black male racialized body to rationalize white supremacy, Jim Crow, and colonialism in the twentieth century.[96]

Some jazz fans initially engaged in a "communal masculinity" typical of black Atlantic cool and African American religious internationalism.[97] Communal masculinity in jazz was embodied in the performances of black men who wore colorful zoot suits to mark their complex masculine identities, representing a counterculture narrative in reaction to white supremacy in the United States. In Boston and New York, zoot suiters expressed possibilities for African American unity and transcendence in the performances of the lindy hop with their black girlfriends. Later, in the golden age of African American Islam, they would draw on their musical and spiritual philosophy of black Atlantic cool and their understanding of African American religious internationalism to reimagine the black male body as an instrument of Allah in the Fruit of Islam and as "a global [communal] body connected to America, Africa, and the Middle East."[98] Jazz provided the creative, experimental, and improvisational culture that encouraged its fans and musicians to experience various presentations of African American and African diasporic masculinities through the performance strategies of black Atlantic cool, African American religious internationalism, and conversion to Islam.

The engagement of musicians and their fans with jazz in Boston also exemplified a number of expressive forms of African American modernism in the Atlantic world, which Paul Gilroy analyzes as performances of black masculinity and femininity: oppositional visions of identity based on a black consciousness constructed outside the realm of post-Enlightenment modernity; a culture of embodied performance that prioritizes orality, gesture, call-and-response, costume, and signifying in African diasporic musics; distinctive ways of using language among African diasporic populations; new cultural elements and performances that result from dislocation, migration, and immigration in the Americas; anti-hierarchical visions of radical democracy embodied in performances that influence critiques of hegemonic structures in European modernism; rhythmic performances that draw on the racial authenticity, power, and authority of the drum in subversive African diasporic musics; and productions of racialized identities of lived blackness that use Pan-African sounds to connect diverse groups of African-descended peoples.[99]

We will see later on how the Islamic communities that jazz people interacted with in Boston and New York City reshaped these expressive aspects of black modernity to construct their own unique religious identities in the golden age of African American Islam. Black jazz musicians in the 1940s took the lead in circulating African American modernist styles and forms that used the black body and the sounds and rhythms of the city to participate in a "new transatlantic cultural dialogue . . . within the larger African diaspora."[100] Indeed, Gilroy's analysis of black music captures the subtle angle of political agency in the zoot suiters' complex masculinity, black Atlantic cool, African American religious internationalism, and attraction to jazz musicians, as well as the musical and religious convergences that they pursued in their journey to Islam. Gilroy, in *The Black Atlantic*, expressed it in this way: "Examining the place of music in the black Atlantic world means surveying the self-understanding articulated by the musicians who have made it, the symbolic use to which their music is put by other artists."[101]

And I might add, religious leaders. For his part, Ramsey also sheds light on how jazz's artistic experimentation with sounds and "masculinist, aggressive, and transformative" cultural practices among black youth in the 1940s influenced a larger African American counterculture encompassing and expressing new representations of style, politics, language, and spirituality.[102] In the jazz world, the countercultures of black youth explored the interplay between African American Islamic and Christian cultural forms in music and religion, and their experimentation rejected systemic racism while asserting the values of black affirmation, freedom, and self-determination.

We saw earlier in this chapter how jazz fans were drawn to the sounds and rhythms of gospel music in Boston's black churches in the 1940s. Modern gospel blues began in Chicago with the songs of Thomas A. Dorsey, a blues pianist from Georgia who brought "something that's jazzy" and modern to Christian worship.[103] This encouraged African Americans to use their music to express their migration consciousness, which involved urban and rural cultures in the North, Midwest, South, and California. However, some jazz fans and musicians quickly critiqued black Christianity. Eventually, their dynamic Boston experiences of coolness, African American religious internationalism, performance, masculinity, and race were deeply influenced by their interactions with a close-knit group of black jazz musicians who worked in the South End bars and ballrooms and stayed in black-owned rooming houses. Duke Ellington was a regular figure in Boston's black community, staying at Myra McAdoo's family house when he performed in the South End. Later on, John Coltrane lived at Eddie Logan's house at 421 Massachusetts Avenue when he played in Boston. Thus, Massachusetts Avenue at the corner of Columbus Avenue was nicknamed the "jazz corner of Boston" and "Boston's 52nd Street."[104]

When the zoot suiters and the lindy hoppers left Boston for New York City, their evolving black masculinities and jazz experiences continued and were reshaped by thriving communities of black musicians whose musical, religious, and political forms celebrated new expressions of art and blackness and influenced new internationalist identities in African American Islamic culture. It is to the description and analysis of these interactions that we now turn.

"Take the 'A' Train": Bebop, Jazz, and Resistance in Harlem

In the 1940s, some zoot suiters and lindy hoppers traveled back and forth between Boston and New York, holding jobs and dancing in the Savoy Ballroom. My analysis here is based on the work of scholars who provided essential information about the musical presentations of Billie Holiday, Dizzy Gillespie, and bebop in New York as well as the Harlem Race Riot, all of which influenced black youth and the goals and values of freedom, racial affirmation, and self-determination that African American Islam and jazz shared during World War II. Manhattan and Brooklyn (the latter of which encompasses the important black community of Bedford- Stuyvesant) were cultural centers for new performances of African American religious internationalism and black Atlantic cool that drew on the creative energies of jazz musicians and their fans. For Boston jazz fans, their experiments with innovative musical forms, dynamic protest strategies against racism, and interactions with diverse African American Muslim movements shaped their attraction to Islamic culture in the Roxbury jazz community to which they returned after their sojourns in Harlem.

Trains were essential to the routes of African American Islam and jazz and to musicians' and fans' lives in the 1940s, and their journeys up and down the Eastern Seaboard resonated with Duke Ellington's signature theme, "Take the 'A' Train." Billy Strayhorn, a pianist in Ellington's orchestra, wrote the music for the song after receiving directions to ride the A train to get to a party at Ellington's house in the famous Harlem neighborhood called Sugar Hill because of the black celebrities who lived there. The song, recorded in 1941, soon became a hit. Originally an instrumental, it opened with a trumpet solo by Ray Nance, after which the orchestra launched into an evocative recreation of the sounds of the New York City subway.[105] Later on, jazz vocalist Joya Sherrill wrote the lyrics that Ellington used in the song: "Hurry, hurry, hurry, take the A train, to get to Sugar Hill, way up in Harlem. . . . If you miss the A train, you'll miss the quickest way to get to Harlem."[106]

As black jazz fans worked, danced, and hustled in the nightclubs, bars, and restaurants of Harlem, they rode the A train uptown and downtown on the West Side of Manhattan. The Ellington Orchestra's performance of "Take the 'A' Train" in the 1943 film *Reveille with Beverly* underscores the significance of railroad trains for defining the routes to freedom, self-determination, and resistance that southern blacks traveled to the northern cities during the Great Migration and World War II. Black jazz musicians' lives were shaped by riding those same trains.

For Boston jazz fans, "New York was heaven . . . and Harlem was Seventh Heaven."[107] The fans who became well known in Harlem were friendly with the most famous jazz musicians in the world, including Duke Ellington, Ray Nance, Cootie Williams, Sonny Greer, Eddie Vinson, Earl Hines, Billy Eckstine, Dizzy Gillespie, Dinah Washington, Ella Fitzgerald, Lionel Hampton, Dexter Gordon, Count Basie, Illinois Jacquet, Cab Calloway, and Billie Holiday. Later on, Yusef Lateef and John Coltrane played jazz and lived in New York City. The literary scholar Farah Jasmine Griffin described the dazzling synthesis of black Atlantic cool forms that delighted the black migrants and jazz artists who expressed the links between African American Islam and their music in the black metropolis of Harlem: "New York beckoned, and they came. . . . They were shaped by this city, . . . the movement of their bodies, their style. . . . The Black Mecca, born of the migration of black peoples from the Caribbean and the American South, . . . was a city of swinging rhythms and bebop changes, . . . a city that danced the Lindy Hop, modern choreography, and African isolations."[108] They were a part of all of this, reveling in their nightlife interactions with the Harlem jazz crowds at the Apollo Theater, the Braddock Hotel, the Savoy Ballroom, Small's Paradise, Creole Bill's, and Jimmy's Chicken Shack, spanning Seventh, Eighth, Lenox, and St. Nicholas Avenues up to 155th Street. They also joined the Times Square jazz crowds at the Lobster Pond nightclub on 42nd Street and frequented the clubs on 52nd Street. In New York in the 1940s, black migrants embraced a jazz metropolis that included famous musicians, lindy hoppers, and hustlers.[109] But the city provided more than a jazz education for black youth. Its key musicians, religious communities, and urban movements also nurtured their radical political perspectives and influenced their eventual embrace of Islam.

In the years when the newcomers were dancing and working in Harlem's bars and nightclubs, black artists and their New York fans were revolutionizing jazz, creating new musical forms and forging identities infused with ideas of black Atlantic cool, the African diaspora, freedom, and militant resistance strategies against lynching, white supremacy, and systemic racism. The artistic and political ferment in New York's jazz community resonated profoundly with many black migrants after their tragic childhoods in the South and the Midwest and planted the creative seeds for their future roles as innovators and practitioners of new religious and political forms in the golden age of African American Islam. Some of the migrants in Harlem had fled their home states in the 1930s and 1940s to escape the devastating impact of racism on their families in the South and the Midwest, the epicenters of the Ku Klux Klan and violent white supremacy in the United States. Tuskegee Institute estimates that at least 4,700 black people were lynched in the United States from 1882 to 1964, and historian Leon F. Litwack explains that the lynching was a "participatory ritual of torture and death, a voyeuristic spectacle prolonged as long as possible . . . for the benefit of the crowd."[110] The Midwest was an extension of the South in this regard, with its violent racism, Ku Klux Klan organizations, and the lynchings in Michigan, Kansas, Minnesota, Indiana, Nebraska, Missouri, Illinois, and Ohio that were photographed and circulated on postcards by the murderers. The National Association for the Advancement of Colored People, led by Walter White, investigated more than ten lynchings in 1940 and eventually accused the US government of human rights violations, but there were no federal, state, or local anti-lynching laws to help black people in this era.[111] As the middle of the twentieth century approached, lynching was one of the core issues that created a revolutionary context in Harlem and popularized the parallel goals and values of social justice that made jazz and African American Islam so attractive to black New Yorkers.

Jazz singer Billie Holiday (1915–1959) eloquently expressed these values as well as the black community's pain and desire for social justice every time she performed her theme song, "Strange Fruit."[112] Although Holiday never saw a lynching, she used the lyrics of this song as collective and individual resistance against the racial injustices she experienced as a black woman in Jim Crow America.[113] Holiday exemplified the powerful transformative aesthetic of black Atlantic cool and created a profoundly defiant spiritual and moral voice to represent the victims of lynching. She performed "Strange Fruit" as a mystic dirge, the vocal line accompanied by the mournful trumpet melodies that usually open jazz funerals in New Orleans:

Southern trees bear a strange fruit,
blood on the leaves and blood at the root.
Black bodies swinging in the Southern breeze,
strange fruit hanging from the poplar trees.

Pastoral scene of the gallant South,
the bulging eyes and the twisted mouth.
Scent of magnolia sweet and fresh,
then the sudden smell of burning flesh.

Here is a fruit for the crows to pluck,
for the rain to gather, for the wind to suck,
for the sun to rot, for the tree to drop.
Here is a strange and bitter crop.[114]

In *Blues Legacies and Black Feminism*, Angela Y. Davis interprets the song's shocking lyrics as a blatant "rallying cry" for activism against the Jim Crow system that supported the lynching murders of black men, women, and children in the United States.[115] Billie Holiday's performances of "Strange Fruit" for racially integrated audiences at the Café Society nightclub in downtown Manhattan challenged her jazz fans to reimagine the horrible crime of lynching, to identify with the humanity of the black victims and their families, and to rally to the anti-lynching human rights message of the song.[116] Davis shows that the song "almost singlehandedly changed the politics of American popular culture and put the elements of protest and resistance back at the center of contemporary black musical culture."[117]

Unfortunately, Holiday's social consciousness and her legacy as a cool black feminist and working-class protest artist fighting against white supremacy were overshadowed by the sexism in jazz scholarship and popular culture that focused on her problems with alcohol and drugs, issues that are peripheral to her artistic genius as a jazz singer.[118] Her New York story, like the story of many Harlem jazz fans and black converts to Islam, unfolded in dance halls, music halls, and bars—places that many black middle-class and white critics judged in opposition to the workplace, church, and home, the preferred locales for black female respectability in the 1940s.[119] Thus, many scholarly and cinematic portrayals of Holiday's performances of "Strange Fruit" were presented in a "web of gendered, classed, and raced inferiority," suggesting that she did not understand the political significance of the song until white men told her to sing it.[120]

In contrast, Davis's research engages the complex agency that Holiday possessed to compare the lynching described in "Strange Fruit" to her own father's death. Holiday's father, Clarence Holiday, a touring jazz guitarist, was denied treatment for pneumonia in several segregated Texas hospitals, and his death in 1937 can be directly attributed to Jim Crow medical practices.[121] As Patricia Hill Collins's *Black Sexual Politics* illuminates, the Great Migration and the World War II era stimulated the exchange of ideas about resistance, freedom, and self-determination across a broad spectrum of African American organizations and cultural institutions. As a result, blacks in the North, including jazz artists and their Muslim fans, "clearly had more political rights than their Southern counterparts," rights they used to protest structural racism.[122] Northern blacks were not systematically deprived of their voting rights, and they used the ballot box to effect political change. Moreover, their grassroots movements for racial protest, civil rights, and economic power were enlarged and reinvigorated by the millions of southern blacks who embraced values of social justice by moving to the North.

Billie Holiday's jazz was exquisitely performed. She transformed her jazz fans' understanding of black Atlantic cool with her elegant, shimmering beaded gowns and the gardenia in her hair. But behind her glamorous image was a woman who used her art to convey a passionate message of protest. Although her publishers chose *Lady Sings the Blues* as the title of her autobiography, her preference was for *Bitter Crop*, a title that connected black musicians and their sounds to the three centuries of enslavement, segregation, and Jim Crow that African Americans had experienced since arriving against their will in the United States.

Billie Holiday's mesmerizing musical performances provided a meditation on American apartheid and inspired her fans to use jazz as a soundtrack for reimagining black artists and their contributions to the African American freedom struggles as they emerged from the terrorism of enslavement and Jim Crow to embrace black Islam and black power in the twentieth century.

Billie Holiday's stardom and her militant black Atlantic performances of "Strange Fruit" expressed the dissident femininity of ordinary African American working-class women in New York during World War II who later converted to Islam and who danced the lindy hop at the Savoy Ballroom on Thursday "Kitchen Mechanics' Night" to establish an identity apart from their jobs as cooks and maids, challenging the dominant standards of white feminine beauty by "reclaiming their bodies for pleasure" with black men.[123]

By 1939, when Holiday launched her singing about lynching in the United States, a Federal Bureau of Narcotics agent initiated patterns of harassment that led to her incarceration on several occasions in the 1940s and 1950s because of her addiction to heroin and her refusal to "be silent about racism."[124] Billie Holiday's transcendent, spiritually inspired coolness and her purifying race-conscious music about violent white supremacy would profoundly influence Muslim converts from Boston's jazz community in the years to come, especially in the golden age of African American Islam, when as ministers in the Nation of Islam, they developed their stringent political analysis of lynching, black internationalism, and domestic colonialism.

But during this period in the New York musical scene, big band swing was giving way to a mesmerizing new jazz form: bebop, which offered new artistic freedom for experimentation among black musicians. With its emphasis on listening, feeling, and black cultural memory instead of dancing, bebop embraced new transnational religious identities and musical styles from the Caribbean, Asia, and Africa, especially Islam. Bebop offered a new way for musicians to deconstruct racial stereotypes and highlight black cultural practices in music, including improvisation. Using smaller combos of four to six players, bebop was known for aggressive rhythm, energy, syncopation, and harmonic changes. Drums played a central role in every aspect of the music, as did "dissonant chord structures" and faster tempos.[125]

Eric Porter's *What Is This Thing Called Jazz?* traces the emergence of bebop to a new emphasis on racial pride, liberal politics, and cosmopolitan intellectual styles in black Atlantic cool culture that resulted from dynamic African American urban life, accelerated migration, and a powerful working class in the World War II economy.[126] At the same time, he writes, "rising black awareness and militancy, combined with shifting class relations, an internationalist perspective, and a dissatis-faction with the limitations of racial identities, fostered a certain kind of oppositional consciousness among African Americans from differ-ent social backgrounds."[127] All these factors shaped the atmosphere in which jazz musicians converted to Islam. Charlie Parker, Dizzy Gil-lespie, Thelonius Monk, Kenny Clarke, Max Roach, Dexter Gordon, Bud Powell, and Mary Lou Williams led the way, exploring bebop in musical collectives and jam sessions at Monroe's Uptown House on 138th Street, Minton's Playhouse on 118th Street, pianist Mary Lou Williams's apart-ment on Hamilton Terrace in Harlem, and in clubs on 52nd Street in New York City.[128] Clarke and Roach engaged with African American religious internationalism and eventually converted to Islam.

Musicologist Guthrie P. Ramsey Jr. explains that bebop's accelerated rhythm was revolutionary for its adoption of "an eighth-note subdivi-sion of the basic jazz beat that was usually in 4/4 meter."[129] Initially, because of the American Federation of Musicians recording ban from 1942 to 1944, the general public was unable to appreciate bebop's mu-sical experimentation.[130] But several Boston jazz fans were insiders at the late-night Harlem spaces where black musicians played and partied privately after the bars and nightclubs closed in New York.[131] This gave them an insider's appreciation not only of the technical aspects of this new musical form, but also its thematic preoccupations.

Dizzy Gillespie's "A Night in Tunisia" exemplified African American bebop's messy but exciting transformation of black Atlantic jazz prac-tices and experimentation with Islamic influences during World War II. It also introduced the theme of religious internationalism, describ-ing the conflict between the Allied forces and the Axis powers in the North African nation in 1942. Gillespie (1917–1993), a trumpeter, com-poser, and bandleader, was a migrant from South Carolina who lived in Philadelphia and New York, and was married in Boston in 1940.[132] His story came out of the Great Migration, but it also drew on the creative energies of black Atlantic cool styles in jazz, highlighting his engage-ment with Islamic and Afro-Latin cultural forms that influenced the black internationalism of bebop musicians and fans. "A Night in Tuni-sia" encouraged cool African Americans to think about their freedom struggle in trans-racial ways shaped by black-brown relations, creating a bebop-inspired sonic dialogue with the North African "Muslim Third

World" during the World War II era.[133] Later on, in the 1950s and 1960s, jazz musicians were mesmerized politically and religiously by the Nation of Islam's trans-racial understanding of blackness, which also envisioned cool "Asiatic" black men and women in the United States with deep historical and spiritual linkages to the larger Muslim international world.

Guthrie explains Dizzy Gillespie's engagement with African American religious internationalism and how he wished to reimagine African American urban life in a modern black Atlantic context by beginning "A Night in Tunisia" with "the repetitive ostinato bass pattern" that connects the composition "to an African past, to his South Carolinian not-so-distant past, and to an Afro-Cuban future for jazz music."[134] Eventually, Gillespie hired the black Cuban Chano Pozo to play the congas in his 1940s band. The African American drummer Max Roach, who was a Muslim, also played with him. Gillespie said, "The music proclaimed our identity; it made every statement we truly wanted to make."[135] Moreover, Charlie Parker (1920–1955), the alto saxophone genius of bebop from Kansas City, known for his modern ideas about rhythm, melody, and harmony, played with Gillespie in a 1944 stint at the Three Deuces Club on 52nd Street after the recording ban ended.[136] Although Parker was known for his compositions "Cherokee" and "Confirmation," he also played with Gillespie's band in performances of "A Night in Tunisia" and "Dizzy Atmosphere" at Carnegie Hall in 1947, a concert that also featured Pozo, who played congas, and Lorenzo Salan, who played bongos, on "Cubano-Be, Cubano-Bop."[137] During the last year of his life, 1955, Charlie Parker stayed in Ahmed Basheer's Greenwich Village apartment after he collapsed in the street. Basheer, who was a convert to Islam, took care of Parker, and explained that "Charlie was interested in the Moslem religion. His Mohamedan name was Saluda Hakim. He knew a little . . . Arabic."[138]

When Boston's black jazz fans were in New York, they experienced the convergence of three important cultural and political developments that influenced the militancy of bebop, its ethos of coolness, religious experimentation among blacks, and the social justice values that jazz and Islam shared. First, the New York Police Department and Licensing Commission closed the Savoy, the elegant interracial ballroom on Lenox Avenue in Harlem, where the most talented black lindy hoppers danced to the music of Dinah Washington and Lionel Hampton, and where white women danced with black men.[139] The doors of the Savoy were locked from April 22 to October 15, 1943, because city officials in the Bureau of Social Hygiene claimed that the ballroom promoted prostitution and was responsible for a venereal disease epidemic among the Coast Guard servicemen who went there for entertainment.[140]

In closing the Savoy, they didn't just close a ballroom, they closed a cultural institution that was central to the artistic freedom, racial affirmation, and self-determination of many black New Yorkers. By 1941, black New Yorkers encompassed a population of 458,000 people, including large numbers of southern and Caribbean blacks who identified Harlem as the global Mecca of political activism and youth culture.[141] The Savoy Ballroom was their most important space for the musical and dance expressions of black Atlantic cool and the experimentation with Islamic and Christian elements in jazz that black residents embraced during World War II.

Black New Yorkers struggled to reopen the Savoy, critiqued the Police Department's stereotypes of African Americans and jazz in Harlem, and cited racism and interracial social interactions as the reasons for closing down the iconic club.[142] NAACP head Walter White, Brotherhood of Sleeping Car Porters leader A. Philip Randolph, and city councilman Adam Clayton Powell Jr. embraced black affirmation and circulated public complaints about the closure of the Savoy Ballroom, and the black newspaper the *Amsterdam News* published an influential article, "Mixed Dancing Closed Savoy Ballroom."[143] Although the Savoy did eventually reopen, the black struggle there was a sign of the World War II times, when African Americans dealt with harsh forms of racism and segregation in the Northeast.

The second development that jazz fans experienced on their journey to African American Islam was the rise of black internationalism. New York had the largest Afro-Caribbean communities in the United States, and black residents of Harlem continued to be deeply moved by the Jamaican-derived Pan-Africanism of the Universal Negro Improvement Association.

Boston and New York jazz fans who washed dishes at Jimmy's Chicken Shack "would talk a lot about Garvey's concepts in terms of how they could benefit us as a people."[144] The co-workers at Jimmy's Chicken Shack included John Elroy Sanford, who was nicknamed Chicago Red (and later on, Redd Foxx) because of his red hair and sly raunchy jokes. During World War II, Chicago Red and his Boston co-worker came under the sway of the black radical leader Vicki Garvin, who influenced them to read communist literature and attend meetings of the Communist Party in Harlem, although they never joined. Red's co-worker, who first met Garvin at Small's Paradise, continued to be drawn to her fascinating discussions about race, politics, and revolution, which placed their local concerns in an international perspective.[145]

Harlem's growing black internationalism, bebop, and anti-black racism inspired black musicians and their fans, including those from Boston, to reimagine black solidarities with Asians, especially with Japan, and to test the political and religious boundaries of African American experiences in the 1940s.[146] Some of the members of the jazz community questioned the wisdom of the progressive politics promoting the Double V Campaign of "Victory at Home and Abroad," which encouraged African Americans to embrace the fight for democracy overseas as a way to win the struggle for racial equality and citizenship rights at home.[147] The systemic racism in jazz that zoot suiters and lindy hoppers experienced in Harlem and Roxbury demonstrated that Jim Crow discrimination and segregation prevailed in the North, despite Franklin D. Roosevelt's 1941 Fair Employment Practices Committee, which was supposed to eliminate racism in federal government and defense industry jobs.[148]

While World War II was being fought, jazz musicians and fans witnessed a resurgence of a global black consciousness and interconnected resistance movements such as the Pacific Movement of the Eastern World, which led some African Americans to support Japan's challenge to American white supremacy, even after the Japanese military bombed Pearl Harbor in 1941. Accordingly, to avoid being drafted into the US military while he was living in New York in 1943, a zoot suiter from Boston "started noising around that I was frantic to join . . . the Japanese Army."[149] This crucial aspect of his act to avoid serving in the military reflected the political spirit of those African American men in Harlem who were reluctant to register for the draft; this group of men included blacks like Robert Jordan, Lester Holness, Ralph Green, James Thornhill, and Carlos Cooks, who were arrested in 1942 because of their pro-Japanese political activities.[150] In nearby Brooklyn, the FBI became aware of Moorish Science Temple member William Briggs-Bey in 1943 when he announced, "We have been warned by the Japanese Government that soon a starvation will take place in Europe. . . . I, myself . . . will leave for Tokyo . . . as soon as I can raise $1000."[151] In the 1940s, the Federal Bureau of Investigation believed that the Moorish Science Temple of America and the Nation of Islam were hatching plans with Japanese organizers in the big cities such as New York, Chicago, and Detroit to unify the darker races of the world and to conquer the United States while white men were fighting the war in Europe and the Pacific, and it planned to break up these movements by investigating African American Muslim men and their sympathizers for Selective Service violations.[152] All of these black internationalist developments resonated with the militancy of bebop musicians and jazz fans in New York City and Boston, and eventually, "their affinity for and conversion to Islam was one of the most important ways in which they protested racism and established their independence and identity."[153]

The third cultural development, one that shaped Boston jazz fan Malcolm Little's black radical thinking about freedom and self-determination as a future Nation of Islam leader, was the Harlem Race Riot (also called the Zoot Suit Riots) that took place on August 1 and 2, 1943.

According to his account, black people began "hollering and running north from 125th street . . . smashing store windows and taking everything they could grab and carry. . . . Within an hour, every New York City cop seemed to be in Harlem."[154] Estimates suggest that the New York Police Department killed five people and arrested 550 Harlem residents, 300 people were injured, and many white-owned businesses were destroyed.[155] The uprising began at the Braddock Hotel when white New York policeman James Collins shot and arrested Robert Bandy, a black Army policeman who was defending his mother. Eventually 3,000 black New Yorkers surrounded the police station on 123rd Street and fought with the police, broke windows, and overturned vehicles to protest the shooting.[156]

The scholarship on the Harlem Race Riot brings to light some of the themes of counterculture protest and power that influenced Boston and New York jazz fans' political ideas on systemic racism and black socioeconomic inequities in the 1940s. George Lipsitz argues that World War II racial tensions between blacks and whites in American cities reached a breaking point because of the successful African American efforts to promote the Double V Campaign, which resulted in resentment among whites about new black economic and political power.[157] Luis Alvarez connects the Harlem Riot to the Zoot Suit Riots in Los Angeles and San Diego, California, and to race riots in Mobile, Alabama; Beaumont, Texas; and Detroit in 1943. The cultural, political, and economic progress made by nonwhite urban youth in black and Mexican communities during the war was considered a threat to the systemic power of white mainstream communities in the United States. The youthful political consciousness of the zoot suiters in Harlem and Boston resonated with the rebellious and oppositional spirit of black and brown youth who were so strongly drawn to jazz, a music that exemplified black Atlantic identity and creativity and its rising interest in Islam. Sociologists Kenneth B. Clark and James Baker interviewed African American zoot suiters who participated in the Harlem Riot and circulated a new concept, "zoot effect" to explain the systemic racism that caused the riot.[158] According to Clark and Baker, "the stability of the individual personality and the stability of the larger society are inextricably interrelated and therefore the socially accepted dehumanization of an individual or group must inevitably manifest itself in societal disturbances."[159]

Some black Boston jazz fans in New York were deeply affected by these events, and they returned to Boston, where they began to explore Islam. The cultural and political power of the zoot suiters and their unique presentations of black Atlantic cool had finally reached beyond the realm of clothing, sounds, dance, and countercultural expressions. Along with many other black urban youth, Boston jazz fans and musicians began to study in earnest the new transnational religious traditions that would lead to the emergence of Islam as the iconic religion of African American religious internationalism later in the 1940s.

Introducing the Ahmadiyya Muslim Community in Boston and India

Sympathetic to expressions of African American transnational spiritual consciousness that had arisen out of jazz, musicians and their fans explored successive presentations of Islam in the United States, beginning with the Ahmadiyya Muslim Community. Boston was one of the key cities in which this exploration took place, as zoot suiters, swing jazz musicians, bebop artists, and fans came under the sway of Ahmadi missionaries from India. The Ahmadiyya Muslim Community, which was established in the 1880s in the Muslim communities of the Punjab in India, established international missions in Africa, Europe, and the United States that offered new ways to reimagine Islam in the modern world of the twentieth century. They distributed translated versions of the Qur'an in a variety of vernacular languages and published literature promoting a jihad of words that refuted misrepresentations of Islam in the modern world.

Hazarat Mirza Ghulam Ahmad founded the movement, emphasizing "continuous prophecy." He presented himself as a prophet of Islam, an avatar of Krishna, Christianity, and Islam's promised Messiah, and a mujadid, a special person sent by God to revive the faith at the commencement of every Islamic century.[160] Sunni Muslims in India opposed the Ahmadis because their belief in continuous prophecy did not conform to the Sunni mainstream belief in the seal of prophecy after Muhammad.[161]

However, the Ahmadiyya Muslim Community accepted the basic tenets of Sunni Islam: the unity of Allah; Muhammad as Allah's Messenger; the Qur'an as the word of Allah; and belief in bodily resurrection, final judgment, angels, and commandments prescribing behavior. The Ahmadis also embraced the ceremonial duties encompassed in the Five Pillars of Islam: (1) the confession of faith, "There is no God but Allah and Muhammad is God's Prophet"; (2) five prayers every day facing Mecca; (3) annual fasting in the month of Ramadan; (4) almsgiving to a fund for the poor; and (5) pilgrimage to Mecca at least once in a Muslim's life.[162] Ghulam Ahmad died in 1908, and the Ahmadiyya Muslim Community eventually separated into two factions in India. The Lahore group aimed to reunite with Sunni Islam. The more powerful Qadian group established missionary work in the United States and continued to circulate the original teachings of Ghulam Ahmad; its members were persecuted by Sunni Muslims in India.[163]

Perhaps more than any other Muslim community in the World War II era, the Ahmadis were able to penetrate the black Atlantic boundaries between race, class, color, religion, and style to establish a significant spiritual presence among black jazz musicians that would continue to inspire African American conversions to Islam later in the twentieth century, when the jazz community began to engage with the Nation of Islam and Sunni Islam. The Indian missionaries and supporters of the Ahmadiyya Muslim Community were wealthy businessmen, profession-als, and property owners who had established a successful missionary infrastructure of publications and outreach programs, with religious leaders well established in England and Ghana in the early twentieth century. As a result, the first Ahmadi missionaries in the United States in the 1920s were able to utilize resources and conversion strategies that were already in place. Initially, they focused their proselytizing work on African American business owners, intellectuals, and Pan-Africanists and discussed the Garveyite themes of black affirmation, freedom, and self-determination in their American Islamic networks and publications such as the *Moslem Sunrise*.

But the Ahmadiyya Muslim Community eventually sought out be-boppers as well. Not only were the beboppers fascinated by the religious internationalism that characterized World War II jazz communities, but they seemed eager to extend their musical innovations like impro-visation and experimentation to their efforts to reconfigure black po-litical and religious identities as well. Malcolm Little and his musician friend Shorty Jarvis were two of the first blacks in Boston's jazz com-munity whom the Ahmadiyya missionaries tried to convert to Islam in the 1940s. Malcolm's backstory and jazz story, which follow below, offer a case study of how the themes of African American religious in-ternationalism, black Atlantic cool, black masculinity, experimentation with Islamic and Christian influences in jazz, and introduction to Islam through an encounter with the Ahmadiyya Muslim Community played out in the life of the young Malcolm Little, who was to become one of the major figures of the mid-twentieth century.

The Formation of Malcolm Little's Jazz Identity: From Pan-Africanism to the Zoot Style and the Ahmadiyya

Malcolm Little was born in Omaha, Nebraska, on May 19, 1925. His father, Earl Little, a Baptist minister from Georgia, and his mother, Lou-ise Langdon Norton Little, a Caribbean UNIA member from Grenada, were dedicated organizers for the Marcus Garvey movement in Canada and the United States. Earl and Louise taught their children, Wilfred, Hilda, Philbert, Malcolm, Reginald, Yvonne, and Wesley, to be proud of their militant Garveyite activism in Omaha, Milwaukee, East Chicago, and Lansing. According to Malcolm's daughter Ilyasah Shabazz, the Little siblings never lost Marcus Garvey's internationalist vision of black liberation and social justice. Thus, Malcolm was a politically self-aware supporter of Pan-Africanism well before his involvement with the Nation of Islam in prison in the late 1940s. His brothers and sisters also converted to the Nation of Islam during the 1940s, and by the late 1950s, Malcolm had become the Nation's chief minister. In the wake of President John F. Kennedy's assassination in 1963, when an ideological rift developed between the Nation of Islam leader Elijah Muhammad and his protégé Malcolm X, the loss of Muhammad's support forced Malcolm to leave the Nation of Islam. He converted to Sunni Islam during his hajj (pilgrimage) to Mecca, adopted the Muslim name El-Hajj Malik El-Shabazz, and became a human rights activist in the global Pan-African liberation struggle. Malcolm established the Muslim Mosque Inc. and the Organization of Afro-American Unity, a secular black human rights group in New York City, and gave speeches in Africa, the Middle East, and Europe in 1964. He was assassinated in the Audubon Ballroom in Harlem on February 21, 1965.

Malcolm Little's autobiography is the first document that unfolds the story of black Islamic and black Christian influences on World War II jazz, influences that originated in Boston at the beginning of what I see as the golden age of African American Islam and jazz. During his late teens and early twenties, Malcolm Little was influenced by new religious and racial identities, musical styles, and protest movements in a world where blacks were increasingly aware of the important role they played on a global stage. As a teenager in the early 1940s, he brought a conscious Christian sensibility and perspective to his participation in Boston's jazz culture. As we saw earlier in this chapter, this Christian sensibility had a fascinating influence on black secular dance such as the lindy hop. But Malcolm would soon abandon Christianity, and he ultimately came to realize that his years in Boston represented a significant turning point in his life: "All praise is due to Allah that I went to Boston when I did. . . . No physical move in my life has been more critical and profound."[164] He was fifteen when in 1941, during World War II, he arrived in Boston's Park Square terminal after a long Greyhound bus ride from Michigan. Here Malcolm Little found a new home with his half-sister Ella Little Collins at 72 Dale Street in Roxbury. He lived in Massachusetts for twelve years, and Boston's close-knit black community (which in the 1940s included a few sections of Roxbury and the South End), as well as New York City, played a key role in introducing him to black Atlantic forms of expression about Christianity and in forming his musical identity, his masculinity, his conversion to Islam, and his thinking about black liberation.

Like numerous other African American musicians and their fans, Malcolm Little was initially associated with Roxbury's churches, where he was introduced to the freedom, equilibrium, and resistance strategies of black Atlantic cool. Malcolm learned about the spirituality of black Atlantic urbanites by taking Sunday walks among the crowds of churchgoers on Blue Hill Avenue, Warren Street, and Humboldt Avenue in Roxbury. In 1941 he attended Townsend Street Baptist Church in Roxbury with his cousins Sas and Gracie. Malcolm sang gospel hymns in the choir and was in the church's Boy Scout troop for a short time.[165] In the same year the young Malcolm sometimes attended forums and youth activities at St. Mark Congregational Church and Social Center in Roxbury, where he came briefly under the sway of the Reverend Samuel Leroy Laviscount, the church's pastor, who was known for his charismatic leadership that inspired black youth to think critically about freedom.[166] St. Mark provided social services, a gymnasium, programs, and clubs that focused primarily on African American and West Indian youth in Roxbury. Even still, like some jazz artists, Malcolm believed that Boston's churches did not support black resistance against racism or the values of liberation, black affirmation, and self-determination that he had learned from his father, a Baptist minister who preached the Pan-African message of the UNIA. Around the time of his initiation in jazz in 1941, he began to question his Christian identity and later on, to explore African American Islam, which was gaining ground among the jazz community. Evaluating his new life in Roxbury, Malcolm explained that Boston had freed him from being "a brainwashed black Christian . . . begging to integrate" with whites.[167] As a result, he rejected Christianity during his first year in Boston and immersed himself in the Caribbean and African American world of jazz.

Roxbury's black Atlantic culture resonated with the internationalist perspectives that Malcolm had learned from his parents, who were dedicated but isolated UNIA activists. During his childhood in the 1930s, he had often accompanied his father, Earl Little, the president of the UNIA branch in Omaha, when he talked about Marcus Garvey in black churches and homes in the Midwest.[168] According to Malcolm's brother Wilfred Little Shabazz, their family read the *Negro World* and Marryshow's *West Indian* paper every day after school and "grew up thinking in an international sense."[169] There were few Caribbean blacks in Lansing, Michigan, where Malcolm had previously lived and where his father was murdered by white supremacists. Now he lived in Boston, a black mecca for Garveyism and swing and bebop jazz, with Afro-Caribbean residents who lived next door to and across the street from their northern and southern black neighbors, and even married them. Malcolm's sister Ella, for example, married Lloyd Oxley, a Jamaican doctor and a member of the UNIA in the 1930s. (The marriage later ended in divorce.) Thus the intermingling of Afro-Caribbean and black southern diasporas and resistance movements, along with the blending of their musical and religious traditions, had deep roots in Malcolm's own Boston family.

However, it was Boston's southern migrants and their northern children who had the strongest impact on the jazz performances of the teenage Malcolm Little, who imitated their cool style, lindy hop dance moves, and zoot suit apparel—all forms of racial affirmation and resistance in the black metropolis. Malcolm "Shorty" Jarvis, a black musician from Roxbury's community of Virginia migrants, introduced Little to some of the famous jazz artists who played in Boston in those years. Jarvis was a teenage trumpeter in Roxbury who performed in Boston's jazz clubs and bars, played one-night stands with Duke Ellington's and Count Basie's bands, and worked for the American Federation of Musicians. Jarvis later explained how jazz shaped these musicians' sense of black affirmation and freedom, as well as his friendship with Malcolm Little: "Jazz was our forum. . . . It was our music. . . . The joints were jumpin'. . . . I was meeting these musicians who traveled the world. . . . I was hearing the influences of the places they'd been, reflected in their music. . . . [They] helped me become open to meeting different kinds of people. One of these people was Malcolm X."[170]

Jarvis was not a homeboy from Michigan, as *The Autobiography of Malcolm X* suggests, but was born in Boston in 1923 and lived in his family's upper Roxbury home on Waumbeck Street. He met Malcolm in a neighborhood pool hall on Humboldt Avenue in 1939, when Malcolm was visiting Boston. Malcolm, who already had a reputation in Boston as a "Cool Daddy-O," schooled Jarvis in jazz's expressive forms of black Atlantic cool and hustling.[171] He preferred to be known as Red, Detroit Red, J.C., or Jack Carleton in those days, and his cool names signified important aspects of his complex identities in the worlds of jazz and African American Islam in which he traveled. As Red, Detroit Red, or J.C., Malcolm hustled, danced, and had the cool presence of body, mind, and spirit to attract and direct the energies of the audiences at the pool halls and Roseland State Ballroom, where he met many of the great jazz artists such as Duke Ellington and Billie Holiday during his stint shining shoes there.

Malcolm's cool was legendary. Sporting a red-conk hairstyle and bold-colored zoot suits, he was a tall, charismatic teenager who looked and danced like a mature black man. His scintillating performances of the lindy hop at Roseland Ballroom involved intricate, syncopated breakaway steps, turns, and lifts, improvised with humor and heroic acrobatics in response to the rhythmic patterns of his African American girlfriend, Gloria Strother (named Laura in the *Autobiography*), and Duke Ellington's swinging orchestra.[172] The brilliance of the musical and dance expressions of these elegant black people shone brighter than the stars in the midnight-blue city sky. They created electrifying communal energy on the dance floor. His immersion in Boston's musical culture influenced Malcolm to experiment with Christian influences in jazz by reshaping the rhythms and sounds of his father's black Baptist religion and the cultural memory of his mother's Afro-Caribbean heritage through his dancing. He described his lived experience of such a performance as follows: "Go, Red, go! . . . It was my reputation . . . that helped to turn the spotlight and the crowd's attention to us. They had never seen the feather lightness that she gave to lindying. . . . I had her in the air, down . . . up again, down whirling. . . . The crowd was shouting and stomping. There was a wall of noise around us. . . . And even Duke Ellington half raised up from his piano stool and bowed."[173] Malcolm's lindy hop performances in Boston and New York exemplified freedom, affirmation, improvisation, call-and-response, composure, balance, and resistance. He loved Duke Ellington's music, with its cool representations of life in the black metropolis, and he enjoyed their friendly conversations when he shined Ellington's and Johnny Hodge's shoes (Hodges was Ellington's alto saxophonist) in Roseland Ballroom.[174] Eventually, he quit his job at Roseland, because he "couldn't find time to shine shoes and dance, too."[175]

Malcolm had been just a teenage boy showing off his first zoot suit when he strutted into Roseland Ballroom in 1941. His relationships with both women and men in the World War II era resonate with the period's larger themes of self-determination and liberation and reflect the black masculinities that he learned from his family, from black Christianity, and finally from African American jazz musicians in the 1940s. His half-brother, Earl Little Jr., who lived in Ella Collins's house in Roxbury, was one of Malcolm's first role models. A professional dancer and singer who performed in Boston nightclubs under the stage name Jimmy Carlton, Earl did not adopt the bourgeois black masculinity of African American Christianity but formulated a black cool style of masculinity that he used on the jazz stage. Earl also served as one of Malcolm's mentors in jazz, introducing Malcolm to Billie Holiday when his act preceded her Boston performance in 1940.[176] Although Earl Little Jr. died from tuberculosis in 1941, when he was only thirty years old, his black cool masculine style continued to influence the development of Malcolm's own identity during the years he spent in Boston and New York.[177]

Another influence was his sister Ella's second husband, Kenneth Collins, who married Ella in 1941 and took Malcolm to Boston's dance halls and jazz clubs in 1941 and 1942. A recent migrant from Lansing, Michigan, the twenty-four-year-old Collins had a reputation in Roxbury as a handsome and cool dancer, and Malcolm emulated those qualities in his representations of masculinities in his chosen zoot suit culture.[178]

The women in Malcolm's life also shaped not only his masculinity but also his interactions with African American religious internationalism and ultimately with African American Islam. Malcolm's half-sister Ella Collins was the central figure in the Little family during Malcolm's years in Boston. She created a home infused with jazz, Garveyism, and a vibrant urban social world that blended southern, northern, and Afro-Caribbean cultural traditions. In this environment, African American men could explore the creative agencies of their masculinities by invoking the social, cultural, and political identities and resistance communities that her family's black Atlantic experiences inspired. Eventually, Malcolm's innovative combination of jazz identity, spirituality, and black masculinities, born in Ella's household, became a paradigm for understanding the conversion experiences of black Muslim youth in the golden age of African American Islam.

When he was fifteen, Malcolm rejected his sister's suggestion that he attend a black church and a private prep school in Boston in order to complete his high school education so that he could eventually become a lawyer.[179] Ella did not approve of Malcolm's zoot-suited friends or his white girlfriend Bea Caragulian, an Armenian American professional nightclub dancer (Sophia in the *Autobiography*), whom he met in Roxbury's pool halls and bars, but she supported him as he found his way into Boston's jazz scene and developed his long-lasting attraction to famous blacks and musicians.[180] Malcolm's new social world included not only talented urban-based musicians, but also political activists, writers, and religious leaders who in the years after World War II influenced his black Atlantic cool style, his masculinity, his conversion experiences, and his interactions with the Nation of Islam and Sunni Islam.

Malcolm Little was involved in a complicated interracial romance and sexual relationship with his white girlfriend Bea Caragulian during his teenage years. Like Duke Ellington and Cab Calloway, he was a light-skinned black, and his skin color defined his black masculinity and jazz identity—as we have seen, he was known for a while as Detroit Red. Although he later became an innovator in the black Atlantic cool practices and African American religious internationalism of jazz that led to his conversion to Islam, the way he performed black masculinity in the 1940s showed his acceptance of the colorism and preference for light-skinned and white women prevalent among African American jazz musicians.

His hustling, exploitation of women, and cocaine habit resonated with the destructive practices and patriarchy of black hypermasculinity. However, in his early years in Boston, Malcolm engaged in a communal masculinity and expressed possibilities for African American unity and transcendence in his elegant performances of the lindy hop with his black girlfriend in Roseland Ballroom.

Later, in New York, Malcolm used the zoot style to highlight a cool countercultural masculinity and his black Atlantic anti-war thinking. He dodged the draft in 1943 by acting crazy and wearing a "wild zoot suit, . . . yellow knob-toe shoes, . . . and a reddish bush of conk" to the Army induction headquarters.[181] He worked out a cool strategy of concentration, performance, improvisation, and humor at the induction office to orchestrate and transform the intentions of his enemies (white doctors and psychiatrists), who ultimately exempted him from military service with a 4-F card. Sometimes, black Atlantic cool is about the drama of exemplifying courage in a crisis by directing an enemy or an audience through performance, style, and humor,[182] as Malcolm did when he whispered to an Army psychiatrist, "Daddy-O, now you and me, we're from the North up here, so don't you tell nobody . . . I want to get sent down South. Organize them . . . soldiers, you dig? Steal us some guns, and kill us some crackers!"[183] His successful plan to avoid the draft reflected the anti-war political thinking of several famous black musicians during World War II, musicians who supported jazz's resistance politics by rejecting systemic racism and embracing the struggles for social justice. Ultimately, Malcolm Little would present several variations of black masculinity during the World War II years and beyond that exemplified the construction of masculinities in jazz and African American Islam.

Hypermasculinity was a militant, disciplined masculine identity that was linked to both self-destructive and redemptive representations of black men. Communal masculinity focused on masculinist practices that exemplified black affirmation and unity. Oppositional masculinity epitomized African American masculine values of respectability, dignity, and bravery that rectified stereotypes of black people. Malcolm began his young years with hypermasculinity, and then experimented with communal masculinity and oppositional masculinity throughout his life.

From 1941 to 1944, Malcolm traveled back and forth between Boston and New York, selling sandwiches on the Yankee Clipper Railroad, waiting tables in Jimmy's Chicken Shack, and bartending in Small's Paradise nightclub in Harlem.[184] His work on the Yankee Clipper, Silver Meteor, New Haven, Hartford, Seaboard, and Atlantic Coast railroads allowed him to travel to black communities in Washington, DC, Philadelphia, Lansing, St. Petersburg, and Miami in the 1940s. He supplemented his official railroad work by selling marijuana to jazz artists who traveled to the East Coast cities to perform their music, and as a result, "was known to almost every popular Negro musician around New York."[185] Malcolm's hustling life was influenced by riding those trains. But his travels to New York also allowed him to witness Billie Holiday's performances at the Onyx Club on 52nd Street, the emergence of bebop jazz at Monroe's Uptown House on 138th Street and Minton's Playhouse on 118th Street, the closure of the Savoy Ballroom, Harlem's growing black internationalism shaped by Garveyism and pro-Japanese solidarity, and the Harlem Race Riot. In this way, his musical perspective, his black masculine identity, and his political perspective about race and class began to merge.

Malcolm's musical values of freedom and improvisation were deeply shaped by these events, and his mind was full of radical political ideas and curiosity about African American religious internationalism and Islamic experimentation even as his participation in street life, hustling, and recreational drug use began to compromise his personal stability toward the end of World War II. From July to October 1944, Malcolm capped his black Atlantic jazz performances in New York by recreating himself as a surrogate for his dead brother Earl Little Jr., taking on his stage name Jimmy Carlton, and dancing and drumming at the Lobster Pond club in Times Square for an audience of cool people.[186] This performance would be the culmination of Malcolm's New York jazz sojourn. A potentially life-threatening conflict with his hustling mentor West Indian Archie later in 1944 forced him to return to Boston.[187]

When Malcolm returned to Boston in 1944 after his sojourn in Harlem ended, his black masculinity continued to evolve, as he embraced bebop's cool new sartorial style. He described in the *Autobiography* the transformation of his definition of a well-dressed jazz man: "I didn't lindy-hop any more now. . . . I wouldn't have been caught in a zoot suit now. All of my suits were conservative. A banker might have worn my shoes."[188] Bebop nightlife was thriving in Boston at the time of Malcolm's homecoming, so he went out to the black clubs around Massachusetts Avenue, Columbus Avenue, and Tremont Street where his old friend trumpeter Shorty Jarvis played.

Malcolm's religious ideas evolved as well, especially after he and Shorty Jarvis were introduced to Islam in Roxbury. Although the *Au-*

tobiography is silent about this important fact, Malcolm and Shorty began to consider conversion to Islam as a cool expression of African American religious internationalism and blackness. In this they joined many black young people whose religious identities emerged from the countercultural musical and political styles of jazz. Jazz musicians, zoot suiters, and beboppers had begun to embrace internationalist perspectives on race and religion that led black people in diaspora to think of themselves as more closely aligned with Africans and the "darker races of the world" than with white Americans and Europeans, allowing them to construct powerful strategies against racial oppression in the United States. Although Shorty and Malcolm resorted to hustling and robbery to support themselves, they were at the same time deeply involved in the study of Islam, specifically as presented by missionaries representing India's Ahmadiyya Muslim Community.[189]

The Islamic spiritual journey of Malcolm Little and Shorty Jarvis began when they saw Abdul Hameed, an Ahmadiyya Muslim from India, in the streets of Boston. "He was a very distinguished man," according to Shorty. "He wore a black fez with a long tassel and a neatly trimmed beard. He looked Asian in some ways, and walking around in Roxbury in that attire, . . . he attracted a lot of attention. . . . One day I introduced myself as a young musician." Hameed lived on Hammond Street in lower Roxbury and had an impressive grand piano in his home.[190]

Shorty initiated the first connections with the Indian Muslim because of their mutual interest in music. When the young jazz musician visited Hameed's house, he was treated to an impressive concert of classical piano music and commented, "I had never heard a finer quality of sound from a piano."[191] Then Hameed showed him fascinating books on Egyptian and Indian history, religion, and music theory. Shorty put it this way: "I felt like I was receiving a college education in one visit. I knew I had to introduce Malcolm to this gentleman."[192]

Shorty spent a lot of time talking about Abdul Hameed's knowledge of music and religion to his "partner in crime," and finally Malcolm visited Hameed's house.[193] Soon a deeper spiritual connection developed between the three men, as Hameed taught the two black youth about Islam. Hameed's lessons influenced Malcolm and Shorty to study the Five Pillars of Islam, Arabic prayers, the Qur'an, and Ahmadi literature.

Shorty remembered, "After meeting Malcolm, Abdul took great interest in us and spent many hours teaching us. He thought we deserved a better way of life than the one we were living. It was Abdul Hameed who presented us our first mention of Islam."[194] Hameed helped Shorty and Malcolm to expand their minds to understand a new spiritual philosophy and a new presentation of African American religious internationalism and coolness based on a new holy book, the Qur'an; a new global Muslim community, the ummah; a new language, Arabic; and new interactions with Asians and Africans involved in transnational religious and political networks. As we shall see in chapter 4, John Coltrane and McCoy Tyner had parallel experiences with Islam, as they embraced a new spiritual commitment that allowed them to explore and circulate new internationalist sounds and musical forms from African and Asian sources.

Malcolm "Shorty" Jarvis took the lead in exploring these internationalist modes of spirituality and cool beyond Hameed's lessons, interacting with Boston's small enclave of Arab immigrants in the South End, including individuals who performed mystical healing rituals. One of these was a black Egyptian named Rashee. Hameed introduced Shorty to him in his Washington Street apartment. At the time, Shorty was lovesick and was looking for a way to contact one of his girlfriends, Jackie Taylor, who had suddenly disappeared. Rashee meditated over a skull illuminated by a lighted candle and asked him to return with a picture of his girlfriend and several silver dollars. During Shorty's second visit the healing ritual continued: chanting a prayer in Arabic, Rashee wrote Arabic words on the photograph of his girlfriend and wrapped the money up in the folded picture. Shorty was instructed to bury the package in the cemetery close to a gravestone. Four days later, Jackie contacted him by telephone and visited his house to discuss their relationship.[195]

Shorty later noted, "My introduction to Abdul Hameed and Rashee had given me a lifetime of food for thought. . . . Malcolm and I at this time were leading very stupid lives. That's why we got locked up."[196] They did not have time to complete their lessons with Hameed or to convert to the Ahmadiyya Muslim Community. In January 1946, Shorty and Malcolm were arrested in Boston on burglary charges, along with Bea Caragulian, Malcolm's white girlfriend, her sister Joyce, and Kora Marderosian.[197] Hameed was persistent in his missionary work in these changing times, when bebop became the main theater for African American religious internationalism and the Ahmadiyya Muslim Community's historic interactions with black jazz musicians. Hameed continued his mentoring of Malcolm X and Shorty Jarvis, visiting them in Massachusetts prisons from 1946 to 1952.[198] Ultimately, however, they embraced a different religious path, in the Nation of Islam, a community that exemplified how the parallel goals and values of African American Islam and jazz became synthesized in the minds of black youth during this period. It is to the description and analysis of the Nation of Islam and its first appearance in American prisons that we now turn.

2

"Turn to Allah, Pray to the East"

Bebop and the Nation of Islam's Mission to Blacks in Prison

In the 1940s and 1950s, the Nation of Islam made its first appearance in American prisons, where the themes of resistance to systemic racism and racial separatism, black masculinity, African American religious internationalism, Asiatic identity, and restoration of the black body evoked by the Islamic message found a ready audience among the many black men incarcerated there. In this chapter we will examine black men's identification with the Nation of Islam in Massachusetts prisons. In particular, we will trace the influence of bebop jazz on incarcerated blacks' spiritual journeys to the Nation of Islam at this time. Bebop was a new musical form quite different from the earlier musical world of swing. Bebop encouraged performances of black masculinities and offered a creative space where new visions of African American religious internationalism flourished due to its heady mix of spiritual philosophy, musical practices, black identities, and Islamic experimentation. This story includes Malcolm X's and Shorty Jarvis's conversions to the Nation of Islam in Massachusetts prisons as well, conversions that exemplify the values of black affirmation, freedom, and self-determination that Islam and bebop shared. The chapter concludes with an examination of the interplay between musical and religious traditions at Boston's Nation of Islam Temple, which Malcolm established along with black jazz musicians and World War II veterans in 1954, two years after his release from prison. For almost eighty years, the Nation of Islam has used its construction of prison masculinities to influence the spiritual awakening of incarcerated black men, a tradition that illustrates the larger ideas and social realities in religion and music that strengthened the Nation of Islam and made it so attractive to black people both in and out of prison during the years after World War II.

Bebop, Prison Masculinities, Black Internationalism, and the Nation of Islam

Ultimately, what the Nation of Islam offered to the many incarcerated black men who converted in the postwar period was a way to rise above their situation, a way not to remain bitter victims of the prison system. The resistance strategies and the agency for freedom and racial affirmation that they and other marginalized African American youth in the jazz community embraced after World War II reflected the self-determination of a new black Islamic counterculture that was emerging among incarcerated and urban blacks, one that critiqued Christianity and systemic racism and expressed the groundbreaking artistic and intellectual creativity of bebop. We discussed in chapter 1 how the quick tempos, the bold intensity in harmony, rhythm, and melody, and the dynamic improvisation of virtuoso bebop soloists such as Dizzy Gillespie and Charlie Parker and their rhythm sections created a new soundtrack for black identities that influenced some blacks in Boston to abandon the zoot suit culture of swing jazz and to explore Islam in the Ahmadiyya Muslim Community in Roxbury. Guthrie P. Ramsey Jr. goes deeper into the roots of the bebop counterculture that inspired this generation, arguing that "it was there in the midst of the give and go of rhythms, subtle timbral shifts, and cagey harmonic developments—that audiences were able to discern that a new day had dawned in popular music, and that new communities and identities were being formed as well."[1] Moreover, bebop's radical black Atlantic experimentation in music, politics, style, and religion inspired a new sense of creativity and African American religious internationalism that young men embraced when they explored Islam in Roxbury's Ahmadiyya Muslim Community or converted to the Nation of Islam in prison.

Ramsey also argues persuasively that the making of jazz musical geniuses like the bebop trumpeter Charlie Parker and the pianist Bud Powell, or a religious and political innovator like some men in the Nation of Islam, goes beyond the story of an extraordinary talent. He writes that musical performers' and religious personalities' experiences in the jazz community are "also the product of a complex social process. Hypersexuality, . . . drug addiction, western and African musical [and religious] priorities, the debates surrounding black . . . intellectual prowess, and bebop as a social and musical paradigm" are also important factors to consider in their stories.[2] These factors figured prominently in the radical reshaping of religious and political virtuosos in the golden age of African American Islam and jazz. Their struggles to evolve from incarcerated youth to Muslim men in the prison spaces of Massachusetts became legendary in the larger jazz and Islamic communities in the United States, and their eventual embrace of the Nation of Islam's prison masculinity followed the lead of the bebop artists whose musical performances and spirituality were deeply rooted in the shared goals and values of Islam and jazz, black internationalism, and the exploration of new militant African American masculinist identities in the late 1940s and 1950s.

In prison and in urban black communities, jazz musicians, their fans, and Muslim converts were attracted to the improvisational discourses and black Atlantic practices that had reshaped the musical and religious traditions they embraced. According to Ingrid Monson, bebop's internationalist "turn toward non-Western modes of spiritual expression and ritual enactment in the jazz world was connected to an identification with both the anticolonial struggles of the emerging non-Western nations (in Africa and Asia) and the cultural heritage of the African continent in particular."[3] Although the Nation of Islam's unique perspective on black internationalism, black masculinity, and non-Western spirituality permeated the African American postwar era, until now its religious passion has not been reconciled with jazz experimentation, prison masculinities, and the common ground it shared with legions of black musicians whose work also exemplified the goals and values of social justice that Islam and jazz shared.

My analysis here is based on the work of scholars who shed light on the prison masculinities like those adopted by incarcerated converts to the Nation of Islam. Rashad Shabazz examines prison spaces, tracing the ways "the deployment of carceral techniques—surveillance, policing, and containment" shaped the construction of black male identities.[4] Black men survived their ordeals, he explains, "through the performance of prison masculinities . . . characterized by 'ultramasculine,' hyperaggressive performance, . . . physical toughness and the willingness to negotiate and survive violence."[5] Thus incarcerated black men who were unable to attain the political and economic power encompassed and expressed in hegemonic white masculinity sometimes used physical domination and hypermasculine presentations of their bodies to ensure their own safety and gain attention and respect in the penal spaces. We will see later on that although a similar kind of hypermasculinity governed some black men's identities during their first months of incarceration in Massachusetts state prison in the late 1940s, their earlier musical identities in bebop jazz had primed them for an embrace of the Nation of Islam in prison.

Shabazz goes on to explore the aesthetics of black music as an important redemptive link between black masculinity, black communities, and prison cultures. In this context, incarcerated black men, like jazz fans and musicians on the outside, used the aesthetics and spirituality of the music to "cultivate their bodies [and minds] to send a variety of messages about the meaning of masculinity to themselves and others."[6] Although prison studies scholars Don Sabo, Terry A. Kupers, and Willie James London insist that "prison is an ultramasculine world where nobody talks about masculinity," the autobiographies of black converts to Islam discuss the links between African American masculinity, the aesthetics of the music, the politics of incarceration, black internationalism, and conversion to the Nation of Islam while incarcerated.[7]

Zain Abdullah points out that performances of black masculinities were fluid and constantly evolving from a militant and disciplined hypermasculinity, to communal masculinity exemplifying black affirmation and unity, and ultimately to oppositional masculinity, which conveyed respectability, dignity, and bravery.[8] Islam's dynamic and creative revisions of African American masculinities attracted new converts to the Nation of Islam's non-Western religious traditions, offering the converts a purifying consciousness that inspired a sense of black redemption, freedom, and self-determination.[9] The Nation of Islam encouraged male converts to adopt new black Atlantic cool standards of religious complexity, power, and virtuosity in their performances of black masculinities, just as "the boppers' . . . ideal of virtuosity and complexity . . . connected instrumental proficiency with standards of excellence, power, and manhood."[10] As we will see, African American Islam and bebop jazz "co-exist in close proximity to one another, listen to one another, and respond in a variety of ways."[11] Moreover, religious and musical presentations of African American masculinities overlapped in some incarcerated black men's experiences, expressing the transcendent sense of balance, purification, and control that characterized Islamic cultures and bebop in the 1940s and 1950s.

As black men experienced their conversion in prison, bebop's and the Nation of Islam's values of freedom, transformative creativity, black Atlantic cool consciousness, and self-determination reshaped their destructive hypermasculine practices of petty criminality, allowing a redemptive and militant black Muslim variety of hypermasculinity to emerge, one that prized "bodily discipline, mental dexterity, and moral fortitude."[12] The Nation of Islam's redemptive hypermasculinity would eventually empower a dynamic transformation of African American converts' lives, one that was linked to the internationalist aspects of black Islamic spiritual conversion, which purified and disciplined the body and the mind and marked the place "where they gained a new tongue, the place where their 'ex'-selves were left behind, and the location where their redemption begins."[13]

The redemptive forms of hypermasculinity that initially helped to transform black men's minds and souls in prison eventually led to their search for religious truth. Lillie A. Thomas-Burgess's research shows that for black Christian men who converted to Islam in prison, seeking the truth was a way to become "enlightened, transformed, and disciplined."[14] According to Thomas-Burgess, "Seeking the truth, to some, was based on a strong desire to have a relationship with Allah. . . . Islam was the religion that afforded them an opportunity to do an in-depth study [of the Qur'an] in order . . . to find the true religion."[15] For some musicians' part, the black Atlantic cool style of purification and conversion to black Islam, which on a broader scale gave dynamic meaning to African American religious internationalism, involved a sense of balance, reshaping their souls, spirits, and thoughts in a way that paralleled bebop, where "line merges with oscillation, motion flows with arrest, naked flesh encloses purity of mind, to make a single leap of faith."[16]

Many incarcerated jazz fans' purification process began when they stopped eating pork. According to Edward E. Curtis IV, rejecting pork, which was a forbidden food for members of the Nation of Islam, played a central role in the "Islamization of the black body."[17] Curtis's research is important because it reveals the Nation of Islam's evolving strategies for transnational Islamization. The Nation of Islam's presentation of an

Asiatic identity "combined certain elements of Afro-Eurasian Islamic traditions, especially Sunni traditions, with African American religious practices . . . creating a form of Islamic practice" that resonated with the global agency, creativity, and improvisational focus of bebop jazz.[18] The Nation's Asiatic notion of blackness gave meaning to the spiritual liberation and economic self-determination of non-European people in the modern world, and its vision of African American religious internationalism appealed to the bebop musicians in New York, who exhibited an affinity for Afro-Japanese solidarity during World War II. The founder of the Nation of Islam, W. D. Fard, and his successor Elijah Muhammad embraced the Afro-Asian ties that encompassed Arabs, Japanese, Chinese, Pakistanis, Indians, Filipinos, Iranians, Latinos, Native Americans, and people of African descent and supported the circulation of pro-Tokyo propaganda among black Americans in the 1930s and 1940s.

The successive presentations of musical identities, non-Western religion, and black internationalism that culminated in the Nation of Islam's unique religious consciousness shaped black jazz men's redemptive and militant hypermasculinity in prison and convinced them to perform prayers to Allah and support the teachings of Elijah Muhammad. Moreover, they were beboppers, and according to jazz studies scholar Eddie S. Meadows, "the Beboppers' affinity for and conversion to Islam was one of the most important ways in which they protested racism and established their independence and identity" during this period.[19] Conversion to Islam also gave them a way to express their disappointment in Christianity. "The rift between Christian and Muslim beliefs and practices was clear for some Beboppers. . . . They viewed Christianity as a religion that preached equality and did not practice it," noted Meadows. In contrast, "they viewed Islam as a solution to their social problems and a religion that both advocated and practiced equality."[20]

The Nation of Islam appealed to beboppers like the black men in Massachusetts prisons because it was a new urban transnational religion that, like jazz, critiqued and challenged Christianity and presented a creative non-Western vision of blackness, freedom, and self-determination. Moreover, its global black religious consciousness resonated with the Pan-Africanism and anticolonialism of "inspirational Garveyism" that emerged in some places after Marcus Garvey's incarceration and exile from the United States in the late 1920s forced him to abandon his executive headquarters in Harlem.[21]

Meadows's assessment suggests another key factor that influenced black jazz musicians and fans to convert to Islam in prison. The beboppers' "musical antagonism that developed . . . because of white appropriation of African American jazz . . . without having direct contact with the community that created it" paralleled the Nation of Islam's critiques of the structural racism that developed because of white American Christianity's links to the sociopolitical networks of colonialism, Atlantic empires, and Jim Crow, and its refusal to practice racial equality in the United States.[22]

The Nation of Islam began with the missionary work of W. D. Fard, or Wallace D. Fard Muhammad, in Detroit, Michigan, in 1930. Fard was a light-skinned Muslim peddler of clothing and silk goods in the black community of Paradise Valley. Although he was not a Muslim of African descent, his specific ethnic origins remain undocumented. Scholar Fatima Fanusie believes that W. D. Fard was a Pakistani Muslim.[23] Historian Z. I. Ansari suggests that Fard was Muhammad Abdullah (1905–1992), a Lahore Ahmadiyya Movement in Islam missionary and imam "from the Indian subcontinent" who resided in Hayward, California, in the 1980s.[24]

According to Edward E. Curtis IV, W. D. Fard's mysterious transnational identity highlights the important theme of black and brown Muslim relations—that "African American Islam was . . . an international discourse shaped in part by contact and exchange with persons from Muslim-majority lands" in Asia and North Africa.[25] As we will see, although the Nation of Islam was a black nationalist movement with programs promoting race pride, racial separatism, and economic prosperity among working-class African Americans, it also employed powerful internationalist religious strategies that resonated with bebop's emphasis on black internationalism, freedom, and political self-determination. Moreover, there was a subtle angle of political agency in Fard's attention to the growing phenomenon of African American religious internationalism and its links to the Islamic world. He impressed his followers by "charting a transnational and transhistorical Blackness"[26] that enabled the Nation of Islam to critique "global racism, imperialism, and colonialism. . . . without ever physically crossing national borders."[27]

As W. D. Fard's religious work evolved in the early 1930s among black southern migrants in Detroit, his presentation of Islam focused on his mission as a prophet of Allah, who "came from the Holy City of Mecca."[28] Moreover, his teachings connected the racist experiences of African Americans to the internationalist struggles of the darker races of the world by convincing black Muslim converts whose ancestors were enslaved that "they were not Americans but Asiatics."[29] Fard argued that the Asiatics are "members of the lost tribe of Shabazz, stolen by traders from the Holy City of Mecca 379 years ago. . . . They are the original people, noblest of the nations of the earth."[30] He declared, "The original people must regain their religion, which is Islam, their language, which is Arabic, and their culture, which is astronomy and higher mathematics. . . . They must live according to the law of Allah. . . . They must clean themselves up—both their bodies and their houses."[31] W. D. Fard established an Afro-Asian identity for his followers and labeled Caucasians the "devil white race" responsible for the enslavement and colonization of the original people, who were all the people of color on the planet.[32]

Eventually, the Nation of Islam's membership would also include Latino and Native American Muslims. The Nation of Islam cultivated its own aesthetics of purification, black Atlantic coolness, and black femininity and masculinity within its patriarchal religious communities. Women captains and lieutenants led the Muslim Girls Training and General Civilization Class to cultivate the Nation's religious and gendered practices among their female counterparts, and Muslim women were the teachers who established and administrated the Muhammad University of Islam, a school for children.[33] Boys and men learned about the Nation of Islam's core religious teachings, black masculine practices, self-defense, and recruitment strategies in the Fruit of Islam, which empowered its impeccably groomed and formally dressed Muslim brothers with the control, calm, and balance of black Atlantic coolness.[34] Both men and women worked in the Nation of Islam's community businesses. In the early 1930s, Elijah Poole (1897–1975), a black migrant from Georgia and an admirer of Marcus Garvey, converted to the Nation of Islam with his wife, Clara. He would soon become W. D. Fard's most trusted Supreme Minister.[35] Fard changed Poole's "slave name" to Elijah Karriem and eventually renamed him Elijah Muhammad.[36] He also gave

Muhammad an Arabic Qur'an and Qur'ans translated into English to use in his religious work.[37]

Fard interpreted the Qur'an for his followers. He introduced his followers to the Islamic dietary practices, which prohibited Muslims from eating pork and drinking alcohol. According to Erdmann D. Benyon, W. D. Fard led the Nation of Islam for four years and converted several thousand blacks to his religion in Chicago and Detroit.[38] He was arrested in Detroit in 1933, and he disappeared on June 30, 1934.[39]

Elijah Muhammad deified W. D. Fard as Allah after his disappearance and designated himself the Messenger of Allah. In the 1930s, Muhammad published a newspaper, the *Final Call to Islam*, and moved to Chicago, where he established Temple No. 2 to escape dangerous factionalism among the other ministers, who wished to assume leadership of the Nation of Islam.[40] Eventually, he traveled between Temple No. 3 in Milwaukee and Temple No. 4 in Washington, DC, to proselytize and to avoid FBI agents and violent encounters with competing ministers.[41] Elijah Muhammad honed the Nation of Islam's black internationalism and its Afro-Asiatic identity during these times, by also fraternizing with a Japanese national, Satokata Takahashi, the founder of Development of Our Own, the leading black American organization for the circulation of pro-Japanese and anti-Western imperialist propaganda during World War II.[42]

In 1942 Muhammad and his son Emmanuel were arrested and convicted "for refusing to register for the draft and for influencing his followers not to register" in Chicago.[43] They were two of the victims of the FBI raids on African American Muslim institutions during World War II and were incarcerated from 1942 to 1946 in the federal correctional institute in Milan, Michigan.[44] Elijah Muhammad's incarceration, according to Clegg, reshaped him to "become the martyr of the Muslims . . . and saintly 'Messenger of Allah'" who came to command "an almost immeasurable loyalty from his small, but growing following."[45] Meadows points out that Muhammad's message appealed to musicians as well as to African Americans impacted by "racism and religious persecution" in the post–World War II era of decolonization and global black liberation.[46] He "taught that blacks were the 'original people' and it was only a matter of time before the oppressors lost their power and blacks regained control of their lives and destinies."[47] Elijah Muhammad also taught that black people must control their own economic destiny and land, and he emphasized the wealth and entrepreneurship of his religious community after his release from prison.[48] The Nation of Islam bought a farm in White Cloud, Michigan, in 1945 and opened a restaurant, bakery, and grocery store in Chicago in 1947.[49] Meadows concludes that "these phenomena coupled with appropriation, innovative and creative approaches to music, and a search for individualism led selective Beboppers and other musicians to Garveyism or Islam" in the 1940s and 1950s.[50]

Elijah Muhammad listened to Count Basie's jazz on the radio during his incarceration in federal prison and developed plans for the Nation of Islam's businesses and farmlands in discussions with other black Muslim men who served sentences in the Milan federal correctional institute in the 1940s.[51] His prison time helped him identify both the radio, with its news and black musical messages, and black men and women in American jails and prisons as two important focal points for the Nation of Islam's missionary work among African Americans.[52] Although Elijah Muhammad did not encourage dance among the members of the Nation of Islam, we will see in chapter 4 that he enjoyed jazz and hired African dancers and drummers and jazz musicians to perform at the Muslims' African Asian bazaars and benefit concerts in the 1960s.

Lillie A. Thomas-Burgess explores the processes of conversion that Muslim leaders such as Elijah Muhammad established to attract incarcerated blacks to Islam. She writes, "Many of the activities in prison da'wah programs focus on making connections between individuals, families, and the community."[53] Muhammad understood that "the Islamic faith considers the family as its central institution and places a high value on family stability."[54] Therefore, the Nation of Islam's missionary work focused on reshaping "social networks that heal and strengthen family ties as a way to assist prisoners to successfully re-enter community life . . . through education, correspondence with prisoners, re-entry support groups, family counseling."[55] From redemptive forms of hypermasculinity to purification to programs that strengthened family ties, the Nation of Islam offered incarcerated beboppers new ways to reshape their identities in prison. As we will see in the next section, the Nation's major themes of resistance, self-determination, and global black religious consciousness were exemplified in the varying forms of masculinity that Malcolm X and Shorty Jarvis adopted during their conversions in Massachusetts prisons.

Malcolm X and Shorty Jarvis: Bebop, Masculinity, and Conversion to the Nation of Islam in Prison

The Boston Police Department arrested Malcolm Little in Roxbury on January 12, 1946. Malcolm confessed his involvement in several household robberies in the Boston suburbs and identified his friends, who were also arrested: his girlfriend Bea Caragulian, her sister Joyce Caragulian, Kora Marderosian, and Malcolm "Shorty" Jarvis. Sonny Brown was also in Malcolm's robbery gang, but he was not arrested.[56] On February 27, 1946, their trial concluded, Malcolm and Shorty were sentenced to serve four concurrent eight- to ten-year prison terms for breaking and entering and larceny. They had stolen jewelry, clothing, silverware, rugs, furniture, and household items that were worth more than $10,000.[57]

At the time of his arrest and trial in 1946, Malcolm's Massachusetts Department of Correction file highlighted his jazz identity by listing "show business" and "entertainer" as two of his occupations and reporting his aliases as Detroit Red, Rhythm Red, and Jack Carlton.[58] However, Malcolm left these identities behind during his prison years, from 1946 to 1952. Ultimately, he came to see his time behind bars as a major turning point in his life, when he and Shorty Jarvis converted to Islam and embraced an innovative spiritual transformation that exemplified the themes of resistance to systemic racism, black masculinity, African American religious internationalism, and purification—themes that are developed in this chapter. This section of the chapter sheds new light on Malcolm's and Shorty's conversion experiences and relies heavily upon Shorty Jarvis's autobiography as well as Malcolm's diary and letters, which did not become available until the twenty-first century, almost forty years after his death. Prior to this, the main source of information on Malcolm's life was the *Autobiography*, co-authored and published by Alex Haley after Malcolm X's assassination in 1965. The new evidence provided by Malcolm's diary and letters is essential to an accurate interpretation of Malcolm's life, because Haley omitted several chapters that Malcolm collaborated on before his death, and seems not to have fully understood the impact of some of the key people who influenced Malcolm's cultural and political life.

Malcolm and Shorty were admitted to Charlestown State Prison after their trial.[59] Malcolm described their first year in Charlestown as "a memory of nutmeg and other semi-drugs, of cursing guards, throwing things out of my cell, balking in the lines, dropping my tray in the dining hall, refusing to answer my number."[60] Although Malcolm stayed high on drugs at the beginning of his seven-year prison stint, he became increasingly more thoughtful, especially about topics such as Christianity's links to systemic racism: "Christianity took me to prison and Islam brought me out . . . because [the crime] . . . was all done when I was part of the white man's Christian world."[61]

During his first year in prison, Malcolm came under the sway of John Elton Bembry, an African American inmate whose wide range of knowledge and sophisticated verbal expression represented the intellectual prowess and countercultural masculinities of the bebop era.[62] This relationship was the prelude to Malcolm's conversion to the Nation of Islam. Bembry, an older burglar who had been an inmate in several prisons, now worked with Malcolm in Charlestown's license plate unit, and began to reshape his new friend's prison masculinity by "dipping into the science of human behavior" and critically interrogating the social processes of violence, hypersexuality, drug addiction, street life, and racism that led to their incarceration.[63] But most of all, he impressed Malcolm with his critical knowledge of religion. Solitary confinement had transformed Malcolm into an atheist who cursed God and the Bible. However, Bembry "put the atheist philosophy in a framework . . . that ended my vicious cursing attacks. My approach sounded so weak alongside his," said Malcolm.[64] Under Bembry's intellectual mentorship, Malcolm took correspondence courses in English, Latin, German, and penmanship.[65] But a soundtrack played behind all this learning as his "ear was glued to the radio" to hear the games Jackie Robinson played for the Brooklyn Dodgers, and to listen to jazz: "My ace girl was Dina[h] Washington. She's still the greatest. I hear some of Sonny [Stitt]'s records. When I was out he was on the alto, but I see he is now giving the tenor a fit."[66]

Bembry's mentorship of Malcolm brought to the fore the inner power and agency of the black intellect and the evolving improvisational identities shaped by bebop's potential to construct redemptive iterations of black masculine identities through critical reflection, new sounds, discipline, study, creativity, and self-improvement. Bembry's black Atlantic cool style of intellectual mentorship in prison, which focused on the transformation of Malcolm's mind, resonated side by side with bebop's evolving improvisational sounds, rhythmic tensions, boundary-breaking artistic identities, and techniques of political disguise, resistance, and performance. Both Bembry and bebop jazz inspired new outlooks on masculinity that emphasized a sense of self characterized by intellectual freedom and independence, even for black men who found themselves in prison. These religious and musical factors played out side by side, not only in Malcolm's evolution from Malcolm Little to Malcolm X and in Shorty Jarvis's initiation into the Nation of Islam, but also in the subtle angle of black Atlantic political agency evident in their embrace of non-Western forms of African American masculinity and religion.

For Malcolm, the self-determination and purifying bodily discipline of the Nation of Islam's redemptive hypermasculinity began in 1948 in Concord Prison, when his brother Reginald sent him a letter that said, "Malcolm don't eat any more pork, and don't smoke anymore cigarettes. I'll show you how to get out of prison."[67] Initially Malcolm believed that his brother's advice was a hustling scheme on the prison administrators. He stopped smoking and eating pork one week after he received Reginald's letter. However, he also began to understand that the process of purification in the conversion of African American men to Islam takes many forms. "Later I would learn, when I had read and studied Islam a good deal, that unconsciously, my first pre-Islamic submission had been manifested," he noted.[68]

For Shorty, purification and the path to Islamic spirituality and intellectual freedom began when he and Malcolm "experienced a transformation of our thought processes."[69] Bebop helped to inspire the intellectual transformation that led to their redemptive black masculinity, racial affirmation, and Islamic conversion. Shorty explained the interplay between religion and music that encouraged conversion: "These thoughts are colored, influenced or filtered by one's experiences (akin to the kinds of things Miles, Dizzy and 'Bird' had done . . . with . . . their 'Bebop' . . . playing their soul, their spirit, as an extension of their thoughts)."[70] As Shorty experienced his non-Western initiation into black Islamic masculinity, his independence and perspective broadened as he searched for religious truth: "I studied Islam, Hinduism, Buddhism, African religion and more. I questioned everything. Soon, I was able to begin formulating ideas about religion that came from my head, not the heads of others."[71]

Indeed, these profound changes in Shorty's thinking about Islam in prison overlapped with the development of Malcolm's masculinity and the freedom of his creative mind, which could now produce critical thoughts as well as original music. Shorty experienced his conversion while serving his sentence in Norfolk Prison Colony in Massachusetts. Malcolm was transferred there on March 31, 1948. Norfolk not only had an extensive library, but also a prison orchestra that influenced Shorty's musical and religious transformation.[72] Speaking of his musical transformation in prison, Shorty pointed out, "Something new . . . and wonderful was going on. . . . For example, . . . while playing the prison piano, I accidently struck a series of chord progressions. . . . I wrote the chords down on a piece of music manuscript paper. . . . I imagined I heard a beautiful melody which blended with these chords. . . . I realized I had composed my first song and all of its beautiful melody."[73]

In Shorty's memoir, *The Other Malcolm—"Shorty" Jarvis*, the freedom and black affirmation that arise from improvisation and composition in bebop are shown to parallel the purification experiences that led to his embrace of the Nation of Islam in prison. According to Shorty, "the incarceration of Malcolm X and me had brought about . . . a psychological metamorphosis—purification, intense self-discipline, the courage to walk an uncharted path through the regions of my mind."[74] He also emphasized his rejection of systemic racism in Christianity, which influenced him "to deviate from the family tradition of practicing Christian beliefs."[75]

Ultimately, evolving together with Malcolm X in Norfolk Prison Colony, Shorty converted to Islam. He noted the racial self-determination of his new religion: "The Nation of Islam has my deepest respect, because they are the only people I see today putting forth a supreme effort to raise the social, economic, and spiritual consciousness of black people from the grave of ignorance and stupidity."[76] Building on the ideas of African American religious internationalism and transnational blackness, Jarvis wrote, "We have to travel back through our 'Middle Passage' tunnels of ignorance to retrieve our identity. . . . Common sense should tell any black person that their religion should be that of the majority of the world's black people, Islam, or some form of African religion."[77]

Malcolm X's path to the Nation of Islam in prison was deeply influenced by Shorty Jarvis's mystical and musical conversion experience, which blended Islam and jazz. But Malcolm's own purification process for conversion began with his family. The fact that Malcolm and Shorty were incarcerated in Norfolk Prison Colony, which allowed music, organized debates and discussions, library books on religion and history, education programs from Boston University and Harvard, and daily visitors for two hours, made it possible for them to embrace the family and social networks that facilitated their conversion to Islam.[78] Malcolm's nephew Rodnell P. Collins discussed the Little family members who joined the Nation of Islam a short time after his uncle's incarceration. The conversions began with Malcolm's brother Wilfred, who was later appointed the minister of Detroit's Temple No. 1.[79] Wilfred's siblings Philbert, Reginald, Wesley, and Hilda, and his wife, Bertha, followed his lead into the Nation of Islam.[80] Collins writes, "The Little siblings didn't just join the Nation; they became some of its most dedicated members and effective proselytizers."[81] Malcolm's sister Ella supported the Little family's plans to convert Malcolm to the Nation of Islam. She explained, "If they believed that the organization could rescue our brother from . . . those influences that had encouraged him to run the streets of Boston and Harlem, I was prepared to strongly support their efforts."[82]

Malcolm's siblings took turns visiting him in prison and sent him daily letters, visits and letters that exemplify the Nation of Islam's contributions to the growing sense among blacks that their search for a spiritual tradition should not be confined within national boundaries.[83] Hilda came to Norfolk Prison from Detroit and explained aspects of "Yacub's History" to Malcolm.[84] "Yacub's History" began when Hilda announced that "Elijah Muhammad teaches his followers that. . . . the first humans, Original Man, were a black people. They founded the Holy City of Mecca."[85] She then told Malcolm the mythic story of the ancient black scientist Yacub, who created the "strong black tribe of Shabazz, from which America's Negroes, so-called, descend."[86] Her recitation of "Yacub's History" concluded with an explanation of the divinity of Master W. D. Fard, who "came from the East to the West, appearing in North

America at a time when . . . non-white people all over the world began to rise, and as the white devil civilization, condemned by Allah, was . . . destroying itself."[87]

"Yacub's History" shows how the Nation of Islam's early converts and leaders, like the boundary-breaking black jazz musicians in the 1940s, 1950s, and 1960s, "mined Africa, as well as Asia and the Middle East, for non-Western sources of new ideas for experimental music,"[88] richer forms of blackness, and demands for freedom, as well as black Atlantic religion. The Nation's swift and militant innovations in the performance of blackness, its presentations of African American religious internationalism, and its formation of urban youth cultures reshaped black identities in a way that paralleled the quick chord changes and fascinating new rhythms and sounds of bebop. Malcolm and Shorty, who were hardcore beboppers, exemplified how new African American Muslim converts improvised, purified, and rebalanced their musical identities, black masculinities, and sense of cool with the new countercultural values and spiritual paradigms of the Nation of Islam, even in prison.

During his time in Norfolk Prison Colony, Malcolm spread the word about African American Islam and jazz through daily letters to his jazz friends in Roxbury and Harlem and to his family.[89] The letters were part of what he called his "homemade education."[90] The letters also documented his religious and musical evolution: "In the street, I had been the most articulate hustler out there. . . . How would I sound writing in slang, the way I would say it, something such as 'Look, daddy, let me pull your coat about a cat, Elijah Muhammad.'"[91] Although Malcolm did not receive any replies from his friends in the hustling and jazz world, he was not discouraged. He continued to write to them "all about Allah and Islam. . . . I had no idea where most of them lived. I addressed the letters in care of the Harlem or Roxbury bars and clubs where I'd known them."[92]

For his part, Shorty Jarvis acknowledged the evolving internationalist impact that the Ahmadiyya Muslim Community missionary Abdul Hameed continued to have on his and Malcolm's conversion to the Nation of Islam. "The Muslim prayer books—written in Arabic—Malcolm and I received were left at the prison for us by Abdul Hameed in 1947," he said. "Our first visit from Abdul Hameed came at the Norfolk Prison Colony in 1947. Abdul Hameed played a very important role in our lives while in prison. . . . Mr. Hameed would explain how to pronounce the Arabic words contained in those prayer books."[93] Although Elijah Muhammad also sent them important information about the Nation of Islam's values of black affirmation and self-determination in his letters from Chicago, Shorty emphasized that they "continued to receive privileged information from both the Honorable Elijah Muhammad and Abdul Hameed" while they were incarcerated in Norfolk.[94] According to his account, Hameed's visits convinced the two beboppers to see themselves as "potential Muslims" and to challenge the prison's mandatory rules about shaving.[95] When Shorty met with a prison deputy, he discussed their right to religious freedom: "Many of us blacks are potential Muslims. Our faith is Islam. Our god is Allah. We are not provided with a facility to worship in. We believe in nature, and what grows by nature on our faces we will not cut or destroy. This is our way of paying tribute to Allah." Jarvis argued successfully that "convicts do have some constitutional and human rights. Freedom of religion is one of them—be it Jesus or Allah." Finally, the prison deputy decided in Shorty's favor and said, "Shaving will not be an infraction of the rules. . . . You are excused, and tell Little he is excused also."[96]

Shorty's experience in prison exemplified how African American men embraced the non-Western spirituality, aesthetics, and political consciousness of the Islamic movements, characteristics these movements shared with bebop. Increasingly, jazz musicians sought out a "patriarchal, heroic performance space," one that forged dynamic connections between "jazz manhood," freedom, self-determination, and black Islamic masculinities.[97] Although the jazz community and the Nation of Islam were "male-dominated . . . and marginalized women, except perhaps in the case of singing" in jazz,[98] black men in bebop and the Islamic movements performed their own gendered identities with representations of countercultural manhood to challenge the marginalization and stereotyping of black men.

Steeped in the masculine consciousness of jazz and black Islam in prison, Malcolm began to write daily letters to the Messenger of the Nation of Islam Elijah Muhammad, who initiated him and Shorty into his teachings about the Muslim religion and the black race. It is useful to remember that Malcolm's and Shorty's conversion to the Nation of Islam occurred at the beginning of the second Great Migration (which lasted from the 1940s to the 1970s), in which more than five million blacks moved from the South to northern cities.[99] As Meadows notes, "In addition to transforming and reinterpreting African American culture in their new urban environment, these [migrants] . . . also faced myriad problems and solutions which they transformed into new social and musical identities."[100] An Islamic identity was one of these; a bebop identity was another. In the 1940s bebop emerged as an innovative performance space, one that "challenged many assumptions about black male creativity and the power of pop and mass culture."[101] As for religion, the Nation of Islam had begun to reshape African American gendered and racial identities in profound ways, transforming the spiritual consciousness of black prisoners by introducing them to the world of Islam.

The following excerpts from Malcolm's prison letters to his family exemplify how bebop's black masculine agency and creativity, the Nation's Islamic consciousness, and African American religious internationalism shaped the final stages of his conversion to Islam and his adoption of a new identity as Malcolm X. In his embrace of spiritual freedom and self-determination, courage, peace, composure, and rebirth during his prison conversion, Malcolm also expressed black Atlantic cool.[102] In November 1948, Malcolm began to preface some of his letters to his brother Philbert with the following Islamic greeting: "In the name of 'Allah,' the Beneficent, the Merciful, the Great God of the Universe . . . and in the Name of His Holy Servant and Apostle, the Honorable Mr. Elijah Muhammad. All praise is due to 'Allah'. . . . As Salaam Alaikum."[103] This greeting, using language from the Qur'an's first surah, expressed Malcolm's global black religious consciousness; his new Islamic religious belief in Allah, the transcendent Creator of the universe; and his theological relationship to the ummah—the global Muslim community, as well as to the Nation of Islam. Such beliefs had important social ramifications as well. For as Thomas-Burgess's research shows, Muslim religious practices and beliefs "were the most important theological, experiential factors that influence[d] [black] inmates to convert. . . . [And] because of the appeal of Islamic beliefs and doctrines, participants . . . were more inclined to reject criminal activities after their conversion experience."[104]

A letter to Philbert in August 1949 sums up the evolution of Malcolm's new devotion to Islamic consciousness, peace, and religious self-determination in prison. "Peace Be Unto You. . . . Always as long as you place Islam first, I shall gladly take second," he wrote. Then he added, "You'd be surprised how many people I correspond with, and how many truth seekers my environment is always crowded with . . . and Islam is the only subject I ever discuss. Those who do not wish to hear the truth, steer clear of me."[105] Later on, he wrote to his brother and discussed the pre-prison roots of his conversion to Islam: "It makes me feel good to . . . hear the Brothers there think I was in contact with Islam before my seclusion . . . for they are correct. We were taught Islam by Mom, . . . for she was a most Faithful Servant of Truth years ago. I praise Allah for her."[106]

Malcolm also used his prison letters to Philbert to consider the Nation of Islam's transnational theme of Asiatic blackness in ancient African history: "If the Black people be Holy, and are from the Nile Valley of Blessed Africa . . . is Africa not the Holy Land?. . . . I pray 'Allah' all of our questions are soon answered."[107] A letter to his sister-in-law in early 1951 was one of the first prison letters in which he signed his name "Malcolm X. Little," signifying his spiritual rebirth as a black Muslim in the Nation of Islam, his acceptance of his original Asiatic identity, and his adoption of the new surname X after his encounter with Elijah Muhammad.[108] The X was a powerful symbol representing Malcolm's "African name that was lost" during enslavement and the Nation of Islam's transnational construction of blackness.[109]

As Malcolm's letters to his family show, jazz was still central to his consciousness as he completed his conversion to the Nation of Islam. His friends included the dancers, musicians, and employers he met during his zoot suit years in Boston and New York, many of whom visited him in prison. In 1949 Malcolm wrote to inform his brother Philbert that "Sleepy Williams, the dancer I mentioned that visits me along with a cousin of ours, . . . was killed in an auto accident Sunday nite. He and another girl." In the same letter he explained that their show business relative, the black Hollywood actor "Jimmy Edwards, the fellow who made 'Home of the Brave' is a cousin of ours."[110] In March 1950, Malcolm sent a letter to a Nation of Islam member that included a poem describing how intertwined jazz and Islam were in his own life and in the life of his people: "Music, Brother is ours—it is us. . . . Music without the Musician is like Life without Allah . . . both being in need of the house—a home—The Temple."[111] But he also acknowledged his attraction to the jazz nightlife: "We have been in the darkness so long. . . . No wonder we so continuously have sought the lures of the nightlife to create some sort of peace within ourselves—no wonder we have so longingly turned so often to music for its comforting effects."[112]

Malcolm also had fond memories of his friendship with the jazz singer Billie Holiday. In March 1951 he wrote to his sister-in-law Henrietta, who was Philbert's wife, asking her, "Does Phil still have that picture of me and Billie Holiday? If so send it. I'll return it to him later."[113] Later on, he wrote to Philbert, "Lionel Hampton was in town last week, and his trombonist, Al Hayne, came by to visit me. T'was the first I'd seen of him in six years. He's from Detroit. . . . He brought me up to date on that particular life, and though he admits they're all dying . . . from fast living, he's still living a fast life himself."[114] Malcolm discussed his conversion to Islam with Hayne during his visit and analyzed the jazz musician's reaction to the Muslim religion in his words to Philbert: "His impression of Islam has been formed from his observations of the various Muslims (so called) in show business who say one thing and do another, thus I did not press the subject. But some day I shall introduce him to some real Muslims (be it the will of Allah). Hamp' too."[115] As Malcolm experienced his conversion to Islam, he blended his musical and religious identities, endorsing the religion and the oppositional values it shared with bebop among jazz musicians and incarcerated blacks who were jazz fans.

On March 23, 1950, Malcolm was transferred back to Charlestown State Prison in Boston. Soon thereafter, Shorty was also transferred there.[116] According to Malcolm's prison file, there was no evidence of disciplinary problems during his years at Norfolk Prison Colony, but as a Muslim he "appeared unnecessarily race conscious [and] he complained of the prejudice of officers['] interference with his religious beliefs."[117] Malcolm and Shorty were uniquely qualified to articulate the connections between the militant identities of the hustling and jazz world and the innovative black internationalism of the Nation of Islam. When they interacted with other incarcerated black men, they stood out as rebellious exponents of those ascendant black countercultural perspectives that fostered a redemptive form of black hypermasculinity, resistance to systemic racism, and the conversion of African American inmates to

Islam. According to Malcolm, this inspiring convergence of powerful oppositional perspectives, which came together in his conversion conversations with black youth, explained his sudden transfer to Charlestown State Prison: "Tis odd how things turned out at Norfolk. The truth spread rapidly and was being grasped by the youths. . . . All of the opposition [by the prison authorities] was . . . helpful toward the spread of Islam there, because the opposition made Islam heard by many who otherwise wouldn't have paid it the second thought."[118] Shorty pointed out that one of the major reasons for their transfer to Charlestown was fear on the part of the prison establishment of African American religious internationalism: "At this time, the major concern . . . among the penologists . . . was the growing rate with which black convicts were embracing the faith of Islam. . . . to become . . . registered Muslim[s]."[119] He also argued that Malcolm's jazz background was an important reason for his adopted Muslim religion's appeal to incarcerated black youth and for the repression of Islam in prison: "The cumulative residual effect of his flamboyant zoot suits . . . was a rare treat anyone would remember—let alone his incredible dancing. . . . [Yet] in Norfolk prison, Malcolm always used to speak of his lifetime ambition, which was to visit Mecca. . . . The prison system is trying very hard not to spawn another Malcolm X, lest they live to regret it even more today."[120]

Clearly, American Islamophobia was on the rise in the 1950s. To understand the final details of Malcolm's conversion to the Nation of Islam as well as the cultural and political implications of his musical and religious identities, we have to examine how he and Shorty dealt with Islamophobia in prison. Islamophobia, or "unfounded hostility towards Muslims which results in fear and dislike of Muslims," often takes the form of attacks on and discrimination against people who practice Islam.[121] Scholars in the social sciences and humanities also describe Islamophobia as a global component of racism that marginalizes and isolates Muslim individuals and communities.[122] When Malcolm and Shorty engaged in their protest against the repression of incarcerated black Muslims in the 1950s, the word "Islamophobia" was not part of common parlance.[123] However, as Sylvester A. Johnson's scholarship has shown, "the history of the FBI's engagement with African American Muslims since the 1930s is the early history of the United States racializing Islam under the national security paradigm."[124] Clearly, the Islamo-

phobic backlash against black Muslims by Massachusetts prison officials
was a racially motivated response driven by the fact that the majority
of the Muslims in the United States from the 1940s to the 1960s were
African American.[125] Also, as Johnson has pointed out, black internationalism played a major role in systemic Islamophobia from 1945 to
the 1960s, when "no fewer than forty nations—composing mostly non-
white peoples colonized by European nations—rebelled against their
conquerors and demanded their freedom, typically through violent military action."[126] Some of these people lived in Muslim-majority nations,
and the exploitation of their natural resources by European nations as
well as the United States was an important aspect of twentieth-century
global imperialism in the Third World.[127]

In April 1950 a local newspaper reported that Malcolm, Shorty, Osborne Thaxton, and Leroy Thaxton were the first Muslims in Massachusetts state prison and that they "grow beards, won't eat pork; [and]
demand east-facing cells to facilitate 'prayers to Allah.'"[128] Shorty and
Malcolm had converted the African American Thaxton brothers to
Islam in prison,[129] and the newspaper article noted that "the guards have
proven co-operative in granting religious freedom, but are keeping the
four under close surveillance."[130] Malcolm believed that their surveillance was based on Islamophobia and anti-black racism, which, as we
have seen, were rampant both in the prison and in the United States
more generally. This lack of support for African American religious freedom led Malcolm to bolster his global Muslim identity, which gave him
the strength to survive the repression of his chosen religion in prison.
On June 29, 1950, he wrote a letter to President Harry S. Truman protesting America's involvement in the Korean War, a letter that expressed
his deepening sense of himself as part of the Nation of Islam's global
Asiatic community: "It looks like another war. . . . I . . . tried to enlist in
the Japanese Army, last war, now they will never draft or accept me in
the U.S. Army."[131] In December 1950, Malcolm protested Charlestown's
repression of the Muslim inmates' nighttime prayers, by threatening to
contact the global Islamic community—"the whole body of Islam" for
support.[132]

During his time in prison, Malcolm X's survival, resistance, redemption, and conversion to Islam depended on his ability to use the skills he
had learned as a jazz man—improvisation, experimentation, and trans-

formation—to express the sense of freedom, self-determination, social justice, internationalism, and black masculinity that his Muslim identity in the Nation of Islam afforded him. Moreover, the aspects of global black religious consciousness that he and Shorty embraced to confront Islamophobia and racism in prison offered a new model for jazz musicians who, after converting to Islam in the 1950s and 1960s, found themselves confronted with these same issues in the music industry.

As we will see in chapter 4, Malcolm X and Elijah Muhammad hired numerous jazz musicians to play during bazaars, rallies, and benefit concerts for the Nation of Islam in the 1960s. The transnational, Islamic sensibilities of the jazz artists they selected resonated with the movement's Afro-Asiatic identity and its links to the Black Power movement. Both men used jazz performances to attract and entertain potential converts during a momentous decade when the Nation "accounted for almost half of all operating Muslim congregations in the United States, and its budget . . . was likely in the millions of dollars," according to Edward E. Curtis IV.[133] Later on, the formation of jazz and Islam in Malcolm's antiracist, Pan-African politics served as a representative metaphor for the political awakening of black urban youth and even John Coltrane during the hard bop and free jazz era.

Fishing for Converts in Boston: Jazz and Islam in Temple No. 11

Malcolm's first petition for executive clemency and pardon was denied on December 19, 1950. The state prison's recommendation to deny his parole emphasized that "he became a follower of the Moslem religion."[134] He was then twenty-five years old and had been incarcerated for four years and nine months. He would not be paroled and released from Massachusetts state prison until August 7, 1952.[135] Malcolm X spent his first year of freedom living with his brother Wilfred and his spouse, Ruth, in Inkster, Michigan, and working in factories and a store in the Detroit area.[136] In the summer of 1953, Elijah Muhammad appointed him assistant minister in Detroit Temple No. 1, after training him for the Nation of Islam ministry in Chicago and Detroit.[137] Malcolm X became a Nation of Islam minister toward the end of 1953.[138] Elijah Muhammad instructed Malcolm X to "go after the young people," with the goal of increasing the Nation of Islam's membership by the thousands.[139]

Following Muhammad's lead, Malcolm went fishing (seeking converts) for the Nation of Islam in Detroit's jazz spaces, in the "bars, in the poolrooms, and on the corners," pointing out the values of black affirmation, freedom, and self-determination that Islam and jazz shared.[140] Malcolm mesmerized potential Muslim converts with the language of the jazz clubs and the streets: "My man, . . . you see me—well, in the streets they used to call me Detroit Red"; as well as the black nationalist message of the Nation of Islam: "We didn't land on Plymouth Rock, my brothers and sisters—Plymouth Rock landed on us. . . . Give all you can to help Messenger Elijah Muhammad's independence program for the black man!"[141]

At the end of 1953, Muhammad sent Malcolm to Boston to establish a new temple in Roxbury, where black jazz musicians were shaping both the Islamic community and music in the city.[142] Malcolm "Shorty" Jarvis had returned to Boston after he was paroled from prison, resuming his career as a jazz trumpeter in the 1950s.[143] After his own return to Boston, Malcolm began a "recruitment drive" in Boston's South End and Roxbury jazz spaces, street corners, and apartments, establishing a successful paradigm for the conversion of black youth to the Muslim religion that would ultimately make this period one that earned the name "the golden age of African American Islam and jazz."[144]

In October 1953, Malcolm X spoke to a small group of potential Bostonian converts to the Nation of Islam in jazz trumpeter Lloyd X's apartment on 5 Wellington Street in the South End.[145] One of the attendees was James Sydney James, a seventeen-year-old student at English High School.[146] He converted to Islam in December, gave up his slave name, and was initiated as James S. X.[147] James was impressed by Malcolm's rejection of systemic racism, his black masculinity, and his global black consciousness, as well as his creative and musically inspired performance when he discussed religion: his improvisational skills, his call-and-response technique, his intimate rapport with his audience, and his ability to create a trance-like state in the room "to captivate you psychologically." "He had the ability to read the audience," James remembered. "Christianity, I could see very clearly, was not the religion of my ancestors."[148] Malcolm preached for the Nation of Islam by using the mesmerizing performance strategies of black Atlantic cool and emphasizing the goals and values of bebop that he had learned during his teenage years in Boston's jazz community. Sometimes, James S. X would meet his religious mentor to discuss the Nation of Islam's views on black liberation, racial separatism, and self-determination at Chicken Lane, a Massachusetts Avenue restaurant that was popular among Muslims and musicians both because of its location between two popular jazz clubs, the Savoy and Wally's Paradise, and because the restaurant's owner, Sylvalia Hyman Sr., "accommodated the dietary restrictions of the growing number of Muslim patrons."[149] Although some, including James, thought it was strange, Malcolm X was clearly comfortable doing his missionary work in the midst of these landmarks that defined Boston's black jazz scene in the 1950s.

Malcolm X's post-prison success in Boston converting blacks to Islam built on the Islamization of the black jazz musicians and fans who had converted to the Nation of Islam in Roxbury and the South End during his incarceration.[150] This group of musicians included World War II veteran Alfred Sutton, who came from Ohio to Boston hoping to study jazz trumpet at Berklee College of Music.[151] He converted to the Nation of Islam in 1948, served as the secretary for Temple No. 11, and fished for converts in South End jazz spaces, where he convinced potential members to attend Malcolm X's meetings at 5 Wellington Street.[152]

Charles X O'Neil had embraced the Nation of Islam in the late 1940s during his incarceration in Norfolk Prison Colony, where he "was known primarily for his love of music."[153] He had learned of Islam through his fellow prisoners and mentors, Malcolm X and Shorty Jarvis.[154] When he was released from prison in 1950, he returned to the South End's jazz clubs, street corners, and restaurants to fish for youth converts on behalf of the Nation with its message of black liberation, self-determination, and global black consciousness, which resonated so naturally with the jazz community. He did his work along with fellow Nation of Islam missionaries Alfred X Sutton and musician Osborne X Thaxton.[155] Thaxton became a Muslim during his own incarceration with his brother Leroy, Malcolm X, and Shorty Jarvis.[156] O'Neil proselytized among jazz musicians, introducing them to the global history of Islam, using as his texts scrapbooks containing *National Geographic* photographs and articles on ancient Asiatic civilizations and the original people in Africa and Asia.[157] In the early 1950s, O'Neil converted Charles Williams, a Boston jazz pianist.[158] Rodney Smith, a saxophonist and a student at Northeastern University, also converted to the Nation of Islam.[159] He influenced the Boston calypso musician and Winston-Salem State University graduate Louis Eugene Walcott (Louis X, Louis Farrakhan), who would eventually convert after he met Malcolm X in Chicken Lane restaurant, visited the Nation of Islam in Chicago, and heard Malcolm speak about black masculinity and the Muslim religion in Harlem.[160] Louis X became the minister of Temple No. 11 in 1957.[161] William Bell, also influenced by Smith, converted to the Nation of Islam and was known as a "progressive Afro-wearing artiste" who fished for black youth by focusing on the "connection of avant-garde jazz artists to young men and women who were influenced by the new music."[162] Jazz drummer Charles Hester joined the Nation of Islam in 1951.[163]

Before Malcolm X returned to Boston, the above-mentioned converts had met periodically at a residence for single black women on Massachusetts Avenue in the South End neighborhood.[164] Charles X Williams's sister Evelyn Williams, an opera student who once dated the teenaged Malcolm Little, lived there, as did Lucille Rosary and Coretta Scott (Martin Luther King Jr.'s future wife).[165] Eventually, the university student Rosary became interested in the Nation of Islam, and Evelyn Williams converted.[166] According to Fatima Fanusie's research, a "love and study of music" was the important shared cultural connection that initially brought these women and men together in Boston's black musical community, to socialize, and later on, to consider conversion to the Nation of Islam.[167] By 1953, Malcolm's missionary work, along with the fishing efforts of the Muslim jazz musicians, "stimulated an intellectual awakening among receptive Boston youth."[168] Moreover, the beboppers Charles X Williams and saxophonist Jimmy X Diamond were mentored by Malcolm to emulate his cool style and purity of body and mind in their own missionary work, and they were invited to speak in many of Boston's black churches in the 1950s about black history and African American religious internationalism in the Nation of Islam, attracting converts to the Nation of Islam including high school student Adnan Shabazz.[169] Because of the successful recruitment work of Malcolm X and the Islamic jazz musicians in Boston, Charles X O'Neil eventually traveled to Atlantic City to support the Nation of Islam community in New Jersey, where he used Malcolm X's jazz model to fish for converts.[170] Atlantic City Temple No. 10 was established in 1953 through the organizing work of African American musicians.[171] Moreover, black Muslims owned an Atlantic City music store that employed O'Neil, and the early recruitment meetings for Temple No. 10 took place in their store.[172] Woodrow X Love became the minister of the Atlantic City temple in the 1950s.[173]

In 1953 the Wellington Street group of Muslims that became Temple No. 11 had fourteen members.[174] But due to the missionary work of Malcolm X and the early Nation of Islam jazz musicians who persuasively reframed bebop's values of black affirmation, self-determination, and freedom in a new religious context, Boston's Nation of Islam community expanded rapidly. Temple No. 11 was officially founded in March 1954, led by Minister Ulysses X.[175] Malcolm X then moved on to establish Temple No. 12 in Philadelphia in May 1954, and became the permanent minister of New York City's Temple No. 7 in June 1954.[176] After moving in and out of several temporary meeting spaces, the Boston members purchased a permanent building in 1957, when Temple No. 11 found a permanent home at 35 Intervale Street in Roxbury, in a building that had previously been a Jewish synagogue.[177] Fanusie's research offers interesting demographic information about Temple No. 11, revealing that the early converts included black internationalists, migrants, and World War II and Korean War veterans who were also academically educated musicians with intellectual ties to Boston and Cambridge colleges as well as universities and conservatories such as Berklee College of Music, Boston Conservatory, New England Conservatory of Music, Boston University, Northeastern University, and Harvard University.[178]

The story of Malcolm X and the Muslim jazz musicians in Boston exemplifies the larger history of the black musicians and fans described in this book. Through their practice of African American religious internationalism, they encouraged blacks in the United States to embrace new identities that honored the spirituality of black Asiatics, Africans, and Islamic people of color all over the world. The Muslim beboppers in Boston used these ideas as a springboard for discussing global perspectives about blackness, masculinity, social justice, resistance, and liberation. In black Boston, a key community in which musicians took the lead in exploring the interactions between Garveyism, black Christianity, the Nation of Islam, and modern jazz, the missionary practices and the life story of Minister Malcolm X powerfully expressed the transforming effects of conversion to Islam. The post-prison Malcolm X was deeply involved with Muslim communities during the rise of African American Islam and the golden age of jazz, and these interactions influenced his embrace of the Nation's "communal masculinity, a general concern for black people and their welfare, and . . . [engagement in] performances based on this premise . . . [that] made the black male a central figure in Temple life."[179] Moving beyond the realm of prison masculinities, Malcolm's new communal masculinity, exemplified in his fishing practices for converts in Detroit and Boston, created a new performative showcase for the conversion of blacks to Islam, "where members and others could witness acts symbolizing black unity, . . . forcing thousands of black men to take on a greater responsibility not merely for themselves, but also for their family and community," both in the Nation of Islam and in the ummah, the global Muslim community.[180] According to Zain Abdullah, the style and ritual of black Islamic communal masculinity represented a new and different African American religious world that helped to transform the image and the consciousness of black men.[181]

The history of this internationalist era, when Islam and jazz shaped new representations of black masculinities and inspired global black religious consciousness, continues in chapter 3, where we will examine the racial, spiritual, and political relationships that encouraged African American jazz musicians to convert to the Ahmadiyya Muslim Community USA in the 1940s and 1950s.

3

The Faith of Universal Brotherhood

The Ahmadiyya Muslim Community's Popularity among Bebop Musicians

Abdul Hameed, the Indian Ahmadi missionary in Boston, introduced Shorty Jarvis and Malcolm X to Islam in Roxbury, although they took another route in prison. Hameed's mentorship of Shorty and Malcolm did, however, exemplify the growing influence that the Ahmadiyya Muslim Community would have on the spirituality and internationalism of bebop musicians outside prison in the postwar era. Malcolm acknowledged this influence in 1950, after he converted to the Nation of Islam, when he talked about the "many who belong to the Ahmadiyya movement."[1] A large number of the Ahmadiyya converts were beboppers, who were attracted by the movement's emphasis on universal brotherhood (the Islamic value of racial and ethnic equality) as well as the worldwide Muslim community's belief in the oneness of God. Unlike Malcolm and Shorty, they accepted the prophethood of Ghulam Ahmad and rejected the divinity of the Nation of Islam's founder, W. D. Fard Muhammad, and the doctrine that Elijah Muhammad was a messenger of God.

Chapter 3 looks at the forces of internationalism, resistance, masculinity, black affirmation, freedom, and self-determination that encouraged black jazz musicians to convert to the Ahmadiyya Muslim Community in the 1940s and 1950s, forces that made it the most popular Islamic community among bebop artists during this period. The chapter explores the transnational experience of the Ahmadi missionaries who migrated from their homeland in India and established their American religious networks in the urban centers where jazz thrived, as well as the transnational journeys of their African American converts. It analyzes the Ahmadi links to the Marcus Garvey movement and Pan-Africanism, and the parallel values found in the jazz community and in the Ahmadiyya presentation of Islam.

Ahmadiyya Influences on Transnationalism, Pan-Africanism, and Black Masculinity in the Jazz World

As the 1950s approached, many bebop jazz musicians (especially those who converted to Islam) began to see themselves in a larger global context, as part of the international liberation struggles of blacks in the African diaspora and Africa, and also, sometimes, in solidarity with the oppositional struggles of people of color who were not black. Ahmadiyya missionaries attracted the attention of the bebop artists because they were exemplars of a universal Islamic brotherhood advocating racial equality, Pan-Africanism, and transnationalism: they circulated their religious message widely across a breadth of countries, including India, Pakistan, England, Nigeria, Ghana, Denmark, Sweden, and the United States, and their mission to blacks transformed the meaning of conversion among African American musicians. Communities like these relied on the global networks created by international migrants whose spiritual and political identities were shaped by their travel and their religious connections to both their countries of origin and their communities in their new host countries.

In 1920 the Ahmadis sent Mufti Muhammad Sadiq from England to work as the first missionary of the Ahmadiyya Muslim Community in the United States. Sadiq, who was a philologist and a graduate of the University of London, started out in New Jersey, where he was incarcerated in a detention facility for two months by US immigration officials until he convinced them that he would not preach polygamy in America. During his incarceration, he made his first convert in the United States, R. J. H. Rochford: "Watching me praying and reciting the Holy Book, Mr. Rochford inquired of my religion, which I explained to him and I gave him some books to study. Very soon he was convinced of the truth of our religion and being converted was named Hamid."[2] The Indian missionary converted nineteen additional men to Islam while he was confined in New Jersey; they were immigrants from British Guyana, Jamaica, France, Italy, Russia, Poland, Portugal, Belgium, and Germany.[3]

Sadiq was a victim of America's virulent racism against Asians that created the climate for the Immigration Act of 1917, excluding workers from the "Asiatic Barred Zone" (Afghanistan, India, Saudi Arabia, and other Asian countries). The Chinese Exclusion Act of 1882 and the Geary

Act of 1902 had already barred most Chinese laborers from immigrating to the United States. A federal law, the Immigration Act of 1924 excluded the majority of non-European immigrants by constructing racist origin quotas that closed the door to Asians and Africans and funded the legal deportation of barred migrants in the United States. Finally, the Immigration and Naturalization Bureau revoked the citizenship of numerous Indian Americans from 1923 to 1926 because a 1923 Supreme Court decision, *United States v. Bhagat Singh Thind*, decided that Indians were not eligible for naturalized citizenship because they were not white.[4]

Upon his release, Sadiq moved to Highland Park, Michigan, opened the Ahmadiyya mission house on the South Side of Chicago, converted Americans to Islam, and established the *Moslem Sunrise*, the first Muslim newspaper in the United States.[5] Before long, the newspaper began to criticize the racial deficiencies of Christianity: "What sad news we came across . . . about the conflict between the Blacks and the Whites in this country. It is a pity that no preaching of equality has so far been able to do away with this evil."[6]

In 1920 Mufti Muhammad Sadiq wrote twenty articles on the Muslim religion that appeared in American newspapers and periodicals, and he presented fifty public talks in US cities.[7] Ultimately, his missionary work in Chicago was successful from 1921 to 1925 and he persuaded 1,025 Americans to embrace Islam with his convincing religious message:

> There is but one God. . . . All others are mere prophets, including Jesus. Muhammad was the last and the equal of the others. None is to be worshiped, not even Jesus or Muhammad. The Trinity is an illusion—the word is not found in the Christian Bible and its principle cannot be sustained. God created all races, all colors. Islam makes no difference between race and class.[8]

The *Moslem Sunrise* urged African Americans to abandon Christianity and embrace Islam's universal brotherhood: "Christian profiteers brought you out of . . . Africa . . . and made you forget the religion and language of your forefathers—which were Islam and Arabic. . . . Christianity cannot bring real brotherhood. . . . Now leave it alone. And join Islam, the real faith of Universal Brotherhood."[9] In 1922 Ahmad Din (P. Nathaniel Johnson), a convert and missionary in St. Louis who wore a fez in his photo, was one of several African American missionaries whose stories and photos appeared in the *Moslem Sunrise*.[10] The *St. Louis Post Dispatch* featured an article about the one hundred converts that he influenced to join the Ahmadiyya Muslim Community in the first months of his work.[11] Brother Omar (William M. Patton) was another new African American Muslim mentioned in the former newspaper for his missionary work in St. Louis, and Sister Noor (Ophelia Avant) was cited as a notable black woman who embraced Islam in the city. Brother Hakim (Dr. J. H. Humphries) was an African convert discussed in the pages of the *Moslem Sunrise*. Born in the Congo Free State (Belgian Congo), he immigrated to the United States as a teenager, studied for several years at Tuskegee Institute, and became a Protestant minister and missionary. When he heard Ahmad Din's lectures, he decided to leave Christianity and became a Muslim and an Ahmadiyya missionary. Brother Hakim's Islamic mentor commended him as a "magnetic healer of extraordinary ability" and "great spiritual powers."[12]

A photo of four African American female converts—Mrs. Thomas (Sister Khairat), Mrs. Watts (Sister Zeineb), Mrs. Robinson (Sister Ahmadia), and Mrs. Clark (Sister Ayesha)—in the *Moslem Sunrise* in 1922 is the first group photograph of Muslim women in the United States. These "four American Moslem ladies" were modestly dressed, wearing hats and shawls that covered their heads, mouths, necks, and shoulders. An important aspect of Mufti Muhammad Sadiq's work as a new missionary in America is the way he presented Islam as a religion that opposed both sexism and racism. The majority of women converts to the Ahmadiyya Muslim Community in the 1920s were black southern migrants. As Sylvia Chan-Malik writes,

> Islam offered [them] . . . a religious and political ethos that rejected the dehumanization of Black working-class women by white society and the Black bourgeoisie and presented expansive and productive concepts of citizenship, belonging, and racial and gendered selfhood in a religious framework that was at once politically empowering and adaptable to their existing knowledge of Christianity. Further, the clear organizational structure of the . . . [Ahmadiyya], along with its emphasis on religious education and moral development, constituted a stabilizing force in wom-

en's lives—a framework that provided safety and sustained them against the harsh and unforgiving environments of Bronzeville and beyond.[13]

In the black Atlantic world of jazz, the Ahmadiyya Muslim Community was known for its racial equality and its Afro-Indian Islamic identity, which was performed through missionary work and political interactions with Pan-Africanists and musicians in African American urban communities. According to Moustafa Bayoumi's understanding of these parallel connections between Asians and black Americans, Ahmadi Islam "is where blacks become Asians and Asians black under color of divine law."[14] Its success in the United States would not have been possible without an early group of black converts in the 1920s, members of Marcus Garvey's Universal Negro Improvement Association in Chicago, Detroit, St. Louis, and Gary, Indiana, who asked African Americans to consider more deeply their links to Africans and the darker races of the world.[15] These Pan-Africanists exemplified the values of black social justice and dignity by promoting the global unification, liberation, and empowerment of people of African descent. Their goals were the decolonization and freedom of Africa through means as seemingly diverse as the recrafting of African culture and identity in the African diaspora and the emigration of diasporic peoples back to Africa.

The Ahmadi missionaries were familiar with the global movements of Pan-Africanism that ultimately impressed black musicians because of their branch in Lagos, Nigeria, established in 1916, and their association during the World War I period with Duse Mohamed Ali, the Egyptian Muslim editor of the *African Times and Orient Review* and a mentor of Marcus Garvey in London.[16] Ali introduced Garvey to Islam and African politics and history during his time in England from 1912 to 1914. The *African Times and Orient Review* was circulated in Europe, the United States, the Caribbean, West and East Africa, Egypt, India, Turkey, Japan, and Ceylon from 1912 to 1920 and focused on the links between Pan-Islamic and Pan-Africanist discourses, anticolonialism, and resistance to the European and white American domination of the world. The journal opened up the international framework of Pan-Africanism to discuss the cases of Moroccans, Egyptians, and additional African and Asian Muslim groups. It featured essays on Islam in India, book reviews, advertisements from Asian and African sources, and for a brief time a section written in the Arabic language.[17] It was owned by Pan-Africanists in Sierra Leone, Lagos (Nigeria), and the Gold Coast.[18] John H. Hanson writes, "Duse Mohamed Ali's influence on the Ahmadiyya extended to the United States, where Mufti Muhammad Sadiq, the first Ahmadi missionary in the United States, concentrated his efforts on African Americans in several northern cities, most likely through Ali's contacts."[19]

In Chicago, Mufti Muhammad Sadiq resisted Western imperialism and supported Pan-Africanism, Pan-Islamic coalitions, and anticolonial movements for black and brown liberation and self-determination. He encouraged Garvey to revise the UNIA motto "One God, One Aim, One Destiny" to connect to "one language which would be Arabic," so that black Americans could find supporters among millions of Muslims in Asia, Africa, and the Middle East.[20] The Ahmadiyya Muslim Community circulated Muhammad Ali's first English translation of the Qur'an among African American Muslim communities, including Sheikh Daoud Ahmed Faisal's Islamic Mission of America and Elijah Muhammad's Nation of Islam, and converted several thousand black Americans by 1940 in its mission houses in midwestern and northeastern cities.[21]

The 1930s and 1940s brought a significant shift in the Ahmadiyya Muslim Community's missionary work, with the successful new programs of a new Indian missionary, Sufi Mutiur Rahman Bengalee, and popularity among jazz musicians in the United States.[22] Black Ahmadi leaders like Omar Cleveland wrote about the "democracy of Islam" in the *Moslem Sunrise*: "Across the threshold of the mosque, in the fold of Islam, all are held to be equal. No distinction is made between men, regardless of race, class, or position. The prince and pauper meet on common ground. . . . The inequality of wealth and opportunity, which makes life so cruel ceases. All are children of Allah."[23] The Ahmadi missionary Bengalee criticized the systemic racism of Christianity and, in his lectures and publications, engaged in a jihad of words, using spiritual and political arguments about the struggle for faith and democracy to promote racial equality:

> Treat the colored people in a truly democratic spirit. Do not shut the
> doors of your churches, hotels, schools, and homes against them. Let

them enjoy all the privileges which you possess. If they are poor, help them. If they are backward, uplift them, but for heaven's sake, do not despise them.[24]

The *Moslem Sunrise* condemned racism as the cause of the Detroit race riots in 1943:

> The Detroit riots have smeared a dark blot on this country's good name. . . . Now the news goes all over the world, to North Africa, among the dark-skinned people in India and the South Pacific Islands, among the yellow-skinned peoples of Malaya, Indochina, Thailand, China, and Korea, that black-skinned people are killing and being killed by white-skinned people in free America.[25]

In the early 1940s, the Ahmadiyya's global population was close to two million adherents in Asia, Africa, Europe, and the Americas. Their most important missions in the United States were in Chicago, Kansas City (Missouri), Cleveland, Pittsburgh, and Washington, DC. The community's twenty years of American missionary work were successful in terms of its converts' faithful practice of the Five Pillars of Islam and their adherence to studying the Qur'an and Arabic. Although the Ahmadiyya Muslim Community in the United States included Asians and whites, most of its converts were black, some were jazz musicians, and it was one of the oldest and most significant Islamic groups among African Americans in the World War II period.

The late 1940s were a period of shifting strategies among some segments of the Ahmadiyya Muslim Community, because the political turmoil in Pakistan forced the Ahmadis to use some of their resources there. When the British government left India and the country became independent, it was partitioned according to religious identities, with Hindus and Sikhs in the new India and Muslims in the new Islamic Republic of Pakistan. These dramatic shifts brought on the persecution and relocation of the Ahmadiyya community in the Punjab. Two months after the partition plan was publicized, 100,000 Muslims were massacred in August 1947 in Patiala, a Sikh state in the Punjab. The violence escalated later in the summer and resulted in 650,000 Muslims reported missing in East Punjab and 5 million Muslims compelled to migrate to

Pakistan. Three-quarters of Pakistan's 70 million people were Muslims in 1948. Rabwah in Pakistan became the new international headquarters of the Ahmadiyya. Yet the Sunni Muslim majority in Pakistan branded the Ahmadiyya community heretical because it believed that prophecy continued with its founder, Ghulam Ahmad. The persecution of the Ahmadis escalated in 1953, when the government of Pakistan declared them "a non-Muslim minority."[26]

Black jazz musicians performed all over the United States in the postwar period, and they were appalled by what they sensed was a growing explosion of white Christian attacks on black Americans. Headlines and newspaper descriptions of such events told only part of the story: "Ex-Marine slain for moving Jim Crow sign" in Alabama; "Cops gouge out Negro vet's eyes" in South Carolina; "Black veteran . . . blow torched until his 'eyes popped out of his head and his light skin was seared dark'" in Louisiana; "Planned lynching of a black veteran who defended his mother from a beating" in Columbia, Tennessee; and "Bound and surrounded, two sisters and their husbands were defenseless against the truckload of firepower brought to the killing fields at Moore's Ford" in Monroe, Georgia.[27] During this era of Jim Crow atrocities, southern politicians and the State Department worked together to prevent the United Nations from investigating lynchings and enforcing human rights in the United States.[28] These racially motivated crimes added fuel to Bengalee's fiery critique of systemic racism in American Christianity and influenced some musicians to consider conversion to the Ahmadiyya, not only to resist racism and to protect their endangered black male bodies in the Jim Crow era, but also to leave the United States and to reject a Negro/colored identity by embracing universal Islamic values of racial equality.

The 1950s began with reinvigorated political perspectives on self-determination and liberation in the Muslim world, perspectives that attracted the attention of African American jazz musicians who were disgusted with racial segregation in America, attracted to the Ahmadiyya, and interested in the international issues that the global Islamic community and the Third World faced. In 1952 Gamal Abdel Nasser became the Muslim president of Egypt and constructed a postcolonial identity for Egyptians that emphasized pan-Arab Islamic unity, socialism, and solidarity with the Third World.[29] Nasser articulated his political and religious perspectives in his 1955 book *Egypt's Liberation: The Philosophy of the Revolution*, which discussed his country's identity encompassed and expressed in three circles of power: "the Arab, the African, and the Islamic."[30] As a result, African American Islamic leaders began to develop religious and political contacts with Egypt. Nasser supported Egypt's participation in the 1955 Bandung conference of Third World nations in Indonesia, and later on, he curried favor with African American leaders again, when he convened an international summit in Cairo, the Afro-Asian People's Solidarity Conference.[31] Then, from 1956 to 1957, Nasser impressed African American Muslims by challenging Western imperialism: forcing Britain to leave the Suez Canal Zone as he nationalized it; overcoming British, Israeli, and French military attacks; opposing American control of Egypt; and affirming Afro-Asian political power.[32]

On the American Islamic front, black musicians in the Ahmadiyya Muslim Community created their own cool language forms that blended Arabic and bebop slang.[33] The black Atlantic coolness of the Ahmadi jazz musicians and fans incorporated Afro-Islamic internationalist styles of political, artistic, and religious consciousness, impressing the hep cats in the working-class youth cultures after World War II. In this period, coolness came to be defined as a profound lived expression of experimentation with Islam—the style, struggle, consciousness, and peace of being a black Muslim in the United States.

The Ahmadi sense of African American religious internationalism differed from the Nation of Islam's vision of a black Asiatic identity. The first wave of Ahmadiyya missionaries were South Asians who supported jazz's values of black affirmation, freedom, and self-determination but also emphasized reading the Qur'an, studying Arabic, practicing the Five Pillars of Islam, and embracing the religious values of the global Muslim community as the pathway to peace and liberation for black musicians. They viewed the struggle for black liberation in a global context, and promoted solidarity with people of color in the Muslim world who were not black.

These ideas were powerfully compelling to post–World War II bebop jazz musicians and fans, who felt stuck in a culture that offered very few pathways to freedom and equality. They were fascinated by the Ahmadis' rejection of systemic racism, as well as their ideas about Muslim identity and masculinities. Although African American converts did not adopt the Nation of Islam's X to replace their slave surnames and to signify an oppositional masculinity that demonized whiteness, the Ahmadi converts changed their Christian names to Arabic names and embraced their own communal masculinity to signal their blackness as well as their religious solidarity with the transnational values and universal brotherhood of the worldwide Muslim community. And as we will see, there were various degrees of spiritual rigor among the jazz musicians who practiced the Ahmadi presentation of Islam.

The Ahmadiyya mission in the United States sent forth South Asian as well as African American male proselytizers to work among prospective bebop converts, whereas the Nation of Islam relied solely on black male missionaries, who canvassed the urban street corners in Boston, New York, Chicago, Philadelphia, Detroit, and other big cities for new members in the jazz community. Moreover, Ahmadi innovations involving the style of clothing and the presentation of the black male body differed from the Nation of Islam's sartorial style for black men, which emphasized Western styles of formal dress such as dark suits and clean-shaven faces for its male members. The black male musicians who joined the Ahmadiyya might mark their new religious identity by wearing Islamic skullcaps such as the kufi or taqiyah, Middle Eastern head scarfs such as the kuffiya, or Islamic robes or tunics, or by growing beards like the Indian missionaries, although some of the converts continued to wear modest Western styles of men's clothing and remained clean-shaven.

In the following sections of the chapter, we will see how the themes of transnationalism, resistance to systemic racism, African American religious internationalism, and masculinity played out among the black jazz musicians who converted to the Ahmadiyya Muslim Community in Boston, New York, Chicago, and Detroit in the 1940s and 1950s. We will look at the spiritual awakening of jazz artists such as Ahmed Abdul-Malik and Yusef Lateef, Kenny Clarke's migration to Paris, the Muslim musicians in Dizzy Gillespie's band, the missionary work of Art Blakey in New York City, his sojourn in West Africa, and the Jazz Messengers and hard bop. As we will see, the Ahmadiyya was a wealthy religious group with worldwide networks and resources to support its African American jazz artists who decided to leave the United States to escape violent racism and to expand their sense of freedom, black internationalism, and global musical collaborations.

Ahmadiyya Beboppers in Boston, New York, Chicago, Philadelphia, Washington, DC, and Detroit: Transnational Journeys and Resistance

Two jazz artists who had studied music at the Boston Conservatory and the New England Conservatory of Music led the way in Roxbury and the South End, converting to the Ahmadiyya Muslim Community just as active missionaries began work there. These musicians expressed the values of black affirmation, liberation, and self-determination not only by accepting Islam, but also by adopting transnational strategies in their musical careers. In 1945 or 1946, the bebop saxophonist and flutist Eddie Gregory, who was a migrant from Georgia and a former student at the Boston Conservatory, embraced the religion and changed his name to Sahib Shihab.[34] He played with Fletcher Henderson, Thelonius Monk, Tad Dameron, Dizzy Gillespie, Illinois Jacquet, Oscar Pettiford, Quincy Jones, and Kenny Clarke in the 1940s and 1950s.[35] Shihab was interviewed in 1953 for an *Ebony* magazine article on Muslim jazz musicians, who were the leaders in the conversion of African Americans to Islam, and the article reported that he changed his religion "because Islam seemed to offer all that Christianity had failed to give him."[36] Tired of the systemic racism he experienced in the New York jazz scene, Sahib Shihab expressed his freedom and resistance as a proud black Muslim man by leaving the United States in 1959. South Asian missionaries had just arrived in the Scandinavian countries in 1956 to recruit new converts for the Ahmadiyya Muslim Community, and Shihab joined them, migrating and performing jazz in Sweden and Denmark until the early 1970s.[37]

In the 1940s tenor saxophonist and World War II veteran Gladstone Scott converted to the Ahmadiyya Muslim Community in Boston and took the Muslim name Ghulam Sadiq, although jazz performance venues in the United States and Canada continued to bill him as Gladstone Scott. He had received a scholarship to study at the New England Conservatory of Music when he was eight years old and played with the tenor saxophone star Coleman Hawkins when he was twelve. His best friend during the 1940s and 1950s was the Nation of Islam member and trumpeter Malcolm "Shorty" Jarvis. Their friendship illustrates that a black Islamic brotherhood was fostering a communal masculinity among Boston jazz musicians, a brotherhood that sometimes crossed the boundaries of the various Muslim communities in the city. Sadiq played the saxophone in USO shows in Japan during World War II, and in 1952 he created his own transnational path by migrating to Montreal and performing with Al Cowan's band the Tramps, although he sometimes came back to Boston to visit his wife and children. Shorty Jarvis was with Ghulam Sadiq in Montreal in 1957, the year he died from cancer. The jazz musicians around Sadiq's hospital bed reported that he was reciting Arabic prayers just before he died.[38]

Bashir Ahmad, an Ahmadi missionary who was born in Philadelphia, proselytized in Boston's black community for new converts during the 1940s and 1950s.[39] Attracted by the transnational Islamic style of Ahmad's South Asian clothing, Stephen Peters, a young professional jazz pianist, came under his sway and converted to the Ahmadiyya Muslim Community in 1945. Using his family's Cambridge home for religious meetings in the 1940s, Peters adopted the new name Khalil Mahmoud. He cultivated his jazz connections in the South End and used his vision of freedom and global black religious consciousness to introduce the Ahmadi message to bebop musicians in Boston.[40] Later on, Mahmoud would abandon his musical career and embark on a transnational religious and educational journey: graduating from Boston University and McGill University in Canada, teaching religion at Lincoln University in Pennsylvania, and working for the Ahmadiyya in West Africa and London.[41] However, from 1947 to 1952, he competed with the Nation of Islam for new converts to Islam among Boston's jazz musicians. Khalil Mahmoud persuaded Jack Byat (Jahmid Ahmad Bashir) and Wilbur Lucas (Waji Lateef) to join the Ahmadiyya and to change their names during this period.[42] Bostonian Eleanor Jumper, a nightclub bartender, was fascinated by the Ahmadi jazz musicians performing at the Savoy Ballroom in Harlem. She converted to the Ahmadiyya Muslim Community along with black musicians in New York City, but she traced the roots of her conversion to the Islamic influences she first encountered in Boston's black jazz world.[43]

Khalil Mahmoud's sense of communal masculinity and Islamic brotherhood, along with his program to propagate Islam among black beboppers, encouraged him to interact with the small community of Syrian and Lebanese Sunni Muslims who eventually built their own mosque in

Quincy, a Boston suburb.[44] However, Mahmoud's relationship with the Arab Muslims in Quincy did not help to advance his Ahmadiyya missionary work in Roxbury and the South End in the 1940s and 1950s, and ultimately the Nation of Islam won the competition for black converts to Islam in Boston, when Malcolm X returned to the city in 1953.

On another religious front, in New York City, the Ahmadiyya missionaries were very successful in their work among the bebop musicians who were drawn to the values of racial affirmation, liberation, and social justice that jazz musicians and Islamic missionaries shared, as well as to African American religious internationalism and the Ahmadi sense of transnationalism and universal brotherhood. In the 1940s, the teenage jazz bassist and violinist Jonathan Tim Jr., whose Afro-Caribbean parents immigrated to Brooklyn from St. Vincent, converted to the Ahmadiyya Muslim Community through the jazz-inflected Muslim Brotherhood in Bedford- Stuyvesant, and changed his name to Ahmed Hussein Abdul-Malik.[45] Abdul-Malik spoke Arabic, played Middle Eastern instruments such as the kanoon and oud, and interacted with Arab musicians on Atlantic Avenue. Among his close friends were pianist Randy Weston, whose Caribbean father was a Garveyite in Bedford-Stuyvesant, and alto saxophonist Bilal Abdurahman, who was also an Ahmadiyya convert.[46] Abdul-Malik's black Atlantic cool vision of modern jazz led him to recreate his musical and religious identities through Islam and to resist the anti-black racism of an American Negro identity. He reached out to Africa by reimagining his West Indian heritage as Sudanese; played with Art Blakey in the 1940s before playing a fusion of jazz, Middle Eastern, and North African musical forms in his own group in Brooklyn and Manhattan; and also played with John Coltrane at the Five Spot Café in New York and with Thelonius Monk's quartet.[47]

Abdul-Malik's contribution to the wave of African American religious internationalism culminated in 1958 and 1959, when he recorded two albums, *Jazz Sahara: Ahmed Abdul-Malik's Middle Eastern Music* and *East Meets West: The Musique of Ahmed Abdul-Malik*, albums that created a new genre of black Islamic music by infusing jazz with Middle Eastern and North African music.[48] In *East Meets West*, Abdul-Malik wrote his own original compositions combining bebop with Arab musical sounds. The "East meets West" idea was also evident in the titles of his compositions: he presented Arabic titles in phonetic English (with English trans-

lations in parentheses) on the album's track list: "El-Lail (The Night),"
"La Ibky (Don't Cry)," "Takseem (Solo)," "Isma'a (Listen)," "Rooh (The
Soul)," "Mahawara (The Fugue)," and "El Ghada (The Jungle)."[49] *East
Meets West* illustrated how the study of Arabic in the Ahmadiyya Mus-
lim Community shaped the spiritual and musical experimentation and
the increasingly international interests of African American and Afro-
Caribbean Ahmadi jazz musicians.

Kenny Clarke, a jazz drummer from Pittsburgh who contributed
to the creation of bebop at Minton's Playhouse during the early 1940s
in New York City, converted to Ahmadiyya in 1946 and adopted the
name Liaquat Ali Salaam. In the story of his resistance to systemic racism and his transnational journey he is much like other jazz musicians
who sought liberation, independence, and racial affirmation through religious conversion. Clarke was in the army during World War II and was
shocked by the racism he encountered in the South as well as the violent
racism against returning black soldiers after the war, in 1946. He had
performed music in England, Belgium, Germany, and Paris during the
war and returned to France to play jazz with Dizzy Gillespie in 1948. By
then, Kenny Clarke was experiencing the brotherhood and racial equality of the Ahmadiyya Muslim Community, but his resistance values and
his plans for migration to Paris were shaped by Gillespie's musical perspectives about self-determination and freedom in bebop. According to
Gillespie, "beboppers . . . refused to accept racism, poverty, or economic
exploitation, nor would we live out uncreative humdrum lives merely
for the sake of survival. . . . If America wouldn't honor its Constitution
and respect us as men, we couldn't give a shit about the American way."[50]

Dizzy Gillespie explained that black bebop musicians like Clarke,
who had converted to Islam, did so to erase the stigma of their colored
Jim Crow identity and to have "'W' for white" printed on their identification cards, to protect them from racial violence.[51] However, Gillespie also admitted in a 1948 *Life* magazine article that although he was
not a Muslim, he was studying the Qur'an, and "in Islam, there is no
color line. Everybody is treated like equals."[52] Indeed, African American musicians identifying themselves as the people they wanted to be,
through their embracing of Islam and new names, could reject Negro
and colored inferiority, and declare themselves to be black international
people—Muslims in the global Islamic community.

Then Gillespie added, "As time went on, I kept considering converting to Islam but mostly for social reasons. I didn't know very much about the religion, but I could dig the idea that Muhammad was a prophet. I believed that and, there were very few Christians who believed that Muhammad had the word of God with him."[53] Impressed by the piety of some of the Ahmadi converts in his band, he reported, "Although I hadn't converted yet, I knew one couldn't drink alcohol or eat pork as a Muslim. . . . I felt quite intrigued by the beautiful sound of the word 'Quran,' and found it 'out of this world,' 'way out'. . . . Most of the Muslim guys who were sincere in the beginning went on believing and practicing the faith."[54]

Kenny Clarke went on to record albums with the Modern Jazz Quartet; pianists John Lewis, Mary Lou Williams, Hank Jones, and Horace Silver; trumpeters Miles Davis and Donald Byrd; bassist Paul Chambers; cornetist Nat Adderley; saxophonists Charlie Parker, Jerome Richardson, Julian Cannonball Adderley, and Sonny Rollins; and vibraphonist Milt Jackson in the United States in the 1950s. Clarke finally migrated to Paris, the city of his teenage dreams, in 1956, a "refugee from racism," escaping white Americans' discrimination against black people and black jazz musicians.[55] He lived there for the rest of his life, with brief visits to America.[56] During the postwar period, Paris was home to a community of African American jazz musicians that included Sidney Bechet, Inez Cavanaugh, Don Byas, and Johnny Griffin, and its neighborhood included jazz-inflected streets such as Rue Armstrong and Rue Bechet.[57] Although Clarke escaped violent racism by migrating to France and merged his religious and musical goals and values in Paris by practicing Islam in peace and forming his own jazz group, the Kenny Clarke/ Fancy Boland Big Band, his evaluation of his journey as a black man in Europe exemplifies the complexities of transnationalism and the limits of Muslim universal brotherhood for some bebop artists who converted to Islam in this era: "I am way out of the European society. I am not accepted. I just stay on the outskirts. In a sense no white society is going to accept a black man. The sooner black people figure that out, the better off they will be."[58]

Jazz musician Maneer Hamid's story involves military sojourns in Muslim-majority countries and may serve as a meditation for thinking about why and how some black Philadelphians decided to convert to the Ahmadiyya Muslim Community instead of Sunni Islam:

My first introduction was around 1954 or 1955. My sister was in a singing group called the Capris. She met Len Hope, and he was a Sunni Muslim and saxophone player who was very well known and had several albums out. He would wear a turban and say "as salaam alaikam." He had some moral qualities the other musicians didn't have. I became interested and started to read as much literature as I could. I was fifteen years old. I met a friend. Instead of hustling money, he gave me a book to read, *Our Promised Messiah*. He was having a meeting in his house in West Philadelphia on Hobart Avenue. The Ahmadi missionaries Nur Haq-Anwar and Muhammad Sadiq were teaching a bunch of brothers in Philadelphia. The rituals made an impression on me so that when I went home I decided to become Muslim. But I hesitated.

In Washington, DC, I was stationed on Andrews Air Force Base. Khalil Nasir, the Ahmadi missionary, invited me to come out for Friday Jumah, 1955. I was sixteen. I converted then. When I got to the mosque in Washington, DC, Islam in America was dominated by African Americans—thirty people in DC were Ahmadiyya, twenty-five were black. I was fortunate to hook up with some brothers. Dr. Bashiruddin Usma, he was going to Howard University at that time studying to be a dentist. He introduced me to E. Franklin Frazier. At that time the Sunni mosque was about to open up.

I was still attached to the US service and really wasn't practicing Islam as it was taught in the Qur'an. One of my friends who was Sunni in the service and a black African, Ali, discouraged me from the Ahmadiyya. I hesitated to sign the Baiyat. But the more I read the literature I saw that what he was saying wasn't true. But our group was the only group that wasn't saying negative things about the other groups in its literature. I was raised Baptist. I didn't pursue being a Sunni anymore.

In 1956 I got an assignment to go overseas to Japan. My roommate in the service had gotten his orders the next day to go to Turkey. We switched. So I went to Turkey to experience a Muslim country. I was stationed in Turkey for three years in the southern part, a small town, about three thousand people. I was able to blend in and practice my Islam. When my time in the service was up, they sent me to Greece for a while—six months; North Africa, Libya—six months.

They let me out in 1960. I went back to the DC mosque on 2141 Leroy Place. I was going to be a missionary, but I was an amateur musician. I was caught sneaking out of the mosque to gig in the bar. The rigidity didn't work out. In 1961 I went back to Philadelphia. . . . A lot of jazz musicians were Muslims. Charlie Parker, they said was Muslim—Abdul Karim.[59]

Dizzy Gillespie's trumpeter from Antigua, Alfonso Nelson Rainey, who was a former Julliard School of Music student, converted to Islam, changed his name to Talib Dawud, and stopped performing jazz to focus completely on his new religion. He married Sayida Faisal, a second-generation black Ahmadiyya woman in Cleveland. By the early 1950s, he founded and led the Muslim Brotherhood USA, a new group that was affiliated with the Ahmadiyya Muslim Community. Dawud and his wife moved to Philadelphia, where he collaborated with the Egyptian-Muslim immigrant Mahmoud Alwan and the Jamaican American journalist and historian J. A. Rogers to establish the Islamic and African Institute. The three men taught Islam, Arabic, and African history to the black community at the institute. Its parades in New York and Philadelphia honored African leaders like Sékou Touré and Kwame Nkrumah when they attended meetings at the United Nations. The organization also supported the Algerian National Liberation Front in the Algerian war of independence from France.[60]

Eventually, the former jazz musician linked the Muslim Brotherhood USA with mosques in Providence, Boston, and Washington, DC, and connected the Philadelphia mosque to Sheik Nasir Ahmad's and Imam Abdul Raheem's International Muslim Brotherhood in Harlem. The organization faced a violent, racist police crackdown in Philadelphia when its members like Sulaiman al-Hadi began using posters and pamphlets to enhance their public missionary work in 1958. Then, theological tensions with the Nation of Islam emerged when Dawud attempted to set up the Muslim Brotherhood in Detroit.[61] According to Robert Dannin, "He claimed the true path to salvation for the American Muslim led toward international solidarity, not racial exclusivity."[62] In 1959 the Muslim leader, who had recently performed the pilgrimage to Mecca, revealed his opposition to Elijah Muhammad's community in a *New York Amsterdam News* article:

Mr. Muhammad's followers do not make prayer properly; they do not face the East and say their prayers five times a day, as all true Muslims do;

their houses of worship are called "temples," while the houses of worship of the true Muslims are called Mosques. . . . All true Muslims believe that the Koran will be here until the day of Judgement, but Mr. Muhammad tells his followers that the Koran will be superseded by a book written for black people.

Another basic difference [is that] . . . the Muslim faith does not teach hatred of any particular group, but on the contrary, welcomes people of all races and colors so long as they abide by and live up to the teachings of Islam. . . . The true Muslims worship Allah, but Mr. Muhammad and his followers claim that Allah is a man named W. Fard Muhammad.[63]

Talib Dawud married the jazz vocalist Dakota Staton in 1959. He met Staton in 1958 and introduced her to Islam; she joined the Ahmadiyya Muslim Community and changed her name to Aliyah Rabia in that year.[64] Born in Pittsburgh, she was one of the leading jazz singers in the United States. Her first album, *The Late, Late Show* (Capitol Records, 1958), which featured her beautiful renditions of jazz standards like "My Funny Valentine," "Misty," and "The Late, Late Show," was one of the best-selling jazz albums in 1958. It was followed by other Capitol Record albums in the 1950s: *Dynamic!* (1958), *In the Night* (1958), *Time to Swing* (1959), *More Than the Most* (1959), and *Crazy He Calls Me* (1959). Although Dakota Staton was a gifted vocalist with her own successful career and money, when she converted to Islam, she viewed her religious experience and marriage as "fundamentally intertwined."[65] She enjoyed preparing meals for her husband and supporting his work as welcome and protective relief from the sexism and drinking that dominated the nightclubs in which she performed.[66] As Sylvia Chan-Malik explains, "For Staton, being Muslim was expressed in negotiations between her career . . . and her self-presentation as a deferential and devoted Muslim wife."[67] However, as the "only non-NOI affiliated woman to publicly identify as Muslim during this period," she followed Dawud's patriarchal lead and joined him in his theological attacks on the Nation of Islam that culminated in an unsuccessful lawsuit against Elijah Muhammad.[68] In a *Pittsburgh Courier* interview, the jazz woman pointed out that "since 1959, we have both vigorously pursued a campaign to make the public aware of the differences between what Elijah Poole preaches and teaches and the actual tenets of that faith in which we believe."[69] Staton emphasized that "my career as a singer has suffered irreparable harm as a result of the fact that the press has linked us with Elijah's organization."[70]

She and her husband signaled their transnational Islamic identities when they took the lead in a 1959 Harlem luncheon for Sékou Touré, the Pan-African, Muslim president of Guinea, an anticolonial nation which became independent from France in 1958.[71] Staton and Dawud used this occasion to verbally attack Elijah Muhammad's followers, who were not invited to the event. Unfortunately, Dawud was "attacked by acid throwers who apparently were members of the Nation," according to Louis A. DeCaro Jr.[72] Later on, in 1962, they filed a legal suit in the Philadelphia US District Court to stop the Nation's leader "from claiming to be Muslim and to prevent him from further use of the terms Islam and Muslim in connection with the sect he heads."[73] Ultimately, their case, which was dismissed, did not help Dakota Staton's jazz career, especially when Malcolm X attacked her: "Ever since she changed her 'tunes' and started singing against Mr. Muhammad, her popularity has been on the downturn."[74] Although she continued to record albums, Capitol Records cut ties with Staton in the early 1960s. She and Dawud relocated to London in 1965 but divorced a few years later, and the jazz vocalist cut all ties with Islam.[75] Dakota Staton's story shows us how Islamic men in the jazz world sometimes shaped "women's constructions of Muslim-ness in both private (e.g., marriage) and public (e.g., the press) relationships, in both positive and . . . negative ways."[76]

Talib Dawud also advanced the religious style of transnationalism and his vision of the "true Islam" by influencing black musicians such as tenor saxophone player Yusef Lateef (William Emmanuel Huddleston) to join the Ahmadiyya Muslim Community in Chicago.[77] The saxophonist remembered his first encounter with the religion:

> My embrace of Islam came about in 1946 while I was working with the Willy Hayes Band in a club on the west side of Chicago. One night a trumpet player named Talib Dawud sat-in with us. He told me that he was an itinerant musician and that he was a practicing member of the Ahmadiyya movement. I expressed interest in learning more about Islam. He said he would give me some literature about Islam. . . . Islam taught that you could realize paradise in this life as well as in the next. The pri-

mary belief was in one God, the Creator of the heavens and earth. All this was very appealing to my rationality.[78]

Yusef Lateef, who was born in Tennessee and raised in Detroit, studied Islam with the Indian Ahmadi missionaries in their Chicago mission house.[79] He attended Ahmadiyya meetings in Art Blakey's apartment when he came to New York with Dizzy Gillespie's band.[80] Yusef Lateef became a devout Muslim in 1948 and noted the universal benefits of Islam in his account of his jazz journey to the Ahmadiyya Muslim Community: "I studied the religion and finally decided to embrace it because" Islam emphasized submission to the will of God, peace, justice, kindness, and compassion and respect for the poor.[81]

Lateef was happy to contribute to the urban musical creativity of bebop, but his religious discipline led to his condemnation of drug addiction in the jazz community. He saw it as a pathological form of black masculinity that destroyed artistic freedom and self-determination.[82] Ultimately, Lateef's spiritual consciousness shaped his music. His respect for the spiritual qualities of bebop sounds fed his resistance to the marginalization of the music: he commented that the music "deserves better venues" than nightclubs that serve alcohol.[83]

His spiritual development as a Muslim was shaped among a network of dynamic black American Ahmadi leaders emerging in the 1950s, such as Mursil Shafeek, who was fluent in Arabic and president of the Dayton community; Muhammad Sadiq, a jazz trombonist who became president of the New Jersey and New York City communities; Bashir Afzal, a New York City leader; and Rashid Ahmed, who studied in Pakistan to get ready for missionary work in New York, Chicago, St. Louis, and Milwaukee.[84]

In the mid-1950s, Lateef studied music at Wayne State University in Detroit and discovered Arab and Middle Eastern reed instruments during his visits to the Syrian store in the city's Eastern Market.[85] Lateef learned to play instruments from all over the world—his works blended the sounds of the tenor saxophone, flute, oboe, shenai, bamboo flute, sarewa, argol, shofar, Taiwan koto, and tambourine. He soon formed his first band, and by 1957, his quintet traveled to New Jersey and New York to record two albums: *Other Sounds* and *Jazz for the Thinker*, which expressed his growing sense of the irrelevance of national boundaries when it came to both music and religion. *Other Sounds* featured Lateef (tenor sax, argol, flute), Wilbur Harden (flugelhorn), Hugh Lawson (Turkish finger cymbals, piano), Ernie Farrow (rebob, bass), and Oliver Jackson (earth-board, drums). Yusef Lateef signaled his Muslim masculinity by wearing a kufi in his photograph, on the album's cover.[86] The liner notes for *Jazz for the Thinker* commented on Lateef's spirituality and his transnational musical forms: "Attempting to bring his audience to a higher level of morality through his music, Yusef Lateef is a . . . consummate musician. . . . [His] music combines elements of the current 'hard bop' approach with Afro-Asiatic tinges. . . . Subtle, abstract touches . . . bring forth Indian effects, the rhythms pulse and force the listener to THINK."[87]

By the late 1950s, Yusef was discouraged by the shortage of jobs for musicians and by a "racial situation" in Detroit in which he was stopped and searched by the police on his way to a performance and was beaten on his hands with a blackjack in the back of a police car.[88] Ultimately he moved to New York City, where he played with jazz men like Charles Mingus, Eric Dolphy, Max Roach, Rashaan Roland Kirk, Randy Weston, and Grant Green, to name a few. He also performed with the Nigerian drummer Babatunde Olatunji's band:

> Playing with Babatunde was an interesting experience, mostly because for the first time I had to perform without a pianist or bassist in the group. It provided me with a lot of harmonic space and freedom. Olatunji's music also provided a wider appreciation for world music. To this extent, he was a pioneer of what is termed today "world music."[89]

The Global Black Religious Consciousness of Ahmadiyya Jazz Musicians and the Emergence of Hard Bop

In the early 1940s, bebop drummer Art Blakey had played at Kelley's Stable in New York City and the Tic Tock Club in Boston, and with Mary Lou Williams, Billy Eckstine, Dizzy Gillespie, Charlie Parker, and Thelonius Monk.[90] Blakey, who was born in Pittsburgh, had begun to question Christianity and protest systemic racism after he was severely beaten by white men while touring with the Fletcher Henderson band in the South in 1943. The beating resulted in a head injury requiring surgery to put a steel plate in his head.[91] By 1947, Blakey had converted to Islam. He took the name Abdullah Ibn Buhaina, and along with Talib Dawud, held Ahmadiyya meetings for jazz musicians in his New York City apartment.[92] When he converted to the Ahmadiyya Muslim Community and experienced Islamic brotherhood, he said, "Islam has made me feel more like a man, really free."[93] Then, in 1947, Blakey decided to travel to West Africa, spending many months on pilgrimage of sorts, traveling to Nigeria and Ghana, where the Ahmadiyya had branches, to study African religions and Arabic languages.[94] When he returned to the United States in 1948, his drumming and his jazz were infused with African rhythms and musical inflections and a sophisticated sense of blackness that influenced a new genre of bebop.

Ahmadiyya jazz musicians like Art Blakey, Kenny Clarke, and Yusef Lateef were among the early leaders in hard bop, a new style of bebop that Samuel A. Floyd described as having "a bluesy, funky delivery, with lots of forceful interaction between trumpet and drums, employing elements from gospel and R&B, . . . characterized by off-beat accents, . . . riffs, call-response vocal inflections, simple melodies, and . . . ostinatos [repetitive melodic or rhythmic phrases]."[95] These musicians often combined emotions from black American, Caribbean, African, and Eastern musical forms with innovative harmonies and compositions.[96] Hard bop musicians played soulful, aggressive, urban sounds that resonated with black Atlantic cool and that expressed communal masculinity, with its concern for black American and African liberation and black notions of self-determination and affirmation. Their music was part of the trend for black men to seek out musical and spiritual inspiration in traditions developed outside the United States. Hard bop quickly became popular in black urban communities from the mid-1950s to the 1960s. Art Blakey's loud and hard-driving drumming and the Islamic, African, and African diasporic musical motifs exemplified by his band the Jazz Messengers led the way in shaping the rhythms and sounds of hard bop in the African American bars and clubs of the northern cities.

The origins of the Jazz Messengers can be traced to 1948, when Blakey established a new band, the Seventeen Messengers, an Islamic brotherhood of bebop artists, which initially included African American artists who had converted to the Ahmadiyya Muslim Community:

Sahib Shihab (alto saxophone), Musa Kaleem and Yusef Lateef (tenor saxophone), Haleen Rasheed (trombone), Abdul Hamid (trumpet), and Ibrahim Ibn Ismail (piano); as well as the following non-Muslim musicians: Sonny Rollins (tenor saxophone), Little Benny Harris and Ray Copeland (trumpet), Bud Powell and Kenny Drew (piano), Gary Mapp (bass), and Cecil Payne (baritone saxophone), among others.[97] In the Islamic world, "Messenger" referred to Muhammad (570–632 CE), the Messenger of God, the Prophet of Islam, and the exemplary Muslim man who expressed Muslim religious goals and values. From Blakey's black perspective, the Messengers incorporated Pan-African motifs into their music that connected the African diasporic, African, and African American sounds of modern jazz, motifs that reminded Blakey of his religious experiences during his sojourn in West Africa.

By the mid-1950s, Blakey was framing hard bop in a larger black global context, incorporating African and Afro-Cuban musical forms, and reshaping his group periodically by including new jazz musicians like Horace Silver, Clifford Brown, Lou Donaldson, Gigi Gryce, Kenny Dorham (Abdul Hamid), Joe Gordon, and Walter Bishop Jr. Many of his musicians were not Muslim during this period, yet the influences of his transnational journey in African American Islam were evident in the Jazz Messengers' spiritual and musical experimentation. For example, in 1956, a newly configured Jazz Messengers recorded an album for Columbia. *Drum Suite* exemplified Art Blakey's new style of African American religious internationalism in hard bop that sometimes used instruments, rhythms, and musicians of diverse religious sensibilities from all over the African and African diasporic world.[98] The atmosphere of the album's first track, "The Sacrifice," was African, featuring West African drumming and a Swahili chant that conguero Sabu Martinez used to recreate the musical spirit of an African religious ceremony.[99] Pianist Ray Bryant's composition "Cubano Chant" featured Afro-Cuban rhythms, Spanish lyrics in a call-and-response chorus, and the Cuban musician Cándido Camero on the bass and congas.[100] The Jazz Messengers recorded *Drum Suite* and another African/African-diasporic-theme album, *Ritual,* just before Ghana's independence celebration on March 6, 1957, and in the first track of *Ritual,* Blakey described the impact of his West African sojourn and the influence of African drum rhythms on his own jazz performances: "I wanted to live among the people and find out . . . about the drums especially. We were in the interior of Nigeria. And I met . . . the Ijaw people. . . . Anything . . . that day that is good, they play about it that night. This particular thing caught my ear for the different rhythms."[101] In these two albums, and in the hard bop musicians' solidarity with Art Blakey, a Muslim bandleader who was a missionary for his faith, we can see how jazz contributed to a growing sense that many blacks in the United States were beginning to see themselves as part of a culture that was increasingly transnational.

But the music would do something else, as well. The African independence and Islamic identities that Blakey and his Messengers celebrated in their albums would come to inform a growing sense of militancy and resistance to white supremacy in the jazz world as the 1950s gave way to the 1960s. As Blakey summed it up, "Islam brought the black man what he was looking for, an escape like some found in drugs or drinking: a way of living and thinking he could choose in complete freedom. This is the reason we adopted this new religion in such numbers. It was for us, above all, a way of rebelling."[102]

In 1961 Blakey and the Jazz Messengers (Jymie Merritt on double bass, Lee Morgan on trumpet, Wayne Shorter on tenor saxophone, and Bobby Timmons on piano) went on to identify with the struggles of the freedom riders who were incarcerated in Jackson, Mississippi, for trying to desegregate interstate public transportation. The liner notes for his album *The Freedom Rider* explained the Muslim bandleader's passionate and militant support of civil rights activism:

> At the time of this recording . . . the battle of the bus terminals had not been won, and there was a feeling of impregnable determination among civil rights actionists to send Freedom Riders into the South until all the jails were filled—if that were necessary to end segregation of interstate travelers. In his absorbing, deeply personal solo, Art Blakey conjures up the whirlpool of emotions at that time—the winds of change sweeping the country, the resistance to that change, and the pervasive conviction of the Freedom Riders that "We Shall Not Be Moved."[103]

From Art Blakey to John Coltrane, through the music, spirituality, and international diversity of black Islamic musicians who were also activists, the urban soundtrack of hard bop as well as free jazz evolved side by side with the global consciousness of the African American Muslim movements during the Cold War, the civil rights struggles, and the Black Power era. As we will see in chapter 4, the Ahmadiyya Muslim Community, the Nation of Islam, and Sunni Islam influenced the religious, artistic, and political identities of jazz artists in this culminating period of the golden age of African American Islam and jazz, from the late 1950s to the 1960s, when the values of the revolutionary times infused spirituality, music, and new interactions with the Third World, all over black America.

4

Hard Bop, Free Jazz, and Islam

Black Liberation and Global Religious and Musical Consciousness in the Late 1950s and 1960s

Chapter 4 explores the intersecting identities of jazz and Islam through the wider lens of Sunni Islam, the Nation of Islam, the Ahmadiyya, and the musical styles of hard bop and free jazz in the late 1950s and 1960s. The conversion of jazz musicians to African American Islam and the links they established between their music and Muslim communities were central to the ascendancy of the religion in the 1960s, a period that saw the rise of the golden age of jazz, independence struggles in Africa, and black liberation movements in the United States. The twentieth century saw the involvement of African Americans with Sunni Islam and its impact on the masculinity and spirituality of jazz artists. The chapter then tells the story of the musicians who used their participation in the State Department's Cultural Presentations Program to influence new connections between music, religious internationalism, and black civil rights consciousness in the Islamic world and Africa. The chapter also traces how gender questions shaped the religious and musical identities of African American women like Etta James, a rhythm and blues and jazz artist and a convert to Islam.

Chapter 4 takes us to Philadelphia, where black artists like saxophonists Lynn Hope and John Coltrane, pianist McCoy Tyner, and drummer Rashied Ali explored rich connections between Islam and hard bop in the late 1950s. Coltrane's spiritual awakening, supported by his Muslim wife, Naima, in 1957 and his later black Atlantic musical practices in hard bop and free jazz, exemplified the emerging Islamic spirit that transformed religion and jazz in Philadelphia and New York. Chapter 4 looks at the religious and musical performances of Jamil Nasser, Grant Green, Lee Morgan, Daoud A. Haroon, Etta James, Max Roach, Abbey Lincoln, Babatunde Olatunji, Ahmad Jamal, Idris Muhammad, Yusef

Lateef, Randy Weston, Pharoah Sanders, and others. The chapter also describes how Malcolm X's and John Coltrane's meditations on jazz, Islam, and African American religious internationalism in the 1960s became so attractive to black musicians and their fans, especially those seeking freedom and self-determination during the civil rights and Black Power era. The biographies of these musicians reveal the many forces—religious, musical, social, and political—that came together in the global consciousness of Muslim jazz musicians.

The African American Journey to Sunni Islam

The involvement of jazz musicians with Islam in the late 1950s and 1960s was shaped by the Sunni practice and the black internationalism of several African American Muslim communities that began in the early twentieth century and that influenced the conversion of blacks to Islam: the Islamic Mission of America, the Addeynu Allahe Universal Arabic Association, and the First Cleveland Mosque. All these communities practiced the Five Pillars of Islam, believed in the Qur'an (in the Arabic language) as the original and final scripture of God, and differed from the Nation of Islam, the Moorish Science Temple, and the Ahmadiyya in their mainstream Sunni belief in Muhammad as God's final messenger and the "seal of the prophets." As we will see, self-determination and racial affirmation were central values embraced by the black Sunni Muslims in these groups as they negotiated the boundaries between immigrant and African American Muslims in the United States and immersed themselves in the spiritual freedom of a global Islamic religious consciousness.

The Islamic Mission of America, which was also called the State Street Mosque, was established by Sheikh Daoud Ahmed Faisal and his wife, Sayedah Khadija Faisal, in Brooklyn in 1939. Faisal (born David A. Donald) was a professional violinist and a Caribbean immigrant. He taught his African American, Arab, Sudanese, Afro-Caribbean, and merchant seamen followers that freedom, dignity, social justice, and human rights are the most important Islamic values after submission to the will of Allah.[1] The converts to the Islamic Mission of America received Muslim birth certificates that affirmed the true identities of "Muslim people of African Asian origin of American descent and of slave ancestry . . .

whose ancestors were unlawfully and forcefully brought to the shores of the Americas against their will, and were enslaved: and were eventually freed."[2] They also signed a Muslim certificate of adoption that verified their mainstream Muslim testimony of faith: "that there is no God but 'Allah' and . . . belief in all of the teachings of the Prophets and Messengers of 'Allah.'"[3] Faisal wrote pamphlets such as *Al-Islam, the Religion of Humanity* and a book, *Islam: The True Faith, the Religion of Humanity*, that formulated the spiritual foundation of his movement's black global religious consciousness, a spiritual foundation based on Sunni Islam in the United States and abroad.[4] His conception of black internationalism was supported not only by his publications and missionary activities, but also by his work in the 1950s with Arab officials at the United Nations who formally bestowed observer privileges in the General Assembly on the Islamic Mission of America. Faisal used his connections in the United Nations to oppose communism's atheism and to show how Islam's global spiritual and economic consciousness could uplift colonized oppressed people.[5] He taught black American Muslims to adopt a new internationalist sense of self that incorporated not just spiritual elements, but also anticolonial transnational styles of dress, custom, and language that were beginning to be popular in Middle Eastern and North African nations.

The Addeynu Allahe Universal Arabic Association was established by Muhammad Ezaldeen (born James Lomax), who was also an early leader of Noble Drew Ali's Moorish Science Temple of America in Chicago and Detroit in the 1920s as well as a public school principal and English teacher. In 1913 Noble Drew Ali had proclaimed that he was a prophet of Islam and that his followers were not Negroes but Moorish Americans with pre-slavery roots that linked them to Muslims in Morocco. Drew Ali moved the national headquarters of his religious movement from Newark, New Jersey, to Chicago in the 1920s. He died in 1929, a momentous year in which he was arrested by Chicago police and was also involved in a leadership struggle with his business manager Claude Greene that split the Moorish Science Temple into factional groups.[6] Muhammad Ezaldeen left the United States and the Moorish Science Temple to sojourn for several years in Cairo, Egypt, while he studied Sunni Islam and Arabic from 1931 to 1936.

When he came home to the United States in the late 1930s, he used his transnational experience to promote the study of Arabic and the Qur'an and to teach his followers about the spiritual relationship between black American Muslim culture and Arab Sunni Islamic consciousness in a new religious community called the Addeynu Allahe Universal Arabic Association, which by 1938 had units in Philadelphia, Camden, Buffalo, and West Valley, New York.

Additional units of this Muslim community emerged later in Jacksonville, Florida; Rochester, New York; Youngstown, Ohio; and Detroit. Muhammad Ezaldeen established the national headquarters of the Addeynu Allahe Universal Arabic Association in Newark in the early 1940s. In the late 1930s and 1940s, Ezaldeen and his African American Sunni followers also founded communal farming communities called Jabul Arabiyyah (Mountain of Arabic-Speaking People) in West Valley and New Jersey (Ezaldeen Village). These rural communes were inspired by Islamic law, black economic self-determination, and the hijra—the migration of Arabian Muslims and the Prophet Muhammad from Mecca to Medina in 622 CE.[7] For the Muslims in Jabul Arabiyyah, embracing the spiritual philosophy and rituals of Sunni Islam and rejecting the values of the white American Christian world connected them to global religious movements as they struggled for racial justice in the United States.

Theological, ethnic, and economic tensions between the African American imam Wali Akram and foreign missionaries from India in the Ahmadiyya Muslim Community led Akram to sever ties with the Ahmadis and to found the Sunni First Cleveland Mosque in 1936. Akram was born Walter Gregg in Texas. Educated as an electrical engineer at Prairie View State College, he had migrated to St. Louis in the early 1920s and joined the Ahmadiyya Muslim Community, where he met and married his wife, Kareema, in 1925. Wali Akram advanced through the Ahmadi missionary ranks in St. Louis and moved to Cleveland in 1927 to convert African Americans to Islam and to establish an Ahmadiyya mosque.[8] By the 1930s, he began to protest his struggling black converts' mandatory financial support of housing, cars, and transnational travel for the Ahmadiyya's Indian missionaries in Cleveland. Moreover, Akram questioned the rigor and the Qur'anic authority of the Islamic religious education that the foreign missionaries provided for black converts. He objected to their custom of sending zakat collected from poor black American Muslims to Qadian, India, as well as the required oath of allegiance to the Ahmadiyya khalifa in India. Then he began to pray with Syrian and Turkish Sunni Muslim immigrants who were members of the Association of the Islamic Union of Cleveland.[9]

Ultimately, Wali Akram came to believe that the African American Ahmadis' dependence on immigrant missionaries from India would undermine their local economic self-determination, their struggle for equal rights in the United States, and their focus on the spirituality of Islam. All of these factors led to his rejection of the Ahmadiyya doctrine about continuous prophecy and his embrace of Sunni Islam, which culminated when Akram and his black followers established the First Cleveland Mosque at 7605 Woodland Avenue.[10] Moreover, he published new missionary materials for his converts to Sunni Islam, converts who were now called dark Americans and were encouraged to "abolish Negro-ism [and] learn the Arabic language, the language of your ancestors, which is . . . used by more than one third of the world's population."[11] Wali Akram emphasized that people of African descent were capable of teaching Sunni Islam in the United States and he believed that the religion's global consciousness would contribute to African American liberation and economic uplift.

In 1937 Wali Akram established the Muslim Ten Year Plan to support Sunni Islamic revivalism, to get his people off welfare, and to promote homeownership and businesses among African American Muslim communities. Then in Philadelphia in 1943, Akram founded a national organization, the Uniting Islamic Society of America, which held conferences from 1943 to 1947, to unify the scattered black American Sunni groups in the areas of universal doctrines and religious practices, empowerment of Muslim women, politics, economic goals, and black leadership. Competing goals and personality conflicts among the leaders of the Addeynu Allahe Universal Arabic Association, the Muslim Ten Year Plan, the First Cleveland Mosque, Harlem's Academy of Islam, Pittsburgh's First Muslim Mosque, and the Wa-Hid Al-Samad Society led to the demise of the Uniting Islamic Society of America in 1947.[12] However, in 1957 Tabligh Jamaat, a missionary organization in Pakistan, sponsored Wali Akram's pilgrimage to Mecca, making him one of the earliest African American Muslims to receive a visa for the hajj in Saudi Arabia.[13]

African American Sunni Muslims put people of African descent at the center of Muslim experiences in the United States and countered the impact of foreign missionaries and anti-black racism on their religious and social lives. Their communal masculinity emphasized racial uplift and unity, empowerment of women, and spiritual, communal, and economic harmony among the African American Muslim movements that embraced mainstream Islam, as well as their ability to achieve these goals through self-reliance and the strength of their own independent Islamic programs, institutions, and networks in America. Although brotherhood among these black Sunnis dealt with the same questions of black manhood, citizenship rights, and Islamic conversion that the Nation of Islam and the Ahmadiyya addressed, their mainstream theological beliefs and practices connected their religious engagement to the study of Arabic and traditions of Islamic knowledge and learning in the ummah (the global Muslim community) as well as travel to Muslim countries in the Third World, such as Egypt and Saudi Arabia. This Sunni Islamic journey intersected with complex representations of black manliness in the 1950s and 1960s, but it also engaged broader frames of spiritual transformation, Islamic revivalism, and anticolonialism. In the bigger picture, it would help lay down the soundtrack that redefined what it meant to be a black, a Muslim, and a jazz musician within the matrix of cool. As we will see, the global significance of Sunni Islam was also a major theme in the decolonizing politics of the Muslim-majority and African countries, to which black jazz artists were dispatched by the US State Department from 1956 to the 1970s.

African American Muslims in the Islamic Third World and Africa: The State Department Jazz Tours during the Cold War and Civil Rights Movement

The State Department fostered rich interaction between the jazz and global Muslim communities when it sent American jazz musicians to the Islamic world and Africa to perform in numerous concerts that would support American diplomatic interests. The political and cultural tensions of the Cold War and the anti-racist values of the civil rights movement intersected in these tours, in which jazz—the music of oppressed African Americans—was used by the US government to represent the values of freedom and democracy to audiences in Asia, Africa, and the Middle East. The United States and the Soviet Union became global superpowers from the end of World War II to 1960, a period during which forty nations in the Third World emerged from colonialism and won independence. American and Soviet political leaders engaged in a struggle to dominate diplomatic relationships with these nations, whose populations included 25 percent of the people on the planet.[14] Almost half of the thirty independent African and Asian countries that attended the 1955 Bandung conference in Indonesia were Islamic-majority nations and the meeting's most important themes were "Third World internationalism [and] . . . cooperation among the newly independent countries."[15] A 1957 American government document explained that "sixteen of the UN's eighty-one members that year had Muslim majority populations, and dozens had Muslim populations larger than fifty thousand. The report concluded that the world's estimated 350 million Muslims could be an important US ally in the Cold War."[16] There were high stakes in the Cold War rivalry between the two superpowers in the Islamic Third World, a region that spanned Africa, Asia, and the Middle East, stakes that reflected US efforts to contain communism, to influence a potential voting bloc in the United Nations, to assert its global economic and military policies, and to shape the public image of democracy abroad.

While the American government challenged communism and monitored anticolonial political and religious movements among Muslims, Asians, and Africans, the Soviet Union attacked President Dwight D. Eisenhower's foreign policy agenda and his global vision of democracy by criticizing the United States as a racist nation because of its Jim Crow system of African American inequality and segregation. And the Soviets were justified in their critique, for although the 1954 Supreme Court decision *Brown v. Board of Education of Topeka* was supposed to end legal support for "separate but equal" public education in the United States, the situation on the ground was quite different. Outrage echoed around the world in 1955, when two white men, Roy Bryant and J. W. Milam, kidnapped, tortured, and killed a fourteen-year-old black boy, Emmett Till, in Mississippi. Till's killers were quickly tried and acquitted. Afterward, they admitted in a *Look* magazine article that they had committed the murder. Moreover, a new phase of the civil rights movement also began in 1955, when the National Association for the Advancement of Colored People (NAACP) activist Rosa Parks was arrested because she refused to give up her seat in the white section of a Montgomery, Alabama, bus. The Baptist minister Martin Luther King Jr. became the leader of the yearlong Montgomery bus boycott, which exemplified his political strategy of demonstrations, marches, boycotts, sit-ins, freedom rides, and rallies based on nonviolent direct action by civil rights organizations such as the Southern Christian Leadership Conference (SCLC), Student Nonviolent Coordinating Committee (SNCC), and Congress of Racial Equality (CORE).

From the violent desegregation of Central High School in Little Rock, Arkansas, which required federal troops to protect black students in 1957, to James Meredith's perilous integration of the University of Mississippi in 1962, to Bloody Sunday in Selma, Alabama, in which six hundred demonstrators were attacked by police using tear gas and billy clubs in 1965, televised civil rights struggles exposed America's system of racism to the world. Global audiences learned about the 1963 assassination of Medgar Evers, the NAACP field secretary in Mississippi; the murder of four black girls, Denise McNair, Carole Robertson, Cynthia Wesley, and Addie Mae Collins, who were bombed by Ku Klux Klansmen in Birmingham's 16th Street Baptist Church in 1963; demonstrators and freedom riders who were arrested and attacked by police dogs, fire hoses, and Klansmen in the Deep South in the 1960s; voter registration workers James Chaney, Andrew Goodman, and Michael Schwerner, who were abducted and killed in Mississippi in 1964; and American cities like Los Angeles, Newark, and Detroit, to name a few, which were disrupted during black urban uprisings before and after King's assassination in 1968. The White Citizens Council of Alabama, which supported segregation, even attacked jazz as an NAACP "plot to mongrelize America."[17] Yet poll takers in the United States Information Agency found that across the board, people in European, African, and Asian nations had consistently negative evaluations of segregation and anti-black activities in the United States.[18]

To deflect the stigma of violent white supremacy during the civil rights movement and to improve America's diplomatic and cultural image during the Cold War, President Eisenhower decided to use the performing arts, launching the President's Special International Program for Cultural Presentations under the auspices of the State Department in 1954. Then in 1956, the State Department, urged by the Harlem congressman Adam Clayton Powell Jr., sent the first jazz musicians to perform in the emerging countries as goodwill ambassadors for the United States. Eventually, the State Department would send jazz artists to perform in nations with significant Muslim populations: Iran, Pakistan, Turkey, United Arab Republic, Malaysia, Ghana, Liberia, Kenya, Tanzania, Ethiopia, Libya, Tunisia, India, Afghanistan, Iraq, Sierra Leone, Mozambique, Malawi, Morocco, Palestine, Jordan, Syria, Cameroun, Congo, Uganda, Togo, Ivory Coast, Senegal, Mali, Niger, Upper Volta, Republic of Dahomey, Guinea, Lebanon, Algeria, Chad, and Mauritius.

Congressman Powell believed that American jazz men like Dizzy Gillespie could use their music to quell racial and political tensions in the Third World and to turn the Cold War into a "cool war," when he announced in Washington, DC, "I'm going to propose to Eisenhower that he send this man, who's a great contributor to our music, on a State Department sponsored cultural mission to Africa, the Near East, Middle East, and Asia."[19] Dizzy Gillespie was honored to become one of the first jazz ambassadors representing the United States, yet he emphasized, "I wasn't going over to apologize for the racist policies of America."[20] He and many of the musicians in his band lived in northern cities in which they could vote and where signs did not designate separate white and black public spaces, as they did in the South.[21] But this did not stop northern civil rights groups from protesting against racism in the areas of criminal justice, housing, and employment, and in hotels, restaurants, stores, theaters, beaches, banks, and schools during the 1950s and 1960s.[22]

Dizzy Gillespie understood the political significance of jazz as a potential tool to build diplomatic relationships with Muslim nations. As he described it, "Our tour was limited to countries which had treaties with the United States or where you had U.S. military bases: Persia [Iran], Lebanon, Syria, Pakistan, Turkey. . . . We opened in Abadan, Iran, and went from there to Beirut, to Damascus, and Aleppo in Syria. . . . Politics was a drag because these were such beautiful places. Beirut is like God's earth."[23] His performances, like those of other jazz musicians who participated in the State Department programs, shaped black internationalism by circulating jazz in their transnational performances and celebrated the intertwined consciousness of the struggles for African American freedom and Third World decolonization. Gillespie's globe-trotting experiences help us to understand how the encounters that developed between jazz musicians and Muslim and African individuals and communities during the tours inspired a warm global reception for new African American art forms, identities, and cultural collaborations in these times.[24] Indeed, the interplay between musicians and local cultures during the jazz ambassadors' travels exemplified the musical and spiritual experimentation and the global diasporic consciousness fostered by African American religious internationalism as well as important black counternarratives describing the struggles and tensions of the Cold War era.

Dizzy Gillespie, who had considered conversion to Islam in the late 1940s, was an ideal musician to play for audiences in the Muslim world, and he and his racially integrated band, which included Quincy Jones, Melba Liston, Dottie Salters, Rod Levitt, Carl Warwick, Charlie Persip, Billy Mitchell, Frank Rehak, Joe Gordon, and others, enjoyed sojourning and bebopping in the Middle East in 1956. As photographs show, while in Syria, Gillespie and his male musicians wore the keffiyeh, the long white headdress that Arab men wear to signify their religion and nationality and to protect their head in desert climates. In Karachi, Pakistan, Gillespie played his trumpet with a local Islamic jazz band, the Rhythm Swingette. He and Quincy Jones relaxed on a carpet while they listened to a circle of local musicians playing their indigenous instruments at Radio Pakistan. Surrounded by Pakistani onlookers in a Karachi park, Gillespie donned a turban while playing his trumpet to charm snakes in a basket. He also enjoyed meeting the sheikh of Kuwait during a party in Beirut, Lebanon.[25]

Overall, after their large official concerts, Gillespie's jazz group reached out to previously colonized Muslim peoples who shared their cool musical interests.

> We heard some marvelous young musicians in Karachi. . . . One guy had an instrument that looked like a violin. . . . But did he play that thing. Sounded like a cello. Then they had a little sixteen-year-old flute player who was beautiful. . . . This was in Pakistan, but they had another brother there, and this cat looked like somebody that I'd seen on the corner of 126th Street and Eighth Avenue. . . . And he had an instrument that he made himself, which was like a piano but the knobs came up and hit the strings. Boy, did he perform. . . . The musicians treated us great. They

played concerts for us . . . and they showed us things. . . . I learned a lot over there. I learned some scales and made some recordings with Stuff Smith using some of those scales in it that came out of Pakistan. One tune was called "Rio Pakistan."[26]

In Dacca, Pakistan, the poor Muslims who attended Dizzy Gillespie's concerts were curious about racism in America because they knew about African Americans who had been lynched and burned at the stake. Although he noted that his band was racially integrated, Gillespie was very frank about the civil rights struggle when he responded to their questions: "A hundred years ago, our ancestors were slaves, and today we're scuffling with this problem, but I'm sure it's gonna get straightened out some day. I probably won't see it, completely, the eradication of racial prejudice in the United States, but it will be eliminated."[27]

Gillespie was especially sensitive to local religious practices. His band played in Damascus, Syria, around sunset during Ramadan, the month-long fast from sunrise to sunset—one of the Five Pillars of Islam that Muslims practice every year. During the concert, he noticed that a feast had been laid out in the rear of the concert hall. When dusk came, he decided to honor the time when the Muslims broke their fast for the day: "We kept playing and then exactly on the minute, the second of sundown, I held up my hand, and boom! We hit a big chord. And I said, 'Food!' and rushed to the back, and everybody rushed back there with me . . . to eat right on the minute that Ramadan ended."[28]

While on these tours, Gillespie considered himself a "world statesman." He saw the parallels between poor black youth in the United States and homeless Muslim children in the streets of Pakistan: "One little raggedy boy in Dacca used to sit on his heels at the stage door. . . . A cute little kid about eleven or twelve years old and he'd sit down there and listen to us every night. When I went out one night I saw him lying down in the back where all those rats had been running. He had on the same clothes, still raggedy."[29] The next day, Gillespie drove the boy to a shop and bought him new clothes and shoes: "That night when I came in backstage, this little guy was shining. He'd taken a bath, had his hair combed. . . . When I came in he snapped to attention, clicked his heals, sharp and clean, man. . . . And I didn't care whether he sold the shoes later to buy himself some food."[30]

When his trombonist Melba Liston traveled to the Middle East with the band, she talked to Muslim women about black women's identities in the United States and her experiences as a traveling jazz artist because "they had things that they felt they were capable of doing and were not permitted to do. And they wanted to know how it happened that I could be out there doing such a thing."[31] Liston, who was also a talented arranger, discussed her experiences in jazz with the Muslim women, experiences that included respect and love as a woman in Gillespie's band in 1956: "When we got into the initial rehearsals, . . . they started playing my arrangements. . . . They say, 'Mama's all right.' Then I was 'Mama,' I wasn't bitch no more."[32] Previously, when she had traveled with Billie Holiday's band touring the South in 1949, she was subjected to sexual harassment from the male musicians as well as opposition to bebop from the southern audiences. The impact of sexism and patriarchy in the black music world in the late 1940s was so disillusioning that she had left it for several years, and worked for the Los Angeles Board of Education and for the Hollywood studios as a film actress in *The Ten Commandments* and *The Prodigal* in the 1950s.[33] However, the talented trombonist decided to return to jazz to work specifically with Dizzy Gillespie during the State Department tours. Although Melba Liston was not Muslim, she believed that her conversations with Middle Eastern women made a difference in their desire for gender equality and inspired "a bunch of sisters over there to demand a little more appreciation for their innate skills."[34]

Finally, during a concert in Ankara, Turkey, a local Turkish Muslim musician, Arif Mardin, gave Quincy Jones a score that he used in the United States, and Jones helped Mardin get a scholarship at the Berklee College of Music in Boston, which specialized in the education of professional jazz musicians. Later on, Mardin worked as an arranger and executive at Atlantic Records.[35]

Although Gillespie and his band came to the Middle East during politically volatile times—several years after the United States had participated in a 1953 coup in Iran, to support the shah and to exploit the country's oil resources—their personal and musical connections with Muslim fans influenced civil rights solidarities with the Third World as well as new black interactions with Islamic gender identities and styles. Ultimately, these transnational connections, exchanges, and collaborations in Africa, Asia, and the Middle East contributed to the pro-Islamic affinities of African American jazz musicians in the 1960s. Later in this chapter, when we discuss Duke Ellington's and Randy Weston's impact on the State Department jazz tours in the 1960s, we will see how their experiences resonated with the values of the Black Power movement in the latter part of a momentous decade.

"These Are Soulful Days": Islam and Hard Bop in Philadelphia in the Late 1950s

If liberation and the synthesis of musical and religious consciousness were among the key themes of the golden age of jazz, Philadelphia was the metropolis in which African American musicians' experiences with Islam and hard bop exemplified these themes in the late 1950s. As noted earlier, hard bop had "a bluesy, funky delivery, with lots of forceful interaction between trumpet and drums . . . elements from gospel and R&B. . . . off-beat accents . . . riffs, call-response, vocal inflections, simple melodies, and . . . ostinatos" and its soulful urban sounds greeted thousands of black migrants who partied in Philadelphia's bars and music clubs.[36] The Great Migration brought thousands of southern migrants to the city in the early to mid-twentieth century to live in black communities like North Philadelphia. By 1950, there were 376,041 blacks in Philadelphia, and their votes helped to elect a Democratic mayor, Joe Clark, who supported governmental civil rights innovations in the city such as a new urban charter with a commission to monitor antidiscrimination laws and provisions and an independent board to support equitable black access to city jobs.[37] By 1960, 529,240 blacks comprised 26.4 percent of Philadelphia's population. It was the fourth-biggest city in the United States, and its Commission on Human Relations had not significantly transformed racism and de facto segregation in its African American neighborhoods.[38] According to historian Matthew J. Countryman, by the late 1950s, "activists in Philadelphia increasingly turned away from state action and biracial coalition politics and toward traditions of black collective action and self-help to achieve substantive advancements in black employment, education, and housing."[39] Among its black movements for uplift and change, the city had a rich African American Islamic culture that included Sunni, Ahmadiyya, and Nation of Islam communities in the mid-twentieth century, and Muslim jazz artists helped to lead the way in challenging white supremacy and making "the physical presence of Muslims" a positive and normative aspect of the cityscape.[40]

Earlier in this chapter, we discussed the missionary work of the black Sunni imam Wali Akram, who established the short-lived Uniting Islamic Society of America in Philadelphia during World War II. By 1953, tenor saxophonist Lynn Hope (El Hajj Abdullah Rasheed Ahmad) led the city's community of African American Sunni Muslims in a mosque called the School of Wisdom of AAUA, which was connected to Muhammad Ezaldeen's Addeynu Allahe Universal Arabic Association. Hope's conversion story and photographs were the centerpiece of an *Ebony* magazine article on Muslim jazz artists who were identified with their religion's significant appeal to black America.[41] He took a break from his music career for a year, during which he intensively studied the Qur'an, Arabic, and Islamic history, and then became a prayer leader and Arabic teacher mentoring new converts to Islam in Philadelphia. After his conversion, the tenor saxophonist explained that the United States needs the racial and social justice philosophy of Islam because "it would wipe out white supremacy and elevate the Negro to equality."[42]

Turning to his religious life, trumpeter Idrees Sulieman introduced Hope to the faith. Hope made his hajj to Mecca in 1952 and was impressed by the peaceful, multiracial spirit of the pilgrimage.[43] After the hajj, he decided to escape racism in American jazz venues "in which band members were forced to enter by the back door and suffer other humiliations."[44] He and his family (his wife and three children) lived for a while in Egypt and Lebanon, where his daughter Barbara Jean said they "learned what it was to be simply human instead of being one of the despised."[45] However, she explained that they returned reluctantly to the United States in the 1950s because forces in the American government believed "it was bad public relations to have black people proclaim to an international audience that they left America because of racism."[46]

Born in Birmingham, Alabama, Lynn Hope and his Muslim band members wore turbans when they toured in the South. They challenged Jim Crow racism and were served in segregated restaurants because they practiced their own version of Islamic identity based on Hope's experiences in the Middle East. Hope explained, "We are not Negroes but members of the Moslem faith. Our customs are Eastern. We claim the nationality of our Arabic ancestors as well as their culture."[47] Sometimes, Hope strutted on the bar while playing the saxophone in the jazz clubs in which he was known as "the amazing man with the turban."[48] The men in his combo signified their own Islamic sense of self by wearing red fezzes.

Photos of Hope's family in Philadelphia were included in the *Ebony* magazine story. His two little sons wore fezzes, his young daughter wore a pretty dress, and his wife wore the hijab. Although little is known about Lynn Hope's spouse, she expressed her Muslim womanhood by covering her head in her own style, moving her family to the Middle East, and sharing her husband's spirituality and resistance to American imperialism and anti-black racism. Although the *Ebony* photo and article did not mention her name or her ideas about Islam, it did show an aspect of her religious experience as a married African American Muslim woman engaging in the preparation of her husband for Friday prayers at the mosque, by helping him to wrap his turban. Her image is one of the first published photos of a black American Sunni Muslim woman in the United States in the 1950s. Lynn Hope's brothers Yunus Ali and Khalil A. Malik were identified as band members and Sunni converts in another photo, while Lynn was described as a family man and a devout Muslim who practiced the Five Pillars of Islam and wore an Arab headdress and agal as he relaxed in his apartment and prayed in the mosque.[49] His sister, a jazz pianist, was also Muslim.[50]

On the musical order, Hope's recorded hits such as "Tenderly" and "Summertime" exemplified the soulful urban rhythm and blues sounds of hard bop, sounds that came from Philly jazz musicians who performed in taverns, clubs, and bars in the 1950s. By the 1960s, club owners had blacklisted Lynn Hope, preventing him from performing on many jazz stages because of his critique of racism in the United States.[51] His daughter Barbara Jean said she saw her father cry for the first time on August 28, 1963, while he viewed the Martin Luther King Jr.–led March on Washington on television and understood that "black and white people had joined to fight the oppression he had fled" in the early 1950s.[52]

The above personal portrait of Lynn Hope provides us with a paradigm for understanding the musical, religious, and political themes of African American religious internationalism among black musicians in

Philadelphia in the 1950s and early 1960s. Hope not only was a talented saxophonist, but also had lived in the Middle East during the decade when Egypt emerged as a global champion of "Afro-Asiatic Third World internationalism" and supported the independence struggles of people of African descent in diaspora.[53] Hope's masculinity, cool style, and resistance practices were infused with the spirit of Pan-African, Pan-Arab, and anticolonial solidarity that Egyptian president Gamal Abdel Nasser encouraged in the Muslim world in the mid-twentieth century.[54] However, Lynn Hope is not the only jazz artist whose testimony about the Philly Islamic scene we can trace. According to Maneer Hamid, a Philadelphian Ahmadi musician, there was a wide spectrum of African American Muslim communities to choose from in his city. Although he was initially influenced by Hope's propagation of Sunni Islam in the urban black musical networks and was stationed in Turkey and Libya during his Air Force years, Hamid decided to embrace the Ahmadiyya Muslim Community in the 1950s. Yet he also acknowledged the impact of the Nation of Islam on the ways he constructed his own religious and political identity:

> The largest group was Elijah Muhammad's group. The most militant Muslims were on the East Coast. We didn't give in to negativism with them. We just remained aloof from them. Most of the people from the Ahmadiyya were all from the 1920s, 1930s, . . . loyal to America. But I was younger, involved in the Black Panthers and all that nationalism. We like to say that Elijah Muhammad was influenced by Mufti Muhammad Sadiq. There is a photograph that exists of Elijah Muhammad and Mufti Muhammad Sadiq sitting together on the stage with Noble Drew Ali and Marcus Garvey. . . . We had one foot in the world and one foot in Islam. Other Muslim Sunnis were doing it, straddling the line. . . . Out there in the big world, a lot of people were Muslims.[55]

The jazz pianist McCoy Tyner provides another perspective about the Ahmadi impact on musicians in his hometown. He was born in Philadelphia in 1938.[56] When Tyner met his future wife, Aisha Davis, she encouraged him to become Muslim and he converted to the Ahmadiyya in 1955, when he was seventeen years old, and adopted a new name, Sulieman Saud, which signified devotion to his new faith.[57] According to the pianist, his Islamic and musical values became linked to one another in a communal black masculinity of discipline, creativity, and strength:

> We talk a lot about freedom in jazz, but there are underlying disciplines too. When you have the discipline of religion, as I have, I think you can meet the demands of music and function better. There are lots of pressures on musicians' lives, and it is easy to see why some fall by the wayside. But you have to strengthen yourself to meet these pressures. You can't wait for them to be removed from your environment. . . . People will usually think of God at a time of tragedy but not when everything is running smoothly. But most musicians believe in God, because most of them are very sensitive individuals.[58]

McCoy Tyner also began a ten-year musical relationship with saxophonist John Coltrane in 1955 and, as we will see later, his spiritual philosophy about jazz illustrated by example the Islamic values that nurtured Coltrane's artistry and personal life during his hard bop years in Philadelphia. John William Coltrane was born in Hamlet, North Carolina, in 1926 and grew up in High Point, where his grandfathers were ministers in the African Methodist Episcopal Zion Church. His grandfather died in 1938 and his father and grandmother passed away in 1939. He learned to play the alto saxophone in high school and after graduating in 1943, migrated to Philadelphia to live with his mother, Alice, and his cousin Mary Alexander, who were already in the city. Eventually, John bought a house for his family on 1511 North 33rd Street and lived there from 1952 to 1958. Coltrane studied the saxophone and music theory for several years at the Ornstein School and Granoff Studios. He was drafted into the navy at the end of World War II, and his early musical education also included a stint playing in the Melody Masters, a navy band in Oahu, Hawaii, from 1945 to 1946.[59]

However, Trane's hard bop sound was also shaped by participating in jam sessions and club performances among the rich network of black musicians playing on Columbia Avenue in North Philadelphia and around South Broad Street in South Philadelphia, musicians such as tenor saxophonists Benny Golson, Jimmy Heath, Odean Pope, John Glenn, Eddie Woodland, and Bootsie Barnes; pianist Ray Bryant; bassists Percy Heath, Jimmy Garrison, Nelson Boyd, Steve Davis, and

Tom Bryant; trumpeters Calvin Massey, Red Rodney, Lee Morgan, and Johnny Lynch; drummers Al Heath and Philly Joe Jones; organist Shirley Scott; and Jimmy Johnson and his Ambassadors, to name a few.[60] According to McCoy Tyner, "You had to attend those classes which were the clubs and sessions"[61] in places like Spider Kelly's, Crystal Ball, Watts' Zanzibar, Emerson's, 820 Club, North West Club, Club Medea, Gay Paree, Red Rooster, the Top, Fan Theater, Downbeat Club, Heritage House, and Music City; the big ballrooms and theaters such as the Earle, the Lincoln, the Tioga, the Venago, and the Colonnade Ballroom; and local musicians' homes and the recreation space in the Richard Allen projects.[62] Coltrane even met his alto saxophone idol Charlie Parker in the 1940s, walking with him on Broad Street and carrying Parker's saxophone case to the Downbeat Club.[63]

Coltrane had his first professional experience playing the tenor saxophone in Eddie Vinson's band in 1947, and the tenor became his primary musical instrument.[64] He played in groups led by Joe Webb, King Kolax, Howard McGhee, and Jimmy Heath during 1947 and 1948. Dizzy Gillespie hired Coltrane from 1949 to 1951. He worked with Earl Bostic in 1952 and 1953, and thereafter, he joined the bands of Daisy Mae and the Hep Cats, Johnny Hodges, Jimmy Smith, and Bud Powell.[65] Some of the engagements with these bands required him to travel, but he always returned to his home in Philadelphia.

Several Muslim musicians influenced Coltrane's musical and religious development during his Philly years, musicians like William Langford (Hasaan Ibn Ali), a talented pianist and composer who played with local groups and with Miles Davis and Clifford Brown in the 1950s and then recorded an album with Max Roach, *The Max Roach Trio Featuring the Legendary Hasaan*, in 1965. Coltrane visited his house, played in jam sessions with Ali, and worked on the pianist's compositions with tenor saxophonist Odean Pope. They were fascinated by Ali's experimentation with extended chords in jazz.[66]

Charles Greenlee, trombonist in Dizzy Gillespie's band, converted to Islam in the 1940s and changed his name to Harneefan Majeed. He married Coltrane's cousin Mary, who moved from Philadelphia to live with him in Brooklyn in 1959. The marriage did not work out, and they divorced. In 1961 Greenlee played the euphonium on Coltrane's album *The Complete Africa/Brass Sessions*.[67]

The drummers Rashied Ali and Muhammad Ali were born in the 1930s in the Patterson family of jazz musicians that included their mother, a vocalist, and their brother Omar Ali, who played African-derived percussion instruments. Their father converted to Islam during their childhood years and changed their family's name from Patterson to Ali, and they developed their musical talents among Philly's brotherhood of Muslim jazz artists. Rashied grew up sitting outside and listening to Coltrane while he played all day in his Philadelphia home in the 1950s. Eventually, all of the Ali brothers performed with Trane in the 1960s, and as we will see, Rashied was one of the key musicians in his group who experimented with free jazz from 1965 to 1967.[68]

C. O. Simpkins points out the religious and political impact on Trane's life of the Islamic jazz drummer Nasseridine, who was a victim of police brutality and Islamophobia:

> Many musicians were searching for a foundation in life. . . . In Philadelphia, Islam was a positive force. . . . Nasseridine, a drummer loved John. . . . He was advanced spiritually, musically, and intellectually. . . . He was a devout Muslim who carried his prayer rug wherever he went, and prayed dutifully five times a day, regardless of where he was. . . . One night he stayed up praying continuously at John's house. The next day on the way to his sister's house he stopped to pray under a tree. . . . Two policemen came by and saw him kneeling nearly motionless. . . . An argument ensued. . . . They beat him savagely. He spent four days in the hospital and died on the last day. Nasseridine's loss sent a shudder through the music community. John, who loved Nasseridine, was hurt.[69]

Coltrane acknowledged his spiritual journey from the black Christian faith of his grandfather in North Carolina to his introduction to Islam in Philadelphia:

> In my early years . . . I was going to church every Sunday . . . under the influence of my grandfather—he was the dominating cat in the family. . . . He was pretty militant, you know. Politically inclined and everything. Religion was his field. . . . So that's where—I grew up in that. . . . And after I'd say my late teens, I just started breakin' away . . . so I questioned a lot of what I find in religion. . . . About two or three years later, maybe

twenty-two, twenty-three, this Muslim thing came up. I got introduced to that. And that kinda shook me. A lot of my friends, you know, they went Muslim. So I thought about that, anyway, it took me to something I had never thought about—you know, another religion?[70]

If we consider Coltrane's later words, "My music is the spiritual expression of what I am—my faith, my knowledge, my being," then we must take a look at the Muslim women who shaped his values.[71] Although he did not officially convert to the religion, Islam made an enduring impression on his religious, musical, and personal life. In 1955 he married a Muslim, Juanita Naima Austin, and their new family included Naima's young daughter Antonia (Syeeda), who was raised in the Islamic faith. Naima's Muslim friends, such as Aisha, McCoy Tyner's wife, and Aisha's sister, Khadijah Davis, a vocalist in Calvin Massey's band and spouse of the Islamic bassist Steve Davis (Luqman Abdul Syeed), became part of Coltrane's social circle and participated in jam sessions in his home.[72]

The Muslim tenor saxophonist and flutist Yusef Lateef recalled, "I met John Coltrane when I was with Dizzy Gillespie's big band, 1949. We were rehearsing in Philadelphia, and we had an engagement at the same time. . . . What impressed me was that he was serious about developing himself as a musician and as a performer."[73] Lateef also discussed the "songs of Islam" that could be traced to John's Philadelphia home: "He was married to a Muslim lady. Naima Coltrane. And of course, as you know, Muslims pray five times a day, and the first chapter of the holy Qur'an, which is the religious book of Muslims, it's called 'Al Fatihah.' . . . Naima would see that various books and things were in his study. She was very essential to his growth."[74]

Lateef indicated that Coltrane lived in an Islamic household in which Naima performed salat facing in the direction of Mecca, prostrating before Allah, and reciting in Arabic the following surah of the Qur'an:

In the name of God, the Merciful and Compassionate. Praise be to God, Lord of the Universe, the Merciful and Compassionate. Ruler on the Day of Judgement. You do we worship and call upon for help. Guide us along the Straight Path, the road of those whom You have favored, those with whom You are not angry, who are not lost. (1:1–7)[75]

Listening to the daily prayers recited with vocal expression and timbre and melodic pronunciation was spiritually as well as aesthetically pleasing. These prayers were the "songs of Islam" that would shape the rhythm and spirit of Trane's sound in the 1960s and later on, his poetry in *A Love Supreme*.[76] In his Atlantic album *Giant Steps*, recorded in 1959, John composed the songs "Naima" and "Syeeda's Song Flute" to express his love and respect for the Muslim women who shaped his personal life. Moreover, Yusef Lateef believed that Coltrane's wife helped to shape his very fast, sweeping musical sound of "superimposing or stacking up chords" in "Giant Steps," by making sure that he had a harp at home.[77] Lateef explained that "you could just set the pedals and pull your fingers over it" to create the "sheets of sound" idea."[78]

Coltrane began a two-year stint as the tenor saxophonist in trumpeter Miles Davis's group in 1955. This new job required John to live in New York City and on the road for a while and created his first opportunities to play on albums, which helped to make him famous. *'Round About Midnight* (Columbia, 1957), the first album on which he was featured with the Davis quintet, composed of Miles on trumpet, Trane on tenor saxophone, Red Garland on piano, Paul Chambers on bass, and Philly Joe Jones on drums, was a combination of bebop, hard bop, show, movie, and standard songs.[79] Trane's solo on "'Round Midnight," the first track on the album, helped to make the song a soulful hit in African American communities.[80] Coltrane was also heard on the Prestige albums that appeared while he worked with Miles: *Two Tenors* with Hank Mobley (1956); *Tenor Conclave* with Hank Mobley, Al Cohn, and Zoot Sims (1957); *Interplay for Two Trumpets and Two Tenors* with Bobby Jaspar, Idrees Sulieman, Webster Young, Mal Waldron, Kenny Burrell, Paul Chambers, and Art Taylor (1957); *Mating Call* with Tadd Dameron, John Sims, and Philly Joe Jones (1957); and *Dakar* with Cecil Payne, Pepper Adams, Mal Waldron, Doug Watkins, and Art Taylor (1957).

Both Miles Davis and John Coltrane struggled with heroin addiction in the 1940s and 1950s. Miles stopped using the drug in 1954, but John continued to get high on heroin and alcohol during his two-year span with the Davis quintet. From Charlie Parker's demise in 1955 to the 1960s, narcotics and jazz artists were linked in the public imagination, when jazz men were seen as representations of a self-destructive black hypermasculinity.[81] Yet substance abuse was a serious problem among both black and white jazz men and women during this period. The bars and nightclubs in which they performed served alcohol and attracted dealers who sold illegal drugs to musicians and fans. William H. James and Stephen L. Johnson argue that the social and psychological consequences of systemic racism contributed to recreational drug addiction in black American communities, as a way to soothe the pain and marginalization of racial discrimination in the United States.[82] This was undoubtedly one of the key factors as well as self-destructive attitudes and peer pressure that influenced narcotics abuse in the post–World War II jazz world.

Tenor and alto saxophonist, arranger, and composer Shafi Hadi (Curtis Porter) was on parole for two years for narcotics possession in Pennsylvania.[83] Philadelphia trumpeter Lee Morgan as well as drummer Art Blakey used hard drugs during this period, as did pianists Tadd Dameron and Bill Evans and saxophonists Sonny Stitt and Dexter Gordon.[84] Sonny Rollins, Davis's tenor saxophonist before Coltrane, had been incarcerated in Rikers Island, New York, for armed robbery in 1950 and for using drugs in 1952; and he decided in late 1954 to stop playing for a while to quit heroin in an institution in Lexington, Kentucky.[85] Drummer Philly Joe Jones, John's bandmate, was also an addict. Eventually, their drug problems affected their performances—they were both nodding on stage—and Miles fired the entire group in April 1957 and rehired a new quintet to play at Café Bohemia in New York City.[86]

Coltrane returned to Philadelphia in May 1957 and relied on support from his Muslim wife and his mother to help him overcome his drug addiction. Heroin, which is usually injected or snorted, is the most difficult narcotic to quit because of its harsh and painful withdrawal symptoms, such as muscle aches, pains, spasms, vomiting, nausea, twitching, cold and hot flashes, shivers, panic attacks, sweating, discharge from nose and eyes, agitation, diarrhea, heart pounding, anxiety, stomach cramps, dilated pupils, and insomnia, symptoms that can last a week or more. It is usually recommended that addicts recover from the acute symptoms of drug detox under medical supervision in a hospital or a rehabilitation facility that uses methadone to treat hard drug abuse.

However, John went cold turkey and kicked heroin with the help of Naima, who brought him water and nursed him while he fasted from food and suffered from the sickness of withdrawal symptoms in a bed in their home. Naima had introduced her husband to the Muslim religion's daily spiritual discipline of ritual prayers and its emphasis on the purification of the black body. These Islamic practices influenced John Coltrane's new identity of communal black masculinity exemplified by a serious concern for harmony and peace in his family and the black community, the links between his religious and musical values, and his spiritual awakening, which he discussed after his recovery from addiction. He believed that God had touched him during his final struggle with drugs and alcohol and had revealed to him that he could speak to people's souls through music. Thereafter, he submitted to God, as can be seen in the following written testimony of faith that resonated with important aspects of a Muslim convert's identity as a believer in the oneness of God: "During the year 1957, I experienced, by the grace of God, a spiritual awakening which was to lead me to a richer, fuller, more productive life. At that time, in gratitude, I humbly asked to be given the means and privilege to make others happy through music. I feel this has been granted through his grace. ALL PRAISE TO GOD."[87]

There were other qualities of John Coltrane's awakening that paralleled the ritual and piety of believers in Islam.[88] Coltrane pointed out that from 1957 on, he was praying when he was playing. Since he practiced the saxophone every day for many hours, his new sense of piety was conveyed by humbling himself before God in daily ritual actions that were encompassed and expressed in his creative musical forms, although he did not perform salat, as far as we know. Moreover, he said, "when you begin to see the possibilities of music, you desire to do something really good for people, to help humanity free itself from its hang ups."[89] This statement revealed Coltrane's shift to a communal masculinity, which highlighted his new black Atlantic cool commitment to unify and uplift humanity as a religious person. In his case, his new sense of masculinity and cool provided identifiable similarities to a "righteous person" as defined by the Qur'an; thus, he created and performed spiritually oriented music that purified and transformed the souls of his fans in the 1960s, music that prayed for them, consoled them, and expressed God's love for them, instead of paying zakat (almsgiving).[90] Because he lived with a Muslim spouse and stepdaughter and had many Muslim friends in Philadelphia, John was undoubtedly exposed to the Five Pillars and the religion's basic articles of faith.

Although he did not go all the way, to recite the shahada among witnesses and to go on record as a convert, we should consider that people embrace Islam in different ways. In the identity that John constructed in 1957, he selectively adopted key aspects of the culture and values of African American Islam and used them in his own personal spiritual journey and in his later music. In the years after he quit heroin, Naima helped her husband to go on "special diets" to remain clean and to maintain his health.[91] Eventually, he experimented with vegetarian diets, which suggested that he was influenced by Islamic food practices, which forbid the consumption of swine and alcohol.[92] During his evolving journey in the late 1950s and 1960s, John Coltrane embraced an "Islamic attitude" that established new paradigms for spiritual transformation and artistic freedom among the intersecting worlds of Muslim converts and jazz men and women.

Free from drugs and alcohol, Coltrane joined bebop pianist Thelonious Monk's quartet at the Five Spot Café in New York City in July 1957. The job lasted for the rest of the year and in August, John, Naima, and Syeeda moved into an apartment on the West Side of Manhattan.

During the engagement at the Five Spot, John continued interacting with Muslim jazz men such as pianist McCoy Tyner, Monk's bassist Ahmed Abdul-Malik, and drummers Art Blakey and Max Roach and saxophonist Sahib Shihab, who sat in with the quartet.[93] He found Monk to be a wonderful teacher: "Working with Monk brought me close to a musical architect of the highest order. I felt I learned from him in every way—through the senses, theoretically, technically. I would talk to Monk about musical problems and he would sit at the piano and show me the answers just by playing them."[94] John's musical reputation and artistry grew enormously in this period, and fans like trombonist J. J. Johnson raved about his performances: "Since Charlie Parker, the most electrifying sound that I've heard in contemporary jazz was Coltrane playing with Monk at the Five Spot. . . . It was incredible, like Diz and Bird."[95]

Coltrane recorded a lot of jazz for Prestige and Blue Note sessions in 1957 and 1958. His albums released in those years, like *Coltrane* (Prestige, 1957), *Blue Train* (Blue Note, 1957), *John Coltrane with the Red Garland Trio* (Prestige, 1958), and *Soultrane* (Prestige, 1958), established him as one of the most exciting hard bop tenor saxophonists in the

United States. Then, Miles Davis invited him to return to his band in early 1958. Coltrane indicated that in this new period of his jazz development, Miles used "fewer and fewer chord changes in songs. He used tunes with free-flowing lines and chordal direction. This approach allowed the soloist the choice of playing chordally (vertically) or melodically (horizontally). . . . Miles' music gave me plenty of freedom. . . . I was trying for a sweeping sound. I started experimenting because I was striving for more individual development."[96] Davis's new musical direction was superbly expressed in his album *Kind of Blue* (Columbia, 1959). *Kind of Blue* exemplified his exploration of modal jazz, which prioritized using scales instead of chord progressions to develop solos; it featured Davis on trumpet, Coltrane on tenor saxophone, Julian "Cannonball" Adderley on alto saxophone, Billy Cobb on drums, Wynton Kelly and Bill Evans on piano, and Paul Chambers on bass.[97]

The job with Miles Davis included a culminating Western Europe tour and ended when Coltrane formed his own group in April 1960. By the fall of that year, his quartet included himself, tenor and soprano saxophone; McCoy Tyner, piano; Elvin Jones, drums; and Steve Davis, bass. His band, with various configurations of sidemen, recorded Atlantic and Impulse! albums that explored African polyrhythms and Indian ragas, experimented with new rhythmic and harmonic concepts, and created sounds inspired by Third World consciousness in the 1960s, an era that was politically and aesthetically defined by revolutionary struggles for freedom in black America.

Later in the chapter, we will examine how Coltrane's Islamic sensibility influenced his support for the civil rights and Black Power movements, his global musical orientation, and his search for religious truth. His music represented the culmination of soul-searching sounds and transnational perspectives that circulated among numerous hard bop artists and fans during the golden age of African American Islam and jazz. In the 1960s, the potent religious internationalism of Sunni Islam, the Nation of Islam, and the Ahmadiyya Muslim Community would reach a high point of influence with the spirituality and musical performances of black jazz musicians who sought out new forms of radical political and social expression at home and abroad. It is to an analysis of their stories that we now turn.

"Freedom Now": African American Islam, Black Power, and the Global Consciousness of Jazz Artists in the 1960s

Hard bop drummer Max Roach's *We Insist! Freedom Now Suite* (Candid CCD, 1960), featuring Abbey Lincoln (vocals), Coleman Hawkins (tenor saxophone), and Babatunde Olatunji (congas), set the tone for the liberation values that Islam and jazz exemplified in the 1960s and the intersecting political strategies of civil rights and Black Power that influenced the global consciousness of musicians. Although Nat Hentoff, the producer of Candid Records, supported the album, it elicited racist and Islamophobic reactions among jazz critics and club owners. The suite's liner notes began with the following call out from the civil rights leader A. Philip Randolph: "A revolution is unfurling—America's unfinished revolution. It is unfurling in lunch counters, buses, libraries and schools—wherever the dignity and potential of men are denied. . . . Masses of Negroes are marching onto the stage of history and demanding their freedom now!" Roach's, Lincoln's, and Olatunji's religious and political stories unfold below. Their stories help us understand the black global struggles to redefine racial, ethical, political, and gender relations in the 1960s.

Max Roach, the composer of the songs on the *Freedom Now Suite* (with singer Oscar Brown Jr.) was clearly riding the wave of African American religious internationalism, as we can see both in his music and in his description of his personal religious identity: "God is my boss. . . . I am definitely a Muslim. To me it's a natural concept, and I fall into it easily. . . . I don't practice as much as I could, but I do my best at it."[98] Roach, who was born in North Carolina in 1925, raised in Brooklyn, and educated at the Manhattan School of Music, was one of the great jazz drummers. In the 1940s and 1950s, he played with Louis Jordan, Benny Carter, Duke Ellington, Dizzy Gillespie, Charlie Parker, Oscar Pettiford, and Clifford Brown. Four years before the *Freedom Now Suite*, the drummer recorded *Max Roach + 4* with Kenny Dorham (trumpet), Sonny Rollins (tenor saxophone), Ray Bryant (piano), and George Morrow (bass), an album that included "Mr. X," a track that he wrote about Malcolm X to signal his political and religious affinities. Oscar Brown Jr. and Abbey Lincoln called Roach "Strong Man," evoking his communal masculinity and musical creativity as well as his social values, which paralleled his spiritual foundation.[99] By the 1960s, he declared, "I will never again play anything that does not have social significance. It is my duty, the purpose of the artist to mirror his times. . . . We American jazz musicians of African descent . . . have to . . . employ our skill to tell the story of our people and what we've been through. . . . Little Rock, New Orleans, . . . sit-in demonstrations, . . . courage of our young people, . . . how can anyone consider my music independent of what I am?"[100]

The vocalist on the *Freedom Now Suite* album was Abbey Lincoln, Roach's girlfriend and future wife (they married in 1962). Her voice used spiritual, blues, and African diasporic forms to deliver the album's black protest messages about the screaming brutality of enslavement in "Driva' Man"; the jubilation of enslaved blacks' liberation after the Emancipation Proclamation in "Freedom Day"; the rage and resistance of oppressed blacks in "Triptych: Prayer, Protest, Peace"; the transnational dialogue with Africa and the call-and-response identification of African ethnic identities with the Yoruba drummer Babatunde Olatunji in "All Africa"; and the tragedy of South African apartheid and the Sharpeville Massacre in "Tears for Johannesburg." The final two songs reveal how the political orientation of the suite resonated with Pan-Africanism. In 1960, known as the "Year of Africa," Pan-African activists were inspired by the emergence of the following independent African nations: Republic of the Congo, Somalia, Nigeria, Ghana, Togo, Cameroon, Senegal, Mali, Niger, Dahomey, Ivory Coast, Upper Volta, Central African Republic, Chad, Mauritania, Gabon, and Zambia.

The album's recording date and its cover photograph of three black men participating in a Woolworths lunch counter demonstration reflected the ongoing CORE and NAACP Youth Council sit-ins to desegregate lunch counters in more than fifty American cities by 1960.[101] Muslim artists like Roach, Lincoln, and Art Blakey played in fundraising events with their jazz colleagues to support civil rights organizations and protests such as the sit-ins in Greensboro, North Carolina, in 1960, the Freedom Rides in 1961, the March on Washington and the Birmingham campaign in 1963, and the Mississippi Freedom Summer in 1964.[102]

However, *Freedom Now*'s anticolonial and proud black Atlantic cultural themes also signaled Max Roach's, Abbey Lincoln's, and Babatunde Olatunji's support for the Black Power movement, which paralleled the civil rights movement from 1954 to 1975.[103] More than a decade before

Stokely Carmichael popularized the term in 1966, Black Power advocates believed that self-defense, economic and political "self-determination, racial and cultural pride, and the global nature of domestic antiracist activism . . . held the key to the promotion of genuine democracy."[104] Many of the internationally aware jazz artists who were influenced by Black Power values respected and supported Martin Luther King Jr.'s legislative strategies and direct-action struggles against poverty, Jim Crow, and black political disfranchisement in states like Alabama, Georgia, Mississippi, and Tennessee, but they had fled racial persecution in the South and resettled in the North, where they became motivated by a new political culture. The global contours of the northern Black Power movement spanned the Bandung Afro-Asian Conference in Indonesia in 1955; Malcolm X's political and religious work in Harlem and his tour of Egypt and Saudi Arabia in the 1950s; his meeting at Harlem's Hotel Theresa with Fidel Castro, prime minister of Cuba in September 1960; his militant speeches challenging global white supremacy and systemic racism; the many successful African decolonization and independence movements; the Algerian Revolution from 1954 to 1962; and the February 15, 1961, demonstration at the United Nations to express opposition to prime minister Patrice Lumumba's assassination in the Democratic Republic of the Congo. It was not coincidental that New York City was a major center for both jazz, Islam, and Black Power in the 1960s.

Members of the Cultural Association for Women of African Heritage participated in the United Nations protest in 1961. Abbey Lincoln had established this new organization, based in New York, with the following black consciousness goals in mind: "that the women would wear African hairstyles and we would explore our culture, our African ancestors."[105] According to Steve Kemple, Lincoln practiced Islam and admired the social and economic autonomy and black pride of the Nation of Islam (although that movement did not encourage its members to take part in civil rights demonstrations).[106] Therefore, it is not surprising that Lincoln, Maya Angelou, and Rosa Guy had a 1961 meeting with Malcolm X at the Shabazz Restaurant in Harlem to solicit his opinion about their participation in the United Nations demonstration. He let them know that he was impressed by their activism against the global imperialism of Belgium and the United States, countries that had supported the murder of Lumumba.[107]

Nigeria-born and New York University and Morehouse College–educated Babatunde Olatunji, who performed the Yoruba-inspired sounds on *We Insist! Freedom Now Suite*, decried the economic underdevelopment of independent African nations and the murder of Patrice Lumumba; he even composed a song about Lumumba, although New York City radio stations refused to play it.[108] Olatunji led the way in shaping the West African musical consciousness of the Black Power movement in the North by introducing African drumming to the jazz world with his best-selling album *Drums of Passion* (Columbia, 1959). He acknowledged that the album "played a major role in all the social change taking place. . . . This meant we were recognized as pioneers in the 'Black is Beautiful' movement. The whole idea of 'black power' came along at this time." His cousin Akinsola Akiwowo wrote the liner notes for *Drums of Passion* with an anticolonial message about African music: "The drum is not only a musical instrument, it is also a sacred object and even a tangible form of divinity. It is endowed with a mysterious power, sort of life force, which however, has been incomprehensible to many missionaries and early travelers, who ordered its suppression and influence by forbidding its use."[109]

Olatunji's spirituality was rooted in Nigeria, where he was exposed to the Yoruba, black Christian, and Muslim religions during his youth. In his autobiography, he noted that although he had converted to the African Methodist Church when he moved to Lagos, "many families had converts from Yoruba to Christianity, or to Islam, and they would still participate in traditional Yoruba practices even after converting,"[110] Thus he came to believe that his primary mission as a master drummer in West Africa and the United States was to play Yoruba polyrhythms to "communicate with the Orisas, spirits of the ancestors" in order to elevate the religious foundation of black Atlantic music and to invoke cool energies for healing and unity, as he did in the *Freedom Now Suite* as well as *Drums of Passion*.[111] The Pan-African aesthetic and political searching that his music helped to inspire among artists encouraged an African American identification with African culture, global independence struggles, and black pride styles like dashikis and afros during the golden age of jazz, as well as a flurry of new recordings such as John Coltrane's "Dial Africa," "Dakar," "Liberia," "Tanganyika Strut," "Dahomey Dance," "Tunji," and *Africa/Brass*; Lee Morgan's "Mr. Kenyatta" and "Search for the New Land"; Cannonball Adderley's "African Waltz"; Max Roach's "All Africa," "Garvey's Ghost," and "Man from South Africa"; Sonny Rollins's "Airegin"; and Randy Weston's *Uhuru Africa*.[112]

Later in the 1960s, Olatunji drummed at Nation of Islam bazaars and concerts for Temple No. 4 in Washington, DC, and Temple No. 7 in New York, played with Yusef Lateef, Randy Weston, and John Coltrane, and befriended Malcolm X.[113] However, he warned that black musicians who publicized their Islamic affinities would be professionally punished by white nightclub and bar owners in the 1960s. He saw how this kind of Islamophobia and racism played out among his friends: "Anybody who associated with Muslims, or Malcolm X, was automatically ostracized—musicians especially. It was an unpleasant situation, even for Max Roach, with whom I recorded a protest album, *We Insist*. . . . For a couple of years after that album, no jazz club in the New York area would book him."[114]

At the height of the Cold War, Roach and Lincoln had clearly aligned their drumming and vocal work in jazz with African American Islam and the black freedom movements in the United States and Africa. They even appeared on a major public stage as the stars at a Nation of Islam benefit concert, "The Muslims Present an Evening with Max Roach and Abbey Lincoln" at Town Hall in New York City.[115] In 1961, inspired by the political and emotional power of Billie Holiday's anti-racist songs and Thelonious Monk's compositions, Lincoln recorded *Straight Ahead* with Max Roach's ensemble of black musicians. The album's proud Black Power themes upset the white jazz critic Ira Gitler, who criticized Abbey Lincoln's singing and objected to her racial consciousness and religious identity. He wrote in *Down Beat*, "*Straight Ahead* is about the slowness in the arrival of equal rights for the Negro. . . . All the musicians on the date are Negro. . . . Pride in one's heritage is one thing, but we don't need the Elijah Muhammed type of thinking in jazz. Apart from the conscious racial angle, the quality of her singing is not consistent nor is her material."[116]

Gitler's critique of Lincoln's album as well as the white critical backlash against the *Freedom Now Suite* led to a series of *Down Beat* articles about race and politics in the music industry in the early 1960s: "Racial Prejudice in Jazz," parts 1 and 2, and "The Need for Racial Unity in Jazz."[117] Jazz historian Frank Kofsky provides a critical evaluation of the racist intent and blacklisting impact of these articles on Abbey Lincoln's recording career:

> To say that the effect on jazz people of *We Insist! The Freedom Now Suite* . . . and *Straight Ahead* . . . was explosive is to be guilty of understatement of almost criminal proportions. . . . No sooner had these recordings hit the street than *down beat*, a publication that has tended to be as much concerned with an artist's politics as with his performance, convened an all white panel of "experts"—critics, journalists, even musicians—to confront the Lincoln-Roach duo and see if the pair could not be made to recant some of their nationalist heresies. . . . While this blatant bit of attempted thought control did not elicit the desired confession of error, . . . it became virtually impossible for them . . . to secure employment.[118]

Although Abbey Lincoln starred in two fine films in the 1960s, *Nothing but a Man* (1964) and *For the Love of Ivy* (1968), she had to confront gender and racial bias throughout her career. Anna Marie Wooldridge was her birth name in Chicago in 1930 and during her childhood in Kalamazoo, Michigan. Before working with Max Roach, she coped with a variety of new names and significations to survive as a supper club vocalist in the patriarchal networks of white nightclub owners and music managers. Her supper club singing career began in the 1950s, when she moved to Honolulu, Hawaii, for two years and then to Los Angeles in 1954, where nightclub owners asked her to take two French-sounding names: Gaby Wooldridge and Gaby Lee. Singing at Ciro's nightclub in Hollywood made her a star and a sex symbol in 1956, the year her first album, *Affair: A Story of a Girl in Love*, appeared. When she became interested in the civil rights movement in 1956, her manager asked her to change her name to Abbey Lincoln, which would identify her with the political legacy of Abraham Lincoln. In 1956 she also sang a song in the film *The Girl Can't Help It* and wore Marilyn Monroe's dress from *Gentlemen Prefer Blondes* in the film. Lincoln wore Monroe's dress again as well as bathing suits in the photos for a 1957 *Ebony* article that compared her to Marilyn and signified her as a sex object who "uses skin-tight gown in night club act."[119]

Max Roach became her mentor in 1957 and encouraged her to become a jazz vocalist: "He was another set of eyes for me. . . . When he saw me in New York wearing a Marilyn Monroe type of dress, he . . . explained, 'You don't have to do that; let the music speak.' . . . When I was given the opportunity . . . to record with Sonny Rollins, Kenny Dorham, Paul Chambers, Wynton Kelly, Sam Jones, and Max Roach . . . it opened my eyes to a whole new world of music."[120] Lincoln recalled, "Their standards were so high, I couldn't help but improve and benefit from their company."[121] Impressed by Roach's masculine performance and commitment to black people expressed in his music and his Muslim identity, Lincoln studied African American and African history, embraced an afro hairstyle, abandoned supper club singing, and married her mentor in 1962 (they divorced in 1970). In the 1970s, she toured Africa with Miriam Makeba, the South African musician and wife of Stokely Carmichael; changed her name to Aminata Moseka; and discussed, in retrospect, her reaction to the racism and sexism she experienced in the 1960s jazz world: "I think I'm very fortunate. I'm still alive and I'm one year older than Billie Holiday was when she passed. . . . I want to make a new version of the *Freedom Now Suite*, one that'll be even better than the first one."[122]

Although Abbey Lincoln's identity as a jazz singer and a Pan-African activist was initially shaped by her husband's Islamic values, she was also a black feminist and a womanist, concerned with addressing the intersections of race, gender, sex, and class oppression as well as the welfare of all black people, female and male.[123] As a black feminist, Lincoln attacked white and black patriarchy in her essay "A Ringing Challenge: Who Will Revere the Black Woman?": "She has been used as the white man's sexual outhouse, and shamefully encouraged by her own ego-less man to persist in this function. . . . Still, she looks upon her man as God's gift to black womanhood."[124] Lincoln revered the black feminist intellectual and political agency of Billie Holiday's life and music. Yes, she was married to a Muslim musician and freedom fighter for eight years and her blackness, respectability, and musical identity also centered on experiences helping to redeem and uplift black manhood by praising and loving Max Roach and his bebop colleagues for their contributions to music and social justice. She admitted that her identity, constructed in the intersecting worlds of African American Islam and jazz, was complex, noting her "awareness of who I am as a human, as a black woman, as an artist and as an entertainer. All these things are me."[125]

Yet, ultimately Abbey Lincoln's artistry and radical politics challenged the masculinist domination of the music industry and demonstrated how women shaped Black Power strategies and Islamic sensibilities in 1960s jazz.

Max Roach became known as the "drummer who dares to dissent."[126] He participated in the protest against Lumumba's assassination at the United Nations and picketed at Miles Davis's Carnegie Hall performance on May 19, 1961, because it raised money for the white-led African Research Foundation, which provided health care for black Africans.[127] In 1962 he wrote two articles for *Muhammad Speaks*, "Max Roach on Jazz: How Whites Made $Billions from Negro Art Form" and "Max Roach on the Future of Jazz: Says Racial Self-Help Is Cure for Whites' Control of Music Negroes Created," which protested the economic exploitation of black musicians in jazz.[128] Roach's involvement in Islam and the militant political movements of the 1960s and his perspective that his music reflected the pain of systemic racism, the black Atlantic cool aesthetic, the freedom struggles of his people, and great art with roots in the African-derived songs of slavery, made it hard for him to make a living as a performing jazz musician. He admitted, "From '63 to about '68 I was hard-pressed really to get anything going. . . . I would talk in a lot in clubs . . . and I remember Max Gordon at the Village Vanguard would say, 'Max, I want you in the club, but I wish you wouldn't make those damn speeches.' . . . We were all kind of caught up in the fever of the moment. I'm happy that I was."[129]

The Nation of Islam's Callout to Jazz and Rhythm and Blues Musicians

Max Roach was not the only Muslim artist featured in *Muhammad Speaks*. The Nation of Islam's callout to jazz musicians supported the values of Black Power, global consciousness, and alternative black masculinities, values that were central to its motto "Freedom, justice, and equality!" and that led to the ascendancy of Islam in the United States in the 1960s. During this period, the Nation of Islam became a wealthy African American religious group with its own temples, dynamic ministers, radio program, newspaper, printing press, bank, factory, meat plant, restaurants, bakeries, stores, schools, farms, houses, barbershops, and apartments.[130] It was a Black Power success story that embodied the values of black pride and community-based economic autonomy, which appealed to African American musicians exploited by white-owned record companies and clubs. Several factors motivated the Nation's musical outreach during the golden age of jazz. First, Louis X, minister of Temple No. 11 in Boston, Malcolm X, national spokesperson and minister of Temple No. 8 in Harlem, and Elijah Muhammad, founder and messenger of the religion, were all jazz fans. Louis X was a violinist and former calypso singer. Malcolm X was a former lindy hop dancer who incorporated the wit and improvisational qualities of jazz into his speaking style. Muhammad's favorite jazz recording was "Poinciana," a hit song on *Ahmad Jamal at the Pershing: But Not for Me* (Chess, 1958). New Orleans-born Vernel Fournier, the drummer on "Poinciana," was part of a jazz group that performed regularly at one of Elijah Muhammad's restaurants in the 1960s. Under Elijah's influence, Fournier converted to the Nation of Islam in the 1970s and changed his name to Amir Rushdan.[131] Abdul Basit Naeem, a Pakistani writer, described in *Muhammad Speaks* the Nation's new policy on music, which began in the late 1950s when "both music and musical entertainment (inclusive of highly interpretive African ethnic dances) . . . played an increasingly significant role in the presentation of American Muslims' overall social and cultural program."[132] Elijah Muhammad was motivated to attract successful jazz men and women to his organization because they created the music he enjoyed, they were local artists as well as celebrities who showcased the religious and economic programs of the Nation, and they helped to attract new African American converts to Islam.

Nation of Islam musicians were expected to embrace the religion's Afro-Asiatic identity, its Islamic dietary rules, and its patriarchal gender politics. According to historian Ula Yvette Taylor, Muhammad's Fruit of Islam promoted a communal masculinity that "promised black women the prospect of finding a provider and a protector among the organization's men, who were fiercely committed to these masculine roles." Yet these Muslim women struggled "to escape the devaluation of black womanhood while also clinging to the empowering promises of patriarchy." Finally, Taylor writes, "Despite being relegated to a lifestyle that did not encourage working outside the home, NOI women found freedom in being able to bypass the degrading experiences connected to labor performed largely by working-class black women and in raising and educating their children in racially-affirming environments."[133] As we will see, black masculinity and femininity among the Nation's jazz artists played out in the context of their individual struggles with the movement's patriarchal values and its emphasis on purification of the black body.

Guitarist Grant Green was Elijah Muhammad's favorite jazz convert. Green, who was born in St. Louis, came under the sway of a local Nation of Islam bass player, Herschel Harris, in the mid-1950s, and converted to the religion because it both appealed to his heart and his intellect and supported his resistance to racism in St. Louis nightclubs. Herschel Harris, Ann and Grant Green, pianist John "Albino Red" Chapman, his wife, Barbara Morris, drummer Albert St. James, his wife, Sarah, and Charles Williams helped to establish Temple No. 28 in St. Louis in the late 1950s. Eventually, they traveled to Chicago to meet Elijah Muhammad and had dinner in his home.[134] St. James pointed out, "Wherever we went it was musicians who were able to understand how the teachings of the Honorable Elijah Muhammad could turn you around and make you do better things."[135] Granted, "Albino Red" Chapman struggled to get off narcotics after he converted to the Nation of Islam and ultimately succumbed to drug and alcohol abuse, freezing to death in a vacant St. Louis house.[136] But Grant Green was widely known as a jazz musician who took Islam seriously, including food prescriptions—he would rather starve than eat pork while on tour. His manager Jay Glover recalled, "We'd be in a small town and Grant would drive all over town looking for a vegetarian restaurant, and if he didn't find one, he'd just go home and go to sleep without eating."[137]

Green left his wife and children in St. Louis and moved to New York City in 1960.[138] He began recording albums for Blue Note such as *Green Street* (1961), *Sunday Mornin'* (1961), *Grandstand* (1961), *Born to Be Blue* (1961), *The Latin Bit* (1962), and *Feelin' the Spirit* (1962), to name a few; and received *Down Beat* magazine's new star award for the best guitarist in 1962.[139] Yet, in the early 1960s, his heroin habit began to affect his money, his health, and his marriage.[140] He spent most of his paychecks on drugs and struggled to send money to his wife, Ann, and their four children. His daughter-in-law Sharony Andrews Green put it this way: "He was becoming a man of pure contradiction. On the one hand, he

would hail the wonders of Islam and eat healthy meals while simultane-
ously destroying his body and mind with a needle and sinister liquid. . . .
While he adhered to certain teachings of his Muslim faith, he rebuked
others, including the one explicitly forbidding the use of drugs."[141] For
a while, the beautiful and creative music that he produced on the guitar
and the numerous albums he recorded protected his career. But by the
mid-1960s, he was strung out on heroin.[142]

In 1968 Grant Green served a prison sentence in New York for narcotics possession.[143] When he was released in 1969, he returned to Brooklyn and lived with his family, and then for a while with Thomas Basir,
a Muslim jazz drummer, who recalled that the guitarist "continued to
cling to the Muslim faith. It showed in his diet. . . . We were always into
eating correctly. . . . It showed in his music. . . . The energy that ignited
his spiritual thinking mirrored the music being heard on the radio across
the country, namely funk."[144] Green had become excited by the music of
James Brown, who was known as Soul Brother No. 1 because of the intensity of his vocal style, dancing, and racial pride, and his band's funky
polyrhythmic drumming. These new musical influences were reflected
in the first two soul jazz albums on which Green performed with the
organist Charles Kynard, *The Soul Brotherhood* (Prestige, 1969), and the
organist Reuben Wilson, *Love Bug* (Blue Note, 1969). Then, Green began
to record his own albums in the soul jazz style for Blue Note, albums
including *Carryin' On* (1969), *Green Is Beautiful* (1970), *Alive!* (1970),
Visions (1971), *Shades of Green* (1971), *The Final Comedown* (1971), and
Live at the Lighthouse (1972). The coda for Grant Green's musical and
religious life spans the 1970s. However, a preliminary summary of his
relationship to Elijah Muhammad's religious community in the 1960s
follows below.

Grant Green moved to Detroit and bought a home on the West Side
in 1970. The city of Detroit was a black mecca for musicians, businesspeople, and Muslims.[145] During this period, he divorced Ann, recon-
nected with his children, remarried, revived his musical career, and
also began using cocaine. On the one hand, because of his reputation
for drug use and womanizing, Green did not go to the Nation of Islam
mosque in the motor city "'cause he knew those brothers [the Fruit of
Islam] were probably gon' whup his head," according to his keyboardist,
Emmanuel Riggins.[146] On the other hand, "the brothers still loved him

and loved his music, so . . . he played a lot of Muslim gigs," said Riggins. "See, Muslims were business men. They would have a bazaar . . . and they would advertise Grant was gon' be playing there. And you know they gon' come hear Grant. They called him Brother Grant!"[147] Green and his band played in black Muslim events in the United States. In the 1970s, St. Louis welcomed him back to officiate with the mayor on Muhammad Ali Day. One of his bandmates, Greg Williams, described the musical significance of the event: "We were at the temple playing and Muhammad Ali walked in. . . . We stood up and gave him a salute. He gave it back. . . . Him and Grant talked for quite a while."[148] Ali was the heavyweight boxing champion and Nation of Islam convert who had been banned from professional boxing for three years for opposing his induction into the armed forces in 1967. Because of his identity as an Asiatic black man, he had famously refused to kill "brown people in Vietnam while so-called Negro people in Louisville are treated like dogs."[149] Green and Williams respected his honesty and his religious and social justice values.

The jazz guitarist hired an African American Muslim manager, Jay Glover, to help recharge his career in 1975. However, they had to deal with religious and racial discrimination from the white executives in the music industry. Glover reported that when Green sent him to discuss his record contracts, the executives would say, "Go back and tell him to give up his religion. And they didn't know that I was a Muslim because I never told anybody."[150] Islamophobia was reportedly widespread in the business end of jazz. Percy James, a conga player in St. Louis who was Green's friend and also a Nation of Islam member, explained that after his band played a successful concert in the Detroit arena, Ahmad Jamal read them a letter from a white music executive that said, "Do not hire these brothers because they are black Muslims." James's wife, Deanetta, believed that Islamophobia in the industry did not make sense because "most of your jazz musicians were Muslims. They were peaceful people. They played peaceful music."[151] Nevertheless, efforts to repress Muslim musicians in the jazz world continued. The FBI practiced domestic surveillance of the Nation of Islam, which it called the "Muslim Cult of Islam."[152] And the US State Department's racism was clearly evident in its imperialist foreign policy toward Islamic Third World countries.

Grant Green's last two soul jazz albums were *The Main Attraction* (Kudu, 1976) and *Easy* (Versatile, 1978). In late 1978 he had a stroke, and while he was recovering in Harlem Hospital, his doctors found a blood clot close to his heart. In spite of his fragile health, Green drove across the United States with his girlfriend Dorothy Malone to perform at the Lighthouse Club in Southern California. Then, in January, they drove back to New York City. Grant Green was forty-three years old when he died from a heart attack on January 31, 1979.[153]

He loved the Nation of Islam, and his musical performances in African American Muslim communities and establishment of a temple in his hometown reflected his deep commitment to the racial uplift of black people and the values of communal masculinity. Green was committed to following Elijah Muhmmad's teachings on "how to eat to live." Although he was proud to practice the Islamic dietary program in his everyday life, he struggled with self-destructive addictions to heroin and cocaine and was unable to comply with the Nation's strict requirements for the purification of the black body. His celebrity status in the jazz world exempted him from selling quotas of the *Muhammad Speaks* newspaper, which was usually a required ritual of black manhood in the religion. Perhaps, because he was Muhammad's favorite jazz musician, he was also able to forgo the Fruit of Islam's severe penalties like a trial, isolation, or suspension for violating its black masculine code of religious ethics and rules for protecting black women.

It is important to note that the leaders of the Nation were never able to totally control the Muslims in their movement; some members adhered to "certain aspects of the N.O.I.'s ritualized behavior, while ignoring others."[154] According to Edward E. Curtis IV, sometimes it was difficult to determine "exactly what the rules [of black masculinity] were" among its jazz artists.[155] For example, the Nation of Islam tenor saxophonist Osman Karriem became a cool exemplar of African American religious internationalism. He studied Arabic at Al-Azhar University in Cairo and returned to Chicago to play with his Egyptian Jazz group at a dinner for Elijah Muhammad in 1966. He cultivated his interest in Bedouin and Amharic music by traveling to Addis Ababa and performing jazz on Ethiopian television with an African rhythm ensemble consisting of drummer German Tsegaye, pianist Sadik Abdul Kadr, and bassist Ato Tusfa in 1967.[156] However, when Karriem's drug addiction was exposed two years later, Muhammad ostracized him in *Muhammad Speaks* and forbade Muslims from associating with him.[157]

The Nation of Islam's many bazaars were grassroots community events free from the exploitative influences of drugs, alcohol, white nightclub owners, and critics, events in which jazz musicians performed in black-controlled contexts emphasizing the movement's Afro-Asiatic style (clothing, art, food, and African drumming) and religious message (speeches and literature). Muhammad's followers constructed their unity bazaars to replicate the ethos of marketplaces in the Middle East.[158] Sometimes, the Fruit of Islam choral ensemble performed in these events, which welcomed Muslims, potential converts, black professionals, businesspeople, artists, and community leaders.[159] The following African and Caribbean musicians and jazz men and women also provided entertainment at the Nation's bazaars, banquets, and concerts in the 1960s: Babatunde Olatunji in New York, 1962, 1963, and Washington DC, 1963; Dinizulu and His African Dancers in New York, 1963, 1967, and Boston, 1963; Abbey Lincoln, Max Roach, Lonnie Smith, Clifford Jordan, and Coleridge Perkinson in New York, 1964; Walter Davis Trio in New York, 1964; Walter Dickerson Quartet in New York, 1964 and 1965; George Price and the Islanders Steel Band in Newark, 1964, and New York, 1964, 1965, and 1967; Samuel 8X and His Jazz Specialists in Newark, 1964; Red Bruce's Jazz Trio in Springfield, MA, 1965; Julian Priester Quintette + 2 and Quartette Tres Bien in Chicago, 1965; Blue Mitchell and Roy Haynes in New York, 1965; Noble Watts Jazz Quintet in Miami, 1966; Osman Karriem in Chicago, 1966; Jiver's Jazz Combo in Washington, DC, 1966; Webster Young Quintet in Washington, DC, 1967; Cecil Payne and group in New York, 1967; Pucho and the Latin Soul Brothers in New York, 1968; and Curtis Amy Quintet in Los Angeles, 1969.[160]

Muhammad Speaks featured photos and articles that documented some of the indigenous Nation of Islam jazz artists who performed at its official events. Their identities and stories illustrate how the conversion of black musicians to Islam contributed to the power of the religion in the 1960s. Bassist Jesse 4X, vibraphonist Harold X, saxophonist John 10X, trumpeter Thaddius X, and pianist Richard X were the "musical men" in the Fruit of Islam in Denver's Mosque No. 26, who played at an affair called "Night with the FOI." They wore FOI uniforms of fezzes, bow ties, and military-style sport coats during a performance that "royally entertained the enthusiastic audience."[161] The Quartet Shahid (guitarist Sonny X Kenner, drummer Edward X Skinner, bassist George X Hudson, tenor saxophonist Ezekial X Cleaves, and vocalist Larthey X Cummings) was organized in Kansas City in 1966 and played at events in St. Louis and New York City.[162] In an article, "Muslim Musicians Reveal Trials of Black Artists," Sonny X described his jazz journey to the Muslim religion and the impact of Islamophobia in the music industry:

> I started playing guitar when I was nine years old. . . . At 19 . . . I joined Sonny Thompson and Lula Reed and traveled with them. . . . Then I was drafted into the army. All the time I was in the army I played. . . . I was discharged in 1958 and . . . during this time I became acquainted with the Nation of Islam in Kansas City and the powerful teachings of the Honorable Elijah Muhammad. . . . From 1959 to 1965, I lived in Los Angeles doing studio recording and television work—with most of the top artists out there, including Jimmy Witherspoon and the Jazz Crusaders. . . . There are many reasons that made me move back to Kansas City in 1965, but mostly, I had become more interested in the Nation of Islam and many of the brothers I had grown up with in Kansas City were now members of the Nation of Islam. Besides that, the whole recording industry out on the West Coast is owned by white people and when they began to find out about my association with the Nation, they began to give me all kinds of trouble.[163]

Larthey X discussed the quartet's Islamic struggle for self-determination, communal masculinity, and respectability in the jazz world:

> Just as Brother Muhammad Ali has cleaned up the world of sports, so we would like to do in music. We hope to specialize in and utilize clean musical material. Music that has dignity and respect, not degrading. I was blessed when I came into the Nation of Islam to have had dinner with the Honorable Elijah Muhammad. Through his guidance and teachings, I have learned how to conduct myself musically, and the inner peace that Islam brings has enabled me to fully concentrate on this area of my music. . . . We feel that since we are unified through Islam . . . we do not suffer the deficiencies of jealousy that plague so many other musicians. . . .

Black musicians need to take control of what is rightfully theirs, as the Messenger points out. The only recognized form of music classified as being American is jazz—and it was created by the black man—but they don't want to recognize jazz because they don't want to recognize the black man.[164]

When the great hard bop trumpeter Lee Morgan became a Muslim in the early 1960s, his severe drug addiction prevented him from embracing the values of communal masculinity that shaped the musical and religious identities of the artists in the Quartet Shahid. Morgan's local jazz career began in the mid-1950s, when he was a sixteen-year-old high school student playing weekend gigs in Philadelphia clubs.[165] His first professional breaks came in 1956, when he played with Art Blakey and the Jazz Messengers during the summer in Philadelphia; moved to New York City in October to play in Dizzy Gillespie's band; and recorded his first two albums, *Introducing Lee Morgan* (Savoy, 1956) and *Lee Morgan Indeed!* (Blue Note, 1957).[166] He developed a distinctive funky and upbeat sound on the trumpet and played as a sideman on John Coltrane's album *Blue Train* (Blue Note, 1957) and Dizzy Gillespie's album *Dizzy Atmosphere* (Specialty, 1957). While he was still a teenage jazz prodigy, Morgan continued to record his own new albums, such as *Lee Morgan Sextet* (Blue Note, 1957), *Lee Morgan Vol. 3* (Blue Note, 1957), *City Lights* (Blue Note, 1957), *The Cooker* (Blue Note, 1958), and *Candy* (Blue Note, 1958). When Dizzy Gillespie's band folded in 1958, Lee Morgan auditioned and was admitted to study at the Juilliard School in New York City, but instead of enrolling, he accepted Art Blakey's invitation to be the trumpeter for the Jazz Messengers in 1958.[167]

Although he recorded new albums, including *Here's Lee Morgan* (Vee-Jay, 1960), *Lee-Way* (Blue Note, 1960), and *Expoobident* (Vee-Jay, 1960), it was during this period that Morgan embraced a self-destructive hypermasculinity that was influenced by street hustling, exploitation of his new Japanese American spouse, Kiko Yamamoto, and drugs: he began using heroin, and his bandleader, Blakey, also used narcotics.[168] Eventually, Lee Morgan's drug habit affected his musical performances and Art Blakey fired him in 1961. His life in New York took a nasty turn during the summer of 1961, when an assailant allegedly hit him in the face with a hammer and knocked his teeth out.[169]

Morgan then decided to return to his hometown, where he converted to the Nation of Islam in Philadelphia's Mosque No. 12.[170] It is unclear how the jazz man's connection to the Nation helped him in his struggle with addiction during his Philadelphia sojourn. According to his biographer, Tom Perchard, he "drifted around the city, apparently still high, still hustling. . . . Keeping in contact with music as much as was possible, he continued to compose."[171] Lee Morgan stayed in Philly for two years, played in a group with tenor saxophonist Jimmy Heath, and made a new album, *Take Twelve* (Jazzland, 1962).[172]

The trumpeter returned to the New York jazz scene in 1963 and produced a new album, *The Sidewinder* (Blue Note, 1964), which became a best-selling hit because of its crossover appeal in the soul jazz, blues, and rhythm and blues genres.[173] Although he was still using heroin, Morgan went back to Art Blakey and the Jazz Messengers in 1964. The stable job and income from *The Sidewinder* helped him get back on his feet as a professional musician, and he began to compose material that identified with black Islamic and African themes.[174] Here we see how Morgan sometimes positioned his intersecting experiences as a jazz man and a Muslim convert in a black Atlantic cool context of anticolonial and anti-racist struggles. He recorded *Search for the New Land* (Blue Note, 1966) with guitarist and Nation of Islam member Grant Green, a record with themes that resonated with Elijah Muhammad's global consciousness and demand for a black nation.[175] The album's song "Mr. Kenyatta" reflected Lee Morgan's respect for Jomo Kenyatta, the anticolonialist and first president of Kenya, serving from 1964 to 1978.[176] He composed "Calling Miss Khadija," a song with a Muslim theme (Khadijah was the Prophet Muhammad's first wife), for Art Blakey and the Jazz Messengers' album *Indestructible* (Blue Note, 1966), on which he was a sideman.[177] With black internationalism in mind, Morgan said he "wanted to name a tune after one of the newly independent African states," and went on to write "Zambia," one of the tracks on his album *Delightfulee* (Blue Note, 1967).[178]

Morgan's success in producing commercially viable jazz records set the stage for his departure from Art Blakey's group in 1965, and Blue Note released many of Lee Morgan's albums from 1966 to 1968, including *The Rumproller* (1966), *Cornbread* (1967), *The Gigolo* (1968), and *Caramba!* (1968). In the late 1960s, he moved into Helen Moore's apartment in the Bronx and tried to change his lifestyle of street hustling and narcotics abuse. Moore became Morgan's new girlfriend and agent, supporting him while he got off heroin and got into a methadone program.[179] According to tenor saxophonist Billy Harper, it was during this time that the trumpeter was drawn to a communal masculinity that reflected his background in the Nation of Islam, his long struggle to kick drug addiction, and his support for militant activism in black political affairs and the jazz world: "He was reading a lot about Malcolm X . . . talking about the kind of philosophies that Malcolm might have."[180] He was regularly going to Harlem to listen to the soapbox speakers in African Square on 125th Street and to buy books in Lewis H. Michaux's National Memorial African Bookstore: The House of Common Sense and Home of Proper Propaganda and World History Book Outlet on Two Billion Africans and Non-White Peoples, which was one of Malcolm X's old haunts.[181] He signaled his black global consciousness among jazz men by talking about books like Jomo Kenyatta's *Facing Mt. Kenya* and Oginga Odinga's *Not Yet Uhuru* with his friends and by expressing his admiration for Stokely Carmichael's Black Power and Pan-African perspectives.[182] Morgan went on to use the Nation's ideal of black economic self-determination to shape his own professional values and his participation in collective protests with other jazz artists, who challenged institutional racism and their marginalization in the white-controlled music and entertainment industries in the 1970s.

Jazz and rhythm and blues singer Etta James, born Jamesetta Hawkins in Los Angeles in 1938, was another celebrity jazz musician who embraced African American Islam in the 1960s. Growing up in Southern California and San Francisco, she learned how to sing in a Black Baptist church choir in South Central, Los Angeles, yet she and her mother, Dorothy, were also fans of Billie Holiday's music.[183] Jamesetta's music career began in 1953, when she quit school and ran away to Hollywood with her teenage singing group, the Peaches, to cut their first rhythm and blues record, "The Wallflower," also known as "Roll with Me, Henry" (Modern Records, 1955). It was produced by Johnny Otis, who changed her name to Etta James.[184] "The Wallflower" and James's song "Good Rockin' Daddy" (Modern Records, 1955) became hit records on the rhythm and blues songs chart.[185] As a solo vocalist in the 1950s, she began touring across the United States, performing with musicians such as Johnny Guitar Watson, Clifton Chenier, Little Richard, the Clovers, the Five Keys, the Shirelles, Harvey Fuqua, Sam Cooke, and Jackie Wilson as well as recording songs as a side vocalist in Fats Domino's studio in New Orleans.[186] In 1960 she moved to Chicago, where she recorded her first album, *At Last!* (Argo, 1960), with her new producer, Leonard Chess. The album included James's signature rhythm and blues songs about the rough struggles of romantic love, "All I Could Do Was Cry" and "At Last," as well as standard jazz songs like "Stormy Weather."[187] At Chess Records, she sang with the famous rock and roll and blues musicians Chuck Berry, Bo Diddley, Muddy Waters, Little Walter, and Howlin' Wolf.

By the early 1960s, James was using heroin and cocaine, partying with pimps and gangsters after her shows, and "liked being compared to Billie Holliday, even if the comparison was based on our common love of dope."[188] However, she pointed out, "Long months would pass when I'd stay clean. It was during one such period that I joined the Muslims. I'd been hearing about the Muslims all my life."[189] Her mother, Dorothy, was impressed with how cool the Nation of Islam brothers in Los Angeles were and she visited their temple in the 1950s.[190] When Etta was a young vocalist living in Atlanta, her manager, John Lewis, took her to Temple No. 15, where she listened to Minister Louis X's preaching. The aspect of his spiritual message that influenced her the most was the cool communal brotherhood among the men, and she experienced it herself when she decided to change her religion: "Let's wear those headdresses and go to temple every night . . . and mostly, let's hang out with those fine-looking clean-cut Muslim brothers. It was the brothers who converted me. I got my X from that temple . . . and called myself Jamesetta X."[191]

Receiving her X allowed her to obliterate her slave name and signified a radical change in the singer's religious, political, and gender self-determination. The name change represented her decision to redefine her identity as "an Honorable Elijah Muhammad Muslim" and as a member of an international, non-European religion.[192] It demonstrated her resistance to racism in Jim Crow America and the music industry and empowered her struggle to attain freedom and respectability as a black woman in the United States. James's Islamic global consciousness developed in the context of a radical, patriarchal religious movement that offered her protection from the self-destructive practices in the jazz and rhythm and blues world.[193] She studied the Qur'an with John Lewis, struggled to purify her body according to the religion's dietary prescriptions, and experienced racial pride as an Asiatic black woman. According to her own testimony about her experience in the Nation, "It was a better way of living, a better way of eating. . . . My religious practices might have been erratic, and my wildness surely overwhelmed my piety, but for ten years I called myself a Muslim."[194]

In 1960, during the period she was living in the Theresa Hotel in Harlem, James's Third World global consciousness expanded. Malcolm X welcomed and met with the Cuban revolutionary leader Fidel Castro while he and his delegation were living in the hotel and took part in the United Nations General Assembly in 1960; she recalled that the Theresa's rooftop area had coops "with live chickens so he could prepare his own food. Fidel worried about being poisoned."[195] Then she began attending Temple No. 7 in Harlem and came under the sway of Malcolm X. "He was incredible. I identified with Malcolm. . . . The cat inspired," said James.[196] She remembered his years as a hustler in Harlem's jazz world, but was now drawn to his Islamic spirituality, his charismatic preaching, his masculine performance, and the cool style that framed his past and present lives in the context of his ministry. The young boxer Cassius Clay was one of her fans when she performed at the Apollo Theater, and she tried, though unsuccessfully, to convert him to the Nation of Islam when he was eighteen years old.[197]

Eventually Elijah Muhammad's religious movement became Etta James's doorway into the Ahmadiyya Muslim Community. After her musical friend John Lewis joined the Ahmadi community, she left the Nation to become an Ahmadiyya Muslim. According to the vocalist, "They were universal Muslims, not separatists. . . . John became pious, praying five times a day. He was also urging me to become more serious. I tried, and for a while I was. At the same time, running around with characters like James Brown, I got distracted."[198]

James had embraced the Nation of Islam because for her, it was an exciting beacon of racial uplift and black consciousness.[199] Its emphasis on respect for black women, sisterhood and brotherhood, purification of the body, dietary health, and black Atlantic coolness appealed to her.[200] However, she explained, "I never changed my stage name, which shows you I never embraced the strict doctrine."[201] As a black celebrity who was economically prosperous and self-sufficient, she avoided the sexist pitfalls of patriarchal protection that could lead to the marginalization and control of women in the movement. But the Nation's appealing gender politics did not stop her from leaving it to join the Ahmadiyya, a community that she believed was more closely aligned with the global beliefs and practices of mainstream Islam in the sixties.

Spiritual, Aesthetic, and Political Influences on Ahmadiyya and Sunni Jazz Musicians in the Late 1950s and 1960s

The jazz pianist Ahmad Jamal exemplified the universal qualities of the Ahmadiyya Muslim Community that attracted Etta James, qualities such as its solidarity with mainstream religious practices in the Muslim world, black internationalism with links to African Islamic networks, spiritual and musical connections with Sunni Muslims, and a sense of global Muslim brotherhood that shaped communal masculinities. Jamal was born Frederick "Fritz" Jones in Pittsburgh in 1930 and started playing the piano and studying music during childhood. He left Pittsburgh after high school to travel with the George Hudson orchestra and also played with the Four Strings. He moved to Chicago after he married Virginia Wilkins in 1949.[202]

During a stint at the Apollo Theater in Harlem, hard bop trumpeter Idrees Sulieman introduced him to Islam; Jamal later remembered their meeting as "a philosophical presentation. . . . It had to do with being all you can be. . . . My philosophy has certainly influenced my music."[203] The pianist also learned about Islam in Detroit and decided to convert to the Ahmadiyya movement in 1950. He and his wife completed the legal paperwork to change their names to Ahmad Jamal and Maryam Mezzan Jamal in Chicago's Cook County court in 1952. According to Jamal, "I haven't adopted a name. It's part of my ancestral background and heritage. I have re-established my original name. I have gone back to my own vine and fig tree."[204] His name change represented a universal spiritual practice among converts to Islam in the wider Muslim world. However, he signaled the influences of Chicago's diverse African American Islamic communities when he talked about going back to his "own vine and fig tree." This expression originated in the Moorish Sci-

ence Temple in the 1920s with Noble Drew Ali's advice in the Moorish
Holy Koran "that every nation shall and must worship under their own
vine and fig tree, and return to their own and be one with their Father
God-Allah."[205]

Following his conversion, Ahmad Jamal formed the Three Strings in
1951, and the group made several albums: *Chamber Music of the New
Jazz* (Parrot, 1955), *Ahmad Jamal Trio* (Epic, 1955), and *Count 'Em 88*
(Argo, 1956). In 1958 his trio made a best-selling album, *But Not for
Me: Live at the Pershing* (Argo, 1958), with drummer Vernell Fournier
and bassist Israel Crosby. The album, which was recorded in a South
Side nightclub in Chicago, made him a rich and famous musician in
the late 1950s and 1960s because it was so popular and commercially
successful.[206] Miles Davis became one of his biggest fans and said he
was impressed by the pianist's lyricism, by Jamal's "concept of space, his
lightness of touch, his understatement, and the way he phrased notes
and passages."[207] The newspaper and magazine articles that discussed
the popularity of Ahmad Jamal's music also deepened the jazz world's
understanding of his religious identity as a devout Muslim.

In a 1958 story in the *Pittsburgh Courier*, the jazz man explained how
his musical success was connected to his Islamic faith: "I feel anyone
needs direction and purpose to become a success and to live with himself. It doesn't matter what faith a person chooses as long as it gives him
direction. I just want them to respect mine. . . . I have my music, my
religion and my family, and I'm really happy."[208] A 1959 *Down Beat* article discussed how Jamal's Muslim values shaped his way of life as a
professional jazz artist and helped him deal with corrupt practices in
the music business.[209] A newspaper story in Newport News, Virginia,
reported that his new name and religious identity had resulted in Jamal's
new faith in his music and his jazz trio, which a *Billboard* poll had rated
thirteen in the category of "Bestselling Artists on LP" in 1958.[210]

Ahmad Jamal decided to expand his global spiritual and political
consciousness in November 1959 by traveling to Egypt and Sudan on a
pilgrimage of sorts, to learn about Africa.[211] A *New York Times* article
provided the following report about his trip: "Ahmad Jamal . . . took
Cairo in tow today without playing a note. He talked of investing his
rising fortune in African real estate and of his devotion to the Moslem
faith. . . . The pianist . . . says Moslem prayers five times a day . . . in Ara-

bic."[212] In Cairo, despite Jamal's religious affiliation with the Ahmadiyya Muslim Community, he also maintained friendly interactions with Arab Sunni Muslims. Ultimately, his fame as a jazz pianist and a potential millionaire attracted the attention of an Egyptian Sunni intellectual who was well known among African American Islamic leaders in the United States in the late 1950s and 1960s. Mahmoud Youssef Shawarbi, professor of agriculture at Cairo University, was his host in Egypt. Shawarbi, who had been a Fulbright scholar at the University of Maryland and Fordham University in the 1950s and a leader of the Islamic Council of New York, went on to write an ethnographic analysis of the Nation of Islam, "Black Americans and the Islamic Organization in Chicago," which was published in his Arabic volume *Islam in America* in 1960.[213] His report discussed his meeting with Elijah Muhammad in Chicago and critiqued the Nation's beliefs as "anti-Islamic," but also encouraged seven selected African American Muslims who had graduated from high school to study Arabic at Cairo University "so that they can be introduced to real Islamic heritage."[214] Shawarbi's report also mentioned that he talked to FBI agents in New York and supported their plans to arrest African American Muslims who resisted the draft.[215]

Apparently, he had mixed motives for supporting the struggle for black liberation and influencing collaborations between the Islamic Third World and Muslims in the United States in the 1960s. He hoped to promote Arab Islamic values in black America through an Egyptian-based organization, Dissemination of Islamic Culture (with branches in New York and Washington, DC), as well as through his friendship with Ahmad Jamal. Shawarbi also attended a New York Afro-Asian bazaar for Temple No. 7 with Malcolm X in 1960.[216] During this gathering of 2,500 followers and friends of Elijah Muhammad, he said, "We are all Muslims and Muslims do not denounce each other. . . . I congratulate you on the work you are doing. . . . We Africans gave civilization to the world thousands of years ago. . . . You Afro-Americans should be proud of us, for we are proud of you. You need us, and we in Africa need you."[217]

Ahmad Jamal's bridge to Africa shaped his political, religious, and musical life and consciousness in the United States in several ways. He returned to Chicago with architectural floor plans for a new house in Cairo, where the pianist planned to eventually live during the winter months of each year. In Africa, he said, "I was home and happy. I had planned to go . . . because my ancestral roots are there; it was a moral obligation for me to go."[218] Visiting the continent and living part-time in Cairo was also a way for him to counteract racism in the United States: "No, I don't like Florida, and I refuse all engagements in southern states. In Africa I have freedom and the sun. In Florida I would only have the sun."[219]

An article in *Ebony* revealed how Jamal's African travels had inspired the layout of his sixteen-room Chicago home in Hyde Park, which was outfitted with its own mosque and a Middle Eastern theme room with art from Africa.[220] The article also took a look at his new supper club AlHambra, an elegant venue on the near South Side for live jazz performances and dining that did not serve alcoholic beverages. Here Ahmad Jamal, who was a businessman as well as a musician, constructed his nightspot and restaurant to conform to the dietary practices of his religion. AlHambra's menu featured foods from the Middle East, India, Pakistan, and the United States.[221] From 1959 to 1961, the short-lived club became the centerpiece of his businesses such as Jamal Export-Import Company, Mazzan Music Publishers, Durrah Restaurant Corp., and Jamal Enterprises, Inc.[222] AlHambra represented Jamal's values of communal masculinity and black Atlantic cool in an African American–owned showplace that purified and nourished the mind, body, and soul by presenting the uplifting music of professional jazz artists and serving the cuisine of global Islamic cultures. His trio recorded their new album, *Ahmad Jamal's AlHambra*, in his supper club in 1961, the year he closed the club.

In 1962 his marriage ended in divorce, and Ahmad Jamal terminated the Three Strings and moved his home and musical base to New York City, where he established a new jazz group with drummer Frank Gant and Muslim bassist Jamil Nasser in 1964. He recorded a series of albums in the 1960s: *Naked City Theme* (Argo, 1964), *The Roar of the Greasepaint* (Argo, 1965), *Extensions* (Argo, 1965), *Rhapsody* (Argo, 1965), *Heat Wave* (Argo, 1965), *Cry Young* (Argo, 1967), *The Bright, the Blue, and the Beautiful* (Argo, 1968), and *Ahmad Jamal at the Top: Poinciana Revisited* (Impulse!, 1969).[223] Although Jamal had embraced the Ahmadiyya community, musical and religious collaborations with Sunni Muslims were always easy for him because of the way he articulated his religious identity: "Yes, I have an Arabic name. . . . Basically, I get my approach to life from the Holy Qur'an. . . . I accepted Islam because it took me from darkness to light and gave me direction."[224]

Jamil Nasser was a Muslim bebop musician who played and recorded frequently with Jamal during the 1960s. He was born George Leon Joyner in Memphis in 1932 and studied music at Arkansas AM&N College in the early 1950s. His early professional career was shaped by gigs in Detroit in 1953 and in the Fort McPherson army band in Atlanta from 1954 to 1955. He played in B. B. King's band from 1955 to 1956. In 1956 Nasser moved to New York City with his Memphis friend and pianist Phineas Newborn Jr. to join the Phineas Newborn Quintet, and he was a soloist on several of Newborn's albums for RCA Victor: *Phineas' Rainbow* (1957), *While My Lady Sleeps* (1957), and *Fabulous Phineas* (1958). The bassist also played on albums recorded by Johnny Ace, Hank Mobley, Red Garland, Lou Donaldson, Gene Ammons, Herbie Mann, Evans Bradshaw, Randy Weston, Melba Liston, Lionel Hampton, and Lester Young in the 1950s.[225]

Nasser toured with jazz men who were victims of heroin addiction, Jim Crow racism, and economic exploitation during this period. When trumpeter Idrees Sulieman introduced him to the Qur'an, he took a critical look at several black Islamic communities. He embraced Sunni Islam in 1957, and officially adopted his new name, Jamil Sulieman Nasser, in 1958.[226] He discussed the pros and cons of conversion: "As an African American Muslim jazz musician, I experienced two levels of discrimination: color and religion. My conversion to Islam . . . cut my work volume in half. Nevertheless, Islam gave me the discipline to eschew self-destructive vices, and the confidence to challenge injustice inside and outside the music industry."[227] The bassist explained that music executives and club owners did not like to employ jazz artists who rejected identification as Negroes and "reclaimed their original identity."[228] He noted that "some Muslim jazz musicians retained their Christian names to sustain their careers. On the other hand, Yusef Lateef, Ahmad Jamal, Ahmed Abdul-Malik, Sadik Hakim, Rashied Ali, Idris Muhammad, Idrees Sulieman, and I legally changed our names and braved the consequences thereof."

Jamil Nasser acknowledged his concern that some of the Muslim communities he considered might try to control his career and personal life. As a result, he embraced Sunni Islam with a non-aligned status and joined the mosque that Dr. Mahmoud Shawarbi led at 1 Riverside Drive in Manhattan's Upper West Side neighborhood. This mosque welcomed Muslim jazz musicians in New York City. As we will see later, Nasser befriended Malcolm X, who also prayed at the 1 Riverside Drive mosque after he left the Nation of Islam in 1964.[229]

Jamil Nasser's religious values supported his political philosophy about social justice and jazz. He pointed out, "Our revolution was a quiet one as it lacked the collective organization and mobilization to dramatize its agenda. It was led by courageous individuals and organizations, who resented the plantation like nature of the jazz business and desired to own their music."[230] Thus, he admired Ahmad Jamal's independent businesses and his demand for respectable performance conditions, as well as his music. Although Nasser attended meetings of the Southern Christian Leadership Conference, the Student Nonviolent Coordinating Committee, and the Black Panther Party to explore their programs of racial liberation, he led the way with the artists who believed that their global consciousness and performances in African Muslim nations were powerful ways to express communal black masculinities in the late 1950s and 1960s.[231] However, he did not hesitate to critique repressive politics and racism in North African Islamic countries.

By 1958, he had joined the New York Jazz Quartet, which also included Idrees Sulieman on trumpet, Oscar Dennard on piano, and Buster Smith on drums. Sulieman was on the "do not call list" among New York City nightclub owners because of his religion.[232] Fed up with the drugs, racism, and mistreatment of jazz musicians in the United States, the quartet traveled abroad to perform. First, they played in Paris for two months in 1959 and connected with the Muslim drummer Kenny Clarke, who lived in the city.[233] The group performed for two months in Tangier, Morocco, and played on Radio Tangier International. Influenced by religious and musical interactions in a Muslim-majority country with two black Muslim artists, Dennard and Smith converted to Islam in Tangier and changed their names to Zaid Abdel Hamid Mustapha and Abu Bakr Salim, respectively.[234] The African American jazz men declined an invitation to play concerts for the United States Information Agency in Morocco—the concerts would have included white managers monitoring their quartet, and they did not wish to get involved with Cold War politics in Africa. According to Nasser, "the consequences of that decision were both far-reaching and tragic, because we encountered sabotage and other difficulties from that point forward."[235]

The members of the quartet played in Casablanca, where they noticed they were being followed, and moved on to Tunisia; then they received an invitation for a lucrative musical engagement in Algeria, where a revolution was going on, and trusted a mysterious African American named Sadler, who fed the hungry artists and claimed he could get work permits for them.[236] Nasser explained that when the quartet landed at the Algerian airport, "immigration officials detained us for twenty-four hours without explanation, denied our visas, and put us on a plane back to Tunisia."[237] The political intrigue continued in Tunisia when "someone told us the Algerian authorities found Sadler's card in one of our passports. Unfortunately, Sadler had been deported from Algeria for spying."[238]

In 1960 the New York Jazz Quartet returned to Europe and played concerts and club engagements in France, Switzerland, Austria, Poland, and Russia.[239] By August 1960, the group had arrived in Cairo, Egypt, to perform in nightclubs and on television.[240] But their Muslim pianist Oscar Dennard suddenly contracted typhoid fever and died in Cairo on October 22, 1960.[241] Jamil Nasser believed that the CIA was involved in Dennard's death "as retribution for not cooperating with them" in North Africa.[242] Faithful to his global Islamic religious philosophy and his black social justice values, he remained adamant about rejecting the State Department's exploitation of bebop musicians in its Cold War programs and propaganda. The quartet disbanded in the wake of the events in Cairo, and Nasser and Buster Smith played gigs in Germany and Italy from fall 1960 to February 1962, when they went home to the United States.[243] As mentioned earlier, Jamil Nasser began playing with Ahmad Jamal's group in 1964, and in 1969 he became vice president of Ahmad Jamal Productions, Jamal Publishing Corporation, and Hema Music Incorporated.[244]

Jazz trombonist and percussionist Daoud A. Haroon was affiliated with the Islamic Mission of America in New York in the 1960s. However, he was born John Mancebo Lewis in 1934 in Boston. His global religious consciousness and introduction to Sunni Islam, which he called "Flow of Baraka," began when he was a young boy in Roxbury's black community in the early 1940s:

I did not convert to Islam from Christianity or any other religion. A better description of what happened to me may be described as "Islamic absorption." No shahada was ever given and none was requested. . . . This may sound strange but it is quite true, taking into consideration the fact that neither of my parents were practicing Christians and were not members of any church. . . . The "church" . . . was described by my mother as . . . a tool by the white man to keep us under his control. . . . What I have described . . . was comparable to being in a "spiritual vacuum"—I have often considered that vacuum a blessing, and an indication of Allah's Barakat, because . . . into that early childhood vacuum came an unsuspecting African traveler by the name of Ali Musa. His birth name was: Hussein Ali bin Musa. . . . Mr. Musa appeared in my father's tailor shop one day shortly after he had "jumped" ship. . . . He had been working as a merchant seaman and had come ashore at the Port of Boston carrying the I.D. of a Yemeni seaman who had died at sea. . . . Musa became a frequent visitor to our home and . . . he became part of the family and thus became my adopted uncle. . . . He spoke what little English he knew with a very heavy . . . African (Somali) accent. . . . When he came to visit he would sit me on his knees and tell me stories with a character called . . . Mustapha Muhammad, who later became known to me as Nabi Mohammed (pbuh). . . . Allah had sent me a gift in the person of Ali Musa. . . . It was through this man's influence that I began to love Islam as a young man and to learn the Fatiha from his lips. The Fatiha eventually led to the Salat and the Salat led me on to ever increasing experiences with different groups of Muslims and the world of Islam—and on to a lifetimes search to gain a closer proximity to Allah.[245]

Daoud Haroon's childhood spiritual story includes two intertwining threads: his embrace of Sunni Islam, influenced by Ali Musa and his mother's stringent critique of the black church, but also by his family's socialization in a rich musical culture. He was brought into Boston's jazz spots as a baby in a shoebox, and as a boy during World War II frequented the dance halls and clubs where his mother and cousins worked as hat checkers, waiters, cooks, and bartenders. He started out working as a downtown shoeshine boy for the jazz artists performing in the city and quit school in the seventh grade. Then he began playing the bongo and conga drums to accompany tap dancers and dance classes in the

Elma Lewis School of Fine Arts in Roxbury in the 1950s. Haroon learned to play the trombone in jam sessions, in the street, and in lessons with professional musicians such as Charlie Connor. By 1958, he was a professional hard bop artist, joining saxophonist Ken McIntyre's band in Boston. He played trombone on McIntyre's album *Stone Blues* (New Jazz, 1962), which was recorded in 1960 and featured McIntyre (flute and alto saxophone), Paul Morrison (bass), Bobby Ward (drums), and Dizzy Sal (piano). The young trombonist moved to New York City with McIntyre in 1962 and continued to perform with him during the 1960s. He played with Ahmed Abdul-Malik as well.[246]

In New York, Haroon came under the sway of Sheikh Daoud Faisal, first at the International Muslim Society at 303 125th Street in Harlem, which he described as "the meeting place of the most diverse Muslims I have ever encountered in my life," including Africans, West Indians, Malays, Chinese, Indians, Arabs, and African Americans.[247] Then, in 1966, at the Islamic Mission of America at 143 State Street in Brooklyn Heights, Faisal encouraged Haroon to purify his life by eliminating major problems that interfered with his spirituality.[248] This advice led to his general education diploma and his hajj to Mecca in 1967 with a Muslim Students Association group that included Warith Deen Mohammed, the son of Elijah Muhammad.[249]

In Mecca, he met African Muslims from Cameroon and Togo who had walked across the continent to the holy city. They thought about trans-Atlantic slavery when they saw him and declared, "Yeah, we were told about our brother[s who] had been taken away."[250] Haroon said, "Women began to put their babies in my arms. . . . They began crying. . . . It was a very moving thing. It happened to me several times when I was there."[251] He went on to study ethnomusicology at Wesleyan University in Connecticut and explored "Africa, Africans in all their diversity. . . . All these different people who are here now come from this diversity."[252] According to Daoud Haroon's spiritual philosophy, which evolved from the intersections of Islam, jazz, and social justice in the 1960s, "Music doesn't discriminate. It reverberates throughout the heavens. . . . It has permeated everything we know."[253]

Sheikh Daoud Faisal influenced a network of Muslim jazz musicians in the 1950s and 1960s, including educator and percussionist Bilal Abdurahman. Born in 1928, Abdurahman was fascinated by the intersec-

HARD BOP, FREE JAZZ, AND ISLAM | 179

tions of African visual art, percussion instruments, and history. These interests led to his work as an illustrator for Brooklyn publications and newspapers and as a jazz percussionist, as well as his exploration of the Muslim religion. Bilal and his wife, Rakhia, converted to Sunni Islam at the Islamic Mission of America in the 1940s. There they met Ahmadiyya oud player and bassist Ahmed Abdul-Malik and trumpeter Rajab Abdul-Wahab. Bilal collaborated artistically with Abdul-Malik, who fused music from the Middle East and Africa in his performances. They played together frequently at Brooklyn's Putnam Central Club, which held regular jam sessions for jazz musicians in the 1960s. Bilal and Rakhia went on to establish the African Quarter, a restaurant that served African food and featured live jazz and African music. Political figures from independent African countries were among its customers, and Malcolm X visited the restaurant in the 1960s. The Abdurahmans created the Ethno-Modes Folkloric Workshops, whose musicians played African instruments for audiences in Brooklyn museums and put on shows to present African and Islamic clothing to the black community. Bilal directed a Brooklyn-based Ethno-Modes community center in the 1960s. He also promoted the global parallels between Islamic spirituality, African music, and jazz as a music teacher in the New York public schools, and he and his spouse used their community-based cultural institutions to contribute to their city's knowledge about Islam. Rakhia and Bilal continued to expand their own sense of African American religious internationalism by visiting Africa several times to learn about African and Middle Eastern musical forms, knowledge that Bilal incorporated into his performances of jazz.[254]

Other musicians in the 1960s were attracted by the values shared by Islam and jazz. Hard bop tenor saxophonist Tyrone Washington was twenty-three years old when he recorded his album *Natural Essence* (Blue Note, 1968) with Kenny Barron on piano, Joe Chambers on drums, Woody Shaw on trumpet, James Spaulding on flute and alto saxophone, and Reggie Workman on bass. Washington converted to Sunni Islam and changed his name to Bilal under the direction of Daoud Faisal at the State Street mosque in Brooklyn in 1968. After the 1960s, he eventually abandoned the jazz world to focus on his religious life in Newark, New Jersey. Bassist and Sunni Muslim Sabu Adeyola was born in Buffalo, New York, and went on to record and play with prominent jazz musicians such as Ahmad Jamal, Dexter Gordon, Abbey Lincoln, Leon Thomas, and Grover Washington. Muslim drummer and music educator Jesse Hameen II began playing bongo and conga drums, tambourines, gospel blues, Afro-Cuban music, rhythm and blues, and jazz as a young boy in New Haven, Connecticut, in the early 1950s. He experienced the London jazz scene and went to his first John Coltrane performance in London during an overseas stint in the service that spanned the late 1950s and early 1960s. Hameen developed his skills as a bebop drummer while performing on the road with musicians in the United States in 1963 and living in Harlem, where he played in its numerous jazz spots in the 1960s. He never experimented with drugs, and his goal as a jazz artist and music teacher was "entertaining and inspiring others to attain a higher level of spiritual consciousness."[255]

Idris Muhammad, who converted to Islam in the mid-1960s, articulates some of the central reasons why jazz musicians sought out Islam in this era:

A Sunni friend of mine showed me the Quran. As I went to pick it up he told me I couldn't touch it until I performed a Wudu. Wudu is the cleansing of one's face, neck, hands, and arms up to the elbows, rinsing out one's mouth and wiping one's feet clean so the contents of what you read can penetrate to one's soul. So I did that. And it did change my life. I read up on the Muslim faith and it changed my life. . . . And the next thing you know, my connection with the Creator becomes close. . . . I decided if I was going to do this, I am going to do it all the way. That's when I stopped using my original name. I am transformed. The man suggested to me my Muslim name. I worked with it and came up with Idris Muhammad. . . . I had been in a lot of trouble. My first wife had left me and I was searching for something to pull me out of this rut. I had become a junkie. . . . Cold turkey. I got hold of myself. I could think more clearly and I felt better about myself. I learned about how to treat human beings. . . . I remember the day I became Muslim and from that day I have always been successful. It's about you as a human being—whatever your religion—you've got to go before the Creator on the Day of Judgement.[256]

Idris Muhammad had a rich musical life as a jazz and rhythm and blues drummer, black Indian tribe member, and second line musician in New

Orleans. His conversion story exemplifies the themes of purification, reconstruction of black masculinity, global consciousness, freedom, and self-determination that attracted thousands of jazz musicians and fans to Islam in the 1960s. But the Islamic jazz brotherhood among black artists was also influenced by the musical performances, religious internationalism, and global travel of non-Muslim musicians, including saxophonist John Coltrane.

Musical and Religious Path to *A Love Supreme*: Afro-Asian Sounds, African Rhythms, and Islamic Spirituality in 1960s Jazz

Earlier in the chapter, we discussed the Philadelphia context in which John Coltrane "repeatedly encountered and considered Islam" in the 1950s.[257] One of the most important artists in the 1960s, Coltrane passionately expressed his African American Islamic spirituality both in his album *A Love Supreme* (Impulse!, 1965) and in his exploration of self-purification, new musical forms, and the Black Arts movement in New York. Coltrane expanded the geographic and religious frame of black internationalism, experimented with new sounds and spiritual traditions from the Third World, played with Muslim artists in his band, and developed a serious interest in Sufi mysticism. He incorporated Islamic themes and Middle Eastern and Indian modal forms into his music, used African polyrhythms and themes in his improvisation, and included what Yusef Lateef called "Islamic poetry" in his iconic album *A Love Supreme*. In this way, he brought together in jazz the liberation values and struggles of African Americans, Asians, and Africans in a "just universal order" whose cultural and racial diversity paralleled that of the global Muslim community—the ummah—itself.[258]

According to Scott Saul, Coltrane represented "the serious side of hard bop . . . [that] established jazz as music of black awakening. . . . [He] aimed to convey the intensity of freedom in a world where . . . the cultural roots of blackness were ripe for rediscovery. . . . He pursued freedom not for the hell of it, but for the heaven of it."[259] The saxophonist pursued an improvisational Afro-Asian, African, and Islamic path to *A Love Supreme* during a period when Black Power activists like Malcolm X and Amiri Baraka demanded a reconstruction of black religious and musical identities drawing on Third World sources, to achieve their revolutionary political goals. Black Power activists admired Coltrane as one of their heavy spirits. Franya J. Berkman sheds light on the heavenly aspect of his spiritual searching that influenced his musical philosophy. By the 1960s, he came to believe that performance of jazz was "personal spiritual expression, and [that] the artist should be fully committed to . . . erasing aesthetic boundaries and proscriptions about style" to explore spirituality in music.[260] The religious and artistic quest that led to the Islamic spiritual themes in his album was inspired by the musicians from the early 1960s who explored new forms of spiritual creativity and sources of sound and expression from India, West Africa, and the Middle East. John Coltrane's provocative musical and religious universalism intersected with his black Atlantic cool style, his sense of independence and liberation, and his transnational vision during an African American cultural revolution, and culminated with his interest in attending Malcolm X's speeches in New York City, his musical and religious projects with Yusef Lateef and Babatunde Olatunji, and his African travel plans at the end of his life.

Trane's revolutionary artistic and religious values helped to create alternative transnational notions of black masculinity in jazz. The transnational musical and religious impressions from Asia, Africa, and the Middle East that animated his new soundscape intersected with the global span of African American Islamic geography expressed in the construction of an Asiatic black masculinity in the Nation of Islam and other Muslim communities. The following narrative takes a selective look at the albums, musicians, and social forces that shaped his Islamic sensibility and black identity and the impact of his perspectives on jazz and the golden age of African American Islam in the 1960s.

Coltrane's monumental influence on jazz in that decade began with *Giant Steps* (Atlantic, 1960), which was distinctive for its synthesis of "third related chord movement"[261] and the very fast improvisations and tempos in "Giant Steps" and "Countdown"; hard bop sounds in "Cousin Mary" and "Mr. P.C."; and Islamic sensibility in the lyrical ballads about his Muslim wife in "Naima" (which the liner notes explain as an "Arabic name") and his stepdaughter in "Syeeda's Song Flute." Trane wrote all the tracks on *Giant Steps*, and the album showed his talent as a composer, a talent that would serve him well in *A Love Supreme*.

African American jazz musicians had been infatuated with the Indian-led Ahmadiyya Muslim Community since the 1940s, so it is no wonder that Coltrane's spirituality and jazz interests branched out to India and modal improvisation in *My Favorite Things* (Atlantic, 1961) and later on in "India." He commented, "I've already been looking into those approaches to music, as in India in which particular scales are intended to produce specific emotional meanings."[262] His notes on Indian scales show how his study of rasa, the Indian idea of attributing emotions, times of day, and moods to ragas (scales), shaped the mystical sounds and impressions in his own compositions and performances.[263] Trane was also drawn to the drone in Indian music and to the modal music making of the Indian sitar player Ravi Shankar, who embraced the spiritual philosophy of Indian classical music that fascinated the saxophonist: "The system of Indian music known as Raga Sageet can be traced back . . . to its origin in the Vedic hymns of Hindu temples. . . . To us, music can be a spiritual discipline on the path to self-realization, for we follow the traditional teaching that sound is God."[264]

The spiritual focus of Qawwali, the Sufi music of Pakistan and India, also helps to explain why John Coltrane chose to use Indian musical ideas in jazz:

> The term Qawwali itself applies both to the musical genre and to the occasion of its performance, the devotional assembly of Islamic mysticism—or Sufism. . . . Qawwali as an occasion is a gathering for the purpose of realizing the ideals of Islamic mysticism through the ritual of "listening to music," or sama. By enhancing the message of mystical poetry, and by providing a powerful rhythm suggesting the ceaseless repetition of God's name (zikr), the music of Qawwali has a religious function: to arouse mystical love, even divine ecstasy, the core experience of Sufism. . . . To the Sufi participant, Qawwali is a "method of worship" and "a means of spiritual advancement"; it is also "a feast for the soul."[265]

John Coltrane read *The Mysticism of Sound and Music: The Sufi Teaching of Hazrat Inayat Khan*, which was published by the Indian Sufi teacher in 1923; Khan believed in spiritual healing through music and wrote that the performance of "each raga has power upon the atmosphere as well as upon the health and mind of man."[266] The saxophonist was not the only jazz artist inspired by Indian music and a synthesis of African, Asian, and Islamic forms of expression. Ahmed Abdul-Malik played the tamboura, the Indian drone instrument, with Trane's group at the Village Vanguard in New York City in November 1961, and the Muslim saxophonist Yusef Lateef began playing the shinai, the Indian woodwind-reed instrument, in 1962.[267] However, as we will see, some of Coltrane's fans came to experience his performances as Sufi-like occasions for collective participation in mystical spiritual rituals of uplift, renewal, and divine love with "the power to make you change your consciousness," and he dominated the fusion of jazz with Indian music and spirituality in the 1960s.[268]

The ensemble for *My Favorite Things* featured, in addition to Coltrane himself on tenor and soprano saxophones, the musicians in his classic quartet: Muslim pianist McCoy Tyner, drummer Elvin Jones, and bassist Steve Davis. His soprano saxophone exploration of hypnotic nasal Indian/Middle Eastern tonality and his haunting modal improvising in "My Favorite Things," which became a jazz and pop hit in the 1960s, resonated with the Islamic sensibility of Yusef Lateef's *Eastern Sounds* and transformed Rodgers and Hammerstein's popular waltz song from *The Sound of Music* into an upbeat but mystical musical experience that was underscored by McCoy Tyner's "repeated piano vamp."[269]

Coltrane's experimentation with African and Middle Eastern sounds, and especially the music in his *Africa/Brass* album, which we will discuss below, paralleled the pianist Randy Weston's spiritual journey and experimentation with "African rhythms," which were influenced by his interactions with Muslim musicians. Born in Brooklyn in 1926, Weston later reflected that his early religious and musical consciousness was shaped by his friendship with the Ahmadiyya bassist Ahmed Abdul-Malik:

> When we were kids he introduced me to the instruments of North Africa and the Middle East, such as the kanoun and the oud. These were instruments where you could play eighth-tones, play in between the standard notes on the western scale. Malik and I used to experiment in local bands as kids. . . . I was already searching for something different. Malik would take me down to the Arab neighborhood around Atlantic Avenue in downtown Brooklyn to hear North African musicians. He spoke fluent Arabic so we had no trouble communicating.[270]

Weston also grew up with the Muslim drummer Max Roach and met emerging bebop musicians as well as jazz stars like Miles Davis at his house in Brooklyn. He was always impressed by the militant and revolutionary political values expressed in Roach's music and his support for black people.[271] In the late 1950s, the pianist hired Muslim jazz musicians such as Abdul-Malik, Art Blakey, Idrees Sulieman, and Jamil Nasser to play with him on many of his own albums.[272]

Randy Weston's father, a Jamaican Garveyite who was born in Panama, raised his son with Pan-African values that shaped his music, masculinity, and spirituality. Eventually, Weston embraced a transnational communal masculinity and declared, "I was always in tune with Africa and I was always upset about the separation of our people . . . who are . . . part of the African diaspora from the Motherland itself. . . . My dad always said that black people would never be free as a people until Africa is free; that's the only time we will be collectively strong."[273] Transnational communal masculinity revolved around his faith in the freedom and unity of black people that led him to forge powerful links between Africa, the Third World, and jazz.

The above Pan-African and Islamic musical influences came together in his classic album, *Uhuru Afrika* (Roulette, 1961), including "Freedom Africa," a four-part suite (including "Uhuru Kwanza," "African Lady," "Bantu," and "Kucheza Blues") that celebrated the decolonization and independence of African nations, from Tunisia, Sudan, and Morocco in 1956 to the liberation of eighteen additional African countries a few years later.[274] The title of the album and the recitation of Langston Hughes's freedom poetry composed for the work were in Kiswahili, an African language that Weston chose to represent the self-determination of the continent after consulting with African ambassadors and petitioners in the United Nations.[275] The pianist said that *Uhuru Afrika*'s universal message is that "we have this commonality, spirituality and great contributions of African society within all of us."[276] He hired Muslim musicians (Yusef Lateef on tenor saxophone, oboe, and flute; Sahib Shihab on baritone and alto saxophones; and Max Roach on drums); Cuban congueros (Armando Peraza on bongos and Cándido Camero on congas); and African artists (including Babatunde Olatunji as percussionist and Tuntemeke Sanga as narrator) to bring together black Atlantic cool performances of the diverse sounds that represented the peoples of the Pan-African musical world. Although music critics and the general public were not yet ready to celebrate the proud African American identity that *Uhuru Afrika* exemplified in 1961, the personnel on this album shows us how Muslim artists played a key role in the jazz collaborations that connected the African diaspora to Africa.[277] Weston created several albums with African themes in the 1960s, performed State Department–sponsored concerts in African Muslim nations, and moved to Morocco in 1967 because Moroccan fans loved his music.[278]

Africa/Brass (Impulse!, 1961) was John's Coltrane's first album for Impulse! Records, and its goal was less ambitious than Weston's in *Uhuru Afrika*. According to trumpeter Freddie Hubbard, "he wanted the African sound."[279] Coltrane said, "I have an African record—they're singing these rhythms, some of the native rhythm, so I took part of it and gave it to the bass and Elvin [Jones]. . . . McCoy [Tyner] managed to find some kind of chords . . . I had to make the melody as I went along."[280] His personnel for the album included not only the musicians in his quartet—McCoy Tyner (piano), Elvin Jones (drums), and Reggie Workman (bass)—but also artists playing trumpet, alto and baritone saxophones, French horn, tuba, euphonium, and bass to achieve a powerful polyrhythmic sound. Finally, Trane pointed out, "I had a sound that I wanted to hear. . . . I wanted the band to have a drone. . . . It's the first time I've done any tune with that kind of rhythmic background. . . . On the whole, I'm quite pleased with Africa."[281] West African drummer Babatunde Olatunji supported and inspired the saxophonist's growing fascination with African rhythms and sounds, and his interest in African music lasted throughout his life and became an integral part of his journey to Islamic spirituality in jazz.

John Coltrane's great fame and success as a spiritually inspired jazz musician and his use of African, Indian, and Middle Eastern sounds and impressions in his records influenced the path of Duke Ellington's Third World journey in the 1960s, a journey that culminated in West Africa. The two collaborated on an album, *Duke Ellington & John Coltrane* (Impulse!, 1963), which included the pianist's compositions such as "In a Sentimental Mood" and "Take the Coltrane." Ellington played State Department concerts in the Muslim-majority countries Jordan, Syria, Indonesia, Afghanistan, Turkey, Pakistan, Ceylon, Lebanon, Iraq, and Iran, as well as India from September to November 1963, and later on in Senegal.[282] Although the State Department briefings on many of these nations demonstrate that its cultural programs aimed to use black jazz musicians to encourage "confidence in the United States as a champion of peace and freedom" and to support "anti-communist programming," photos of Duke Ellington show the pianist playing an Arabic string instrument with a street musician in Baghdad, listening to the music of a sitar player in India, and performing for a large audience in the Roman amphitheater in Aman, Jordan, where he marveled at the country's music, dance, and food traditions.[283] In Damascus, Syria, he acquired knowledge about fasting during Ramadan and the larger collective meal that is eaten to break the fast at night.[284] Beautiful photos and drawings of him were used in an Arabic-language program for one of his Middle East concerts in 1963.[285] The photographic evidence from his State Department tours shows Ellington expanding his musical horizons by interacting with Middle Eastern musicians and learning about their indigenous sounds and instruments.

When he and his orchestra received an invitation from President Leopold Senghor and performed for an African Muslim audience at the First World Festival of Negro Arts in Dakar, Senegal, in April 1966, the local newspaper *Dakar-Matin* published the following review of his concert: "All those for whom jazz is a friend, a confidant, a consoler, Duke Ellington brought each one what he was expecting. . . . He is able with easy gestures and unequaled sounds, to transform the gaiety of a crowd into delirium . . . at the Friendship Stadium where his success was enormous. . . . Thanks for coming."[286] For Ellington's part, the good feelings were mutual in Islamic Senegal. He commented, "Every night, on the balcony of the ninth floor of the Engar Hotel, I sit and listen to the sea singing her songs of the historic past on the island from which slaves were shipped. Farther in the distance, I can hear the tribes that have gathered on another island to rehearse for their show the next day. . . . After writing African music for thirty-five years, here I am at last in Africa!"[287]

"Afro Blue" and "Alabama," two tracks on *Coltrane Live at Birdland* (Impulse!, 1964), brought together Trane's global musical consciousness and his black liberation values during the civil rights and Black Power era. "Afro Blue" was his recreated rendition of the Afro-Cuban conga drummer Mongo Santamaria's Latin jazz song that was based on "blues forms" and African polyrhythms. Coltrane's arrangement maintained the musical roots of "Afro Blue" in African-Cuban rhythms but launched the song with the Indian/Middle Eastern sounds of his soprano saxophone, which were galvanized by hypnotic call-and-response piano improvisations, dramatic crashing cymbals, and the passionate drumming of the musicians in his quartet. Ultimately his new presentation of "Afro Blue" expanded "the form of the song, dilating its sense of time" and imbued it with a sense of religious ritual "infused with a militant spirituality" that paralleled and expressed the spirit of the soul-searching times, times that saw the emergence of many Muslim converts, resurgent black internationalism, Afros and dashikis, Vietnam War protest, inner-city blues, and picket signs and lines across the United States.[288]

"Alabama" was Coltrane's elegy to the four African American girls who were killed in Birmingham's 16th Street Baptist Church when Ku Klux Klan members bombed the building with dynamite on September 15, 1963. He recorded the track on November 18, 1963, and his mournful saxophone voice and introspective melody in "Alabama" were inspired by the words of Martin Luther King Jr.'s eulogy for the girls in a funeral several days after the bombing: "May the flight of angels take thee to thy eternal rest." "Alabama" was Trane's political message condemning anti-black hate crimes and systemic racism in the United States. He said, "It represents, musically, something that I saw down there translated into music from inside me."[289] Drummer Max Roach explained, "I heard many things in what Trane was doing. . . . I heard the cry and wail of the pain that this society imposes on people, and especially black folks."[290] Many complex emotions and "freedom sounds" motivated "Alabama," and they influenced Coltrane's political values, which intersected with his exploration of Islamic spirituality and other non-Western religious traditions.

Just as Trane's "interest in spiritual ideas from around the world was accompanied by listening to the music of India, the Middle East, and Africa," as Ingrid Monson has noted, his embrace of Islamic spirituality was influenced by listening to Malcolm X.[291] Coltrane met jazz pianist Alice McLeod in 1963 and they married and raised four children together in their Huntington, Long Island, home. Alice Coltrane remembered, "As for Malcolm, I know he would go downtown and attend some of the talks that were in [New York]. Once he came back and I asked him how was the lecture, and he said he thought it was superb."[292] In a 1966 interview in Japan, he was asked, "What do you think about Malcolm X?," and the saxophonist answered, "I admired him. I admired him."[293]

Why was John Coltrane impressed with Malcolm X in 1964? First, they were kindred spirits in terms of their conversion experiences, which turned them away from drug addiction in the jazz world and led them to embrace Islamic and Eastern spirituality on Coltrane's part and the Nation of Islam and then Sunni Islam on Malcolm's part. They were both jazz brothers in spirit who became known for their "openness to self-transformation" on an international level.[294] Malcolm X left the Nation of Islam in March 1964, made the hajj to Mecca in April 1964, and changed his name to El Hajj Malik El-Shabazz. "He went to Mecca as a black Muslim and there he became only a Muslim," adopting a universal understanding of his religion, which paralleled Coltrane's universal ideas about the power of non-Western religious and musical forms to uplift humanity.[295] Malcolm received certification as a Muslim missionary from Al-Azhar University and the Muslim World League after completing Islamic training in Egypt and Saudi Arabia in 1964.[296] His human rights group, the Organization of Afro-American Unity, which he established in June 1964, supported the Pan-African values that Coltrane exemplified in his later collaborations with Olatunji and Lateef: freedom, self-defense, black economic and political power, education in community-based alternative schools and cultural centers, the significance of Afro-American history, social uplift of youth, freedom from drug addiction and alcoholism, reconciliation with Martin Luther King Jr. and other civil rights leaders, connections with the United Nations and the Organization of African Unity to support black liberation in the United States, and "workshops in all the arts . . . [as] an indispensable weapon in the freedom struggle."[297] These forces culminated in the revolutionary politics of Malcolm X's transnational communal masculinity as he cultivated pan-Islamic, Pan-African allies like the Egyptian president Gamal Abdel Nasser to support his opposition to anti-black racism in the United States. On July 27, 1964, he spoke to Cairo's Young Men's Muslim Association and argued that the Egyptian leader's "concept of Islam forces him to fight for the liberation of all oppressed people, whether they are Muslim or otherwise, because Islam teaches us that all humanity comes from Allah, and . . . has the same God-given right to freedom, justice, equality—life, liberty, and the pursuit of happiness."[298] Malcolm's opposition to the Vietnam War and his trips to Africa and Europe to promote his new religious and human rights agenda were also of great interest to the saxophonist, who was headed on a similar international path to perform his music, which eventually was called "a revolution in sound . . . that would release the true universal God he sensed lurking beneath the layers of confusion and hangup that American society stuffs all black folk with."[299]

A Love Supreme (Impulse!, 1965) was recorded in 1964. John Coltrane's autobiographical conversion story, which he told in the liner notes, mirrored the austere themes of Malcolm's narrative of submission, deliverance, conversion, and pilgrimage to Islam that he narrated with Alex Haley in his autobiography. Coltrane wrote,

> Dear Listener:
> All Praise Be To God To Whom All Praise Is Due. Let us pursue Him
> in the righteous path. . . . During the year 1957, I experienced, by the
> grace of God, a spiritual awakening which was to lead me to a richer,
> fuller, more productive life. At that time, in gratitude, I humbly asked to
> be given the means and privilege to make others happy through music.
> I feel this has been granted through His grace. . . . As time and events
> moved on. . . . I entered into a phase which was contradictory to the
> pledge and away from the esteemed path; but thankfully . . . through
> the unerring and merciful hand of God, I do perceive and have been
> duly re-informed of His Omnipotence, and of our need for and depen-
> dence on Him. At this time I would like to tell you that NO MATTER
> WHAT . . . IT IS WITH GOD. HE IS GRACIOUS AND MERCIFUL.
> HIS WAY IS IN LOVE, THROUGH WHICH WE ALL ARE. IT IS
> TRULY—A LOVE SUPREME—.

The jazz man's articulation of the "righteous path" in the above conversion narrative is noteworthy for its intersection with Islamic spirituality. When Muslims offer prayers to God they ask to be guided on a righteous path, and this request is expressed in the Qur'an: "Guide us to the straight path—the path of those upon whom You have favor, not those who have evoked anger or those who are astray" (Al-Fatiha: 6–7).

The album's building "drama of spiritual perfection" unfolds in a suite divided into four parts: "Acknowledgement," "Resolution," "Pursuance," and "Psalm."[300] Throughout most of the first part, Coltrane played a strong, lyrical, and surging tenor saxophone melody supported by the steady and vigorous background music of McCoy Tyner (piano), Elvin Jones (drums), and Jimmy Garrison (bass). Toward the end of "Acknowledgement," he put his instrument down and repeatedly chanted the riff, "A Love Supreme" with his bandmates. Moustafa Bayoumi provides the following Islamic interpretation of Coltrane's performance in "Acknowledgement": "This piece is an attempt to unify and capture the rapture of the divine. Listen how . . . Coltrane meanders around the simple theme in every key, as if to suggest the manner in which God's greatness truly is found everywhere, and then the ways in which the band begins to sing the phrase 'A Love Supreme,' like a roving band of Sufi mendicants singing their dhikr."[301] He continues, "The words could change. As the love is extolled, the phrase begins to include the sounds of 'Allah Supreme.' . . . Coltrane makes the connection from 'A Love Supreme' to 'Allah Supreme' for his entire listening audience, forever delivering a sound of Islam to the world of American music."[302]

In "Resolution," Trane's surging and searching hard bop playing embellishes the Indian-flavored melody of the suite and intensifies the pulsing energy of the piano, bass, and drum improvisations of his bandmates. "Pursuance" begins with Elvin Jones's brief drum solo, which introduces Trane's dense and wailing tenor saxophone improvisation and McCoy Tyner's piano and Jimmy Garrison's bass solos.

According to Elvin Jones, the saxophonist bared "his soul on the back of *A Love Supreme*, in . . . that prayer. . . . It's the last part of the suite."[303] In "Psalm," John Coltrane played his poem, his prayer of self-purification and dedication to God through his saxophone. The final movement of his musical performance recreates the flow, speech patterns, and emotions of his poem, which appears in the album's liner notes, and dramatizes through rhythm and ritual the elegant power and peace of God. Some excerpts from the poem follow:

> I will do all I can to be worthy of Thee O Lord. . . . Peace.
> There is none other. . . .
>
> We know. God made us. . . .
>
> God is. He always was. He always will be. . . . The universe has many
> wonders.

God is all. . . . Thoughts-deeds-vibrations, etc.
They all go back to God and he cleanses all.
He is gracious and merciful. . . .

God will wash away all our tears. . . . Let us sing all songs to God
To whom all praise is due. . . .

No road is an easy one, but they all go back to God. . . .
Obey the Lord. . . . Blessed be His Name. . . .
God breathes through us so completely . . . so gently we hardly feel
    it . . . yet,
it is our everything. . . .

ELATION-ELEGANCE-EXALTATION-

All from God.

Thank you God. Amen.

A continuously rolling drum and piano, a gentle throbbing bass, tympani, and crescendos of crashing cymbals in the background created the tension around Coltrane's lyrical and urgent saxophone voice, which sounds like a muezzin's call to prayer during the dramatic conclusion of "Psalm."

Yusef Lateef described how he heard "semantically the songs of Islam" in Coltrane's poem and prayers for *A Love Supreme*:

When John would say in this poem—I'm paraphrasing—"God is the greatest, no matter what" . . . and this keeps repeating. It reminds me of the second sentence of the Holy Qur'an which says, "All praises to God, the Lord of all the worlds." And so it seems as though he was imbued with this love of God in this poem. Islam teaches that he who is grateful to God is grateful to mankind. And in this poem, he thanked all those people who recorded and played with him. . . . He picked them out one by one and said how gracious he was. And this is an Islamic attitude. . . . Spiritual experiences . . . are between the individual and the Creator. . . . Another thing that the Holy Qur'an teaches is that God creates things in pairs . . . for example, when a man hears . . . a beautiful sound, in being drawn towards it, it's not the person who the sound is coming to. It's the Creator who has invested, impregnated this sound with this particular quality that only he can give. And I think that's what John was talking about when he spoke about spirituality. It is the spirit of God, which can be seen in the universe. . . . You see one cannot induce spirituality. . . . It has to be the will of Providence that one becomes anointed with that. That's what I think John was striving for, and one could feel certain moments of this Providential experience in listening to some of his music.[304]

The final section of this chapter considers how *A Love Supreme* shaped discussions about the interplay between African American Islamic identities and Coltrane's jazz among his fans and musical colleagues during the 1960s and beyond. Sold in American stores for the first time in February 1965, the album quickly became a hit among jazz fans and musicians. Malcolm X was assassinated on February 21, 1965, in the Audubon Ballroom in Harlem, and *The Autobiography of Malcolm X* was published that year. Malcolm's hajj to Mecca, conversion to Sunni Islam, Black Power speeches, travel to Africa, and provocative representations of black manhood made him the most famous Muslim in the United States and the world. Because of the tenor of the times in which the golden age of jazz and the golden age of African American Islam collided in a burst of creativity, thousands of black Americans critically considered Islam and converted to the religion, and among black youth in Philadelphia and other American cities, "there was a spiritual response" to the album, "a response to *A Love Supreme* like you would have to Malcolm . . . like you have with the emergence of black consciousness," according to a jazz radio deejay in Philadelphia.[305]

Amiri Baraka, the black poet, playwright, music critic, and author of *Blues People: Negro Music in White America*, sensed similar themes of black consciousness, Islamic spirituality, and Third World creativity in Malcolm X's and Coltrane's work and explained that "so much is made of Trane's link with Malcolm in the sixties, because those periods are when art of that kind does emerge. You have social upsurges, and for every social upsurge, there's an artistic upsurge that corresponds with that."[306] The day after Malcolm's death, Baraka publicized his plans for the establishment of the Harlem-based Black Arts Repertory Theater/

School (BARTS), which used black art forms and artists to promote a racially and culturally affirming African American identity through workshops, performances, and cultural center activities focusing on music, drama, history, and visual art.[307] To generate money for BARTS, he put together a March 28 fundraising concert at the Village Gate in Manhattan that included performances by his jazz musician friends such as John Coltrane, Archie Shepp, Sun Ra, Albert Ayler, Marion Brown, and Sonny Murray.[308] The concert was recorded and became an album, *The New Wave in Jazz* (Impulse!, 1965), with a photo of Trane on the cover. This important East Coast wing of the Black Arts movement was inspired by Malcolm X's political ideas, which we discussed earlier, and was committed to exploring free jazz, a style in which saxophonist Ornette Coleman led the way with his album *This Is Our Music* (Atlantic, 1960), and the Third World roots of jazz, of which John Coltrane became the driving force.

African American jazz musicians were emphasized in BARTS and other Black Arts collectives like Chicago's Association for the Advancement of Creative Musicians and Los Angeles's Union of God's Musicians and Artists Ascension as key activists and heroes in reconstructing the spiritual and historical consciousness of their people in the evolving Black Power era.[309] Iain Anderson writes that "Black Arts theorists insisted on the revolutionary implications of the musicians' intent . . . and emphasized the role of ritual in conveying messages of black solidarity and communal uplift" to advance the ultimate goals of freedom, unity, and self-determination.[310] Islamic artists and musicians who experimented with new forms of expression based on African sources were important figures in this new black aesthetic. A free jazz saxophonist like Coltrane became an attractive icon for this new movement not only because of his link to Malcolm, but also because "free improvisation's stylistic traits, especially collective creation, Afro-Asian inferences, and vocalized instrumental lines, appeared to embody a black aesthetic."[311]

In the context of the Black Arts movement, which reshaped blackness through political activism, poetry, style, community festivals, and "music as serious as your life,"[312] Trane's jazz and religious journey from 1965 to 1967 "played a critical role in redefining concepts of spirituality and black masculinity in the search for an elevated consciousness" that included Islam, African rhythms, and impressions from Asian re-ligions.[313] His Muslim pianist McCoy Tyner contributed to the Islamic significations of Coltrane's African American religious internationalism when he said, "Individuals like John and Bird seem to have been like very strong freers of the music method. John and Bird were really like messengers, but I'm pretty sure there will be other messengers. In other words, God still speaks to man."[314] Tenor saxophonist Archie Shepp, who played on a recorded track of *A Love Supreme* that was not released on the original album, also pointed out his jazz mentor's ability to give clear expression to the frustration of those who felt shut out in 1960s America but who found a new community in Islam: "Some of his solos have exactly the rage that was being expressed in the streets, by the Mus-lims and the Panthers."[315]

Black Arts critic and jazz scholar A. B. Spellman commented that "most of Trane's records since . . . *A Love Supreme*, which could well have been called *Allah Supreme*, attempt to create a religious experience."[316] Spellman went on to discuss the saxophonist's searching experiments with larger ensembles and the dissonant sounds, screams, honks, intense percussion, and unpredictable improvisation of free jazz, experiments in which Trane added spiritual expressions from Hinduism to his final albums:

> Coltrane and others looked for their mystic articulations where they could find it . . . [such] as Om, the all pervasive spirit of the Hindu religion, after which Coltrane named one of his last recordings. And he deepened his meditation with *Expressions* and *Cosmic Music*. This last record Coltrane produced himself and it was first issued on the Coltrane Records label with a simply designed cover which beautifully conveyed John's spirituality. One photograph in particular, showed the man with his head bowed and his palms upraised in the peace-ful posture of Islamic prayer. Here was John in his total commitment: making a spiritual-political statement in the band dedicated to Martin Luther King, Jr. and a further spiritual statement in the band called Manifestation.[317]

Transition, which was recorded in June 1965, was Coltrane's last album with his classic quartet. Turned off musically by Trane's free jazz explorations and the inclusion of new musicians in the band, McCoy Tyner left in 1965, and Elvin Jones and Jimmy Garrison quit in 1966. They were replaced by Rashied Ali, the Muslim drummer from Philadelphia, pianist Alice Coltrane, saxophonist Pharoah Sanders, and guest musicians (Garrison came back to record with the band in 1967). Tyner said, "At times I couldn't hear what anybody was doing! All I could hear was a lot of noise."[318] During this period, John was listening to music from Africa, Japan, Brazil, and even Buddhist temple music for free jazz inspiration. In 1966 his quintet played concerts in Japan. He visited the American atomic bombing site in Nagasaki to pray, to understand the bombing sounds and the suffering of the Japanese victims, and to make an anti-war and world peace statement with his music.[319] Although Ravi Shankar invited him to travel to India to study with him, the sitarist did not understand his music, as he admits in his reaction to a set performed by Coltrane's band at the Village Gate in New York City in November 1965: "The music was fantastic. . . . Here was a creative person who had become a vegetarian, who was studying yoga, and reading the *Bhagavad-Gita*, yet in whose music I heard much turmoil. I could not understand it."[320]

Yet many Black Arts activists, Afro- and dashiki-styled blacks, and African American Muslims, who "dug themselves as a new kind of man [and woman] with a self-defined dignity," spiritually identified with the countercultural sensibilities and the deep spaces in the soul of black America that motivated Trane's later musical forms.[321] Playing a harsher tone and freeing his group from chord, pitch, and intonation restrictions allowed his horn to imitate the passion, anger, cries, screams, and hollers of the human voice that defined the sounds of the urban uprisings and mass demonstrations, and echoing Malcolm's speeches about black liberation, Africa, and the Afro-American revolution in the 1960s. "Makes you want to holler the way they do your life" was the black mantra of the times in which he lived. A. B. Spellman wrote that "a man like Coltrane was playing about something consciously black, no matter how abstract his formulation may be."[322] His music, Spellman explained, created a "revolution in sound . . . that can feed organically into black people's lives."[323]

As for his Islamic and African connections, John Coltrane was headed back in that direction during the last year of his life. He had formed a musical group with Babatunde Olatunji and Yusef Lateef and had planned to travel to Africa with the Nigerian drummer. Lateef played at one of Coltrane's last "Roots of Africa" concerts at Olatunji's Center of African Culture on 125th Street in Harlem in spring 1967. Lateef recalled their plans together:

> We did one concert, but we planned another at Lincoln Center. In fact, we got the hall, and . . . it was going to be an anthology of our music, starting in Africa, the Americas, its development. . . . At that time John wanted to buy a location in New York . . . without alcohol—sandwiches and teas so children could come and hear the music. And he asked to see my realtor. . . . So he came to my house that day—this is about two weeks before he passed—and he went out and found a place that he liked.[324]

Trane, a spiritual and musical leader in the golden age of African American Islam and jazz, died from cancer on July 17, 1967. He was forty years old. His funeral was at St. Peter's Lutheran Church in Manhattan on July 21. The Albert Ayler Quartet began the service, which was called "A Love Supreme," by performing "Truth Is Marching." Twice during the performance, Ayler stopped playing and screamed two times. The Reverend John Garcia Gensel, minister to the jazz community, closed the service with the following excerpts from Coltrane's poetry: "May we never forget that in the sunshine of our lives, through the storm and after the rain—it is all with God in all ways and forever. All praise to God. With love to all, I thank you." The Ornette Coleman Quartet played "Holiday for a Graveyard" as the mourners left the church.

In the late 1950s and 1960s, black jazz musicians traveled to the Muslim world, converted to Islam, and infused hard bop and free jazz with Islamic sounds and sensibilities. Their musical and religious identities were intertwined with the global consciousness of the civil rights and Black Power movements and the anticolonial politics of Third World nations in Africa, Asia, and the Middle East. Numerous jazz artists and their urban fans were attracted to Islam as America's most anti-racist religion, with an ethos supporting dignity and social justice for people of African descent. Muslim jazz men and women exemplified a matrix of coolness, communal masculinity and femininity, and purification of the black body that offered a new Islamic frame for religious life. Their music and spirituality contributed to the ascendancy of the Nation of

Islam, the Ahmadiyya Muslim Community, and Sunni Islam during the golden age of jazz.

The conclusion will complete our exploration of African American Islam and jazz by analyzing the black Atlantic visions of Islamic jazz artists and their musical and religious legacies among jazz and hip hop musicians in the post-Coltrane era.

Conclusion

Last Days and Times: Islam and Jazz in the Post-Coltrane Era

The main goal of this book has been to examine the historical interplay between jazz, African American Islam, and black internationalism during what I have termed "the golden age of African American Islam and jazz" from the 1940s to the 1970s. Drawing on the musical and political creativity of black musicians and their fans in swing, bebop, hard bop, and free jazz, we have traced their Islamic spirituality, alternative masculinities and femininities, anti-racist consciousness, and black Atlantic cool expressiveness in cities including Boston, Philadelphia, and New York. The overarching argument has been that African American Islam and jazz shared intersecting goals and values of black affirmation, liberation, and self-determination and that the conversion of jazz musicians to Islam was central to the ascendancy of the religion from World War II to the beginning of the Black Power movement. Black Muslims and jazz musicians expressed these social justice values by developing a sense of African American religious internationalism—envisioning themselves in the context of a global black religious consciousness as part of the worldwide freedom struggles of blacks in the African diaspora and Africa, and sometimes in solidarity with the anticolonial struggles and spirituality of people of color who were not black.

Unlike many other studies, this book has not focused solely on the Nation of Islam; the incorporation of the interactions of other strands of Islam with jazz and politics during this time period is significant. This book has made the case that the involvement of jazz men and women with the Muslim religion contributed to the success of the Nation of Islam, the Ahmadiyya Muslim Community, and the African American Sunni communities. These artists composed and played some of the greatest music in the twentieth century, music that was influenced by their religious experience and interactions in a variety of American Islamic communities.

As we saw at the outset, this book has been motivated by several research questions. What is the historical relationship of jazz to Islam and African American religious internationalism in the lives of black jazz musicians? How does the identification of important jazz figures with African American religious internationalism and black masculinities in Boston, New York, and Philadelphia help us to document the golden age of African American Islam and jazz? How are their performances of music and religion connected to resistance in the internationalist black Christian and black Islamic communities and to intercultural perspectives about Africa, the African diaspora, and African American freedom? What musical, religious, and political factors influenced the diasporic constructions of blackness and the transformations of racial identity representations in the golden age of African American Islam and jazz? What are the identity claims surrounding Islamic jazz musicians' black Atlantic legacies in the late 1960s and early 1970s?

Given the history we have just traced, we can address these questions with the following answers. Many of the artists in this book found Islam useful in reconstructing gender relations with new forms of black masculinities and femininities that brought dignity and creativity to their musical and religious lives. We have seen how the relationship of swing, bebop, hard bop, and free jazz to Islam and African American religious internationalism shaped the spirituality, black Atlantic cool, and political ideas of famous black jazz musicians and their fans in the northeastern cities during the post–World War II period and beyond. Moreover, the jazz artists who performed in the Muslim world and enriched their international perspectives by participating in the US State Department's jazz tours during the Cold War and continuing to the civil rights and Black Power movements brought their intercultural perspectives about Africa, the African diaspora, and African American freedom to musicians and jazz fans in the Third World. A myriad of black jazz musicians who became Muslim went on to play new Middle Eastern and African sounds and instruments and also embraced Black Power identities that influenced the diasporic constructions of blackness and the transformation of racial identity representations in the golden age of African American Islam and jazz. Many of the identity claims and controversies surrounding Islam, jazz, and black Atlantic religious and musical legacies in the late 1960s and 1970s are related to John Coltrane's spirituality and creativity in particular.

The saxophonist John Coltrane led the way for those African American musicians who infused hard bop and free jazz with Islamic sensibilities and musical and religious forms from Asia and Africa in the 1960s. His sacred music and Islamic poetry in *A Love Supreme* spoke to listeners' souls. Coltrane created a revolution in spirituality and sound that resonated with the Third World aesthetic of the Black Arts movement and the freedom quests of African American Muslims and Christians. Although he did not convert to Islam, the religion's influence on him was nonetheless clear in his exploration of Indian, African, and Sufi musical themes, his marriage to a Muslim woman, his Philadelphia spiritual awakening that led him to kick drug addiction, his numerous collaborations with Muslim musicians, and his political attraction to Malcolm X's ideas. *A Love Supreme* and *The Autobiography of Malcolm X* appeared during the same period, helping to showcase the links between jazz and Islam.

The golden age of African American Islam and jazz culminated in the 1970s, during the aftermath of Coltrane's and Malcolm X's deaths. Coltrane's tragic demise in 1967 meant that the golden age of jazz had lost its major innovator who was on a free jazz "path toward deeper spiritual truth, universality, and internationalism."[1] Even *Muhammad Speaks* acknowledged the climax of an important musical period when he passed: "The 'Trane' that died was to the Black and the Wise World a greater treasure than all . . . the H-Bombs and Polaris Missiles so treasured by the white world. . . . 'Trane' moved more souls than their Beethovens or Bachs or Wagners. . . . His phenomenal performances opened special spheres for untold millions in this world and in the world to come."[2]

Although new African American Sunni Muslim communities including Darul Islam, Mosque of Islamic Brotherhood, Islamic Party of North America, and Imam Warith Deen Mohammed's World Community of Al-Islam in the West were established after Malcolm X's assassination, the 1965 Immigration and Naturalization Act brought more than a million Muslim immigrants to the United States in the 1970s, and these new "foreign-born Muslims" began to change the racial, ethnic, and leadership dynamics of American Islam.[3] Eventually, "there would be over a thousand Muslim American mosques and hundreds of Islamic parochial schools," yet many of these religious institutions were established outside African American communities.[4] Religious studies scholar Edward E. Curtis IV sums up the impact of these changes on jazz: "Malcolm X's radical vision of global black liberation," which had inspired the musical and spiritual creativity of Coltrane and other hard bop and free jazz musicians, "was not adopted by the [new] Muslim American majority."[5]

During the post-Coltrane era, the links between Islam and jazz were explored in a number of albums, including by Alice Coltrane and Pharoah Sanders. In the liner notes of *A Monastic Trio* (Impulse!, 1968), which was pianist and harpist Alice Coltrane's first album after her husband's death, she explained, "I hope to use some of the work thought of by John, with recordings, concerts, and whatever community work, but there is a higher culminating idea in the mind of John, which I hope will become a reality during my lifetime."[6] Musicians from Trane's last quintet, like tenor saxophonist Pharoah Sanders, bassist Jimmy Garrison, and drummer Rashied Ali, played on the LP. Alice also paid tribute to John's musical and spiritual legacy in *Cosmic Music* (Coltrane Records, 1968, and Impulse!, 1969) and *Universal Consciousness* (Impulse!, 1971). Although she exemplified a "feminist politics of interdependence," by acknowledging the positive impact of her family and her husband on her spirituality and music, she also went on to follow a new religious path in Hinduism with Swami Satchidananda, which involved traveling to India in 1970, establishing Vedantic centers in California in the 1970s, becoming a Hindu swami, and working as spiritual director for her own Sai Anantam Ashram in Agoura Hills, California, from the 1980s to 2007.[7] Although Alice Coltrane's music during this period of her life reflected her devotion to Hindu spirituality, her later album *Translinear Light* (Verve Music, 2004) featured her son, Ravi Coltrane, playing the tenor saxophone on "Crescent," one of his father's compositions with an Islamic theme.

Saxophonist Pharoah Sanders led the way in spiritual jazz in the 1970s with a number of albums on the Impulse! label: *Karma* (1969), *Jewels of Thought* (1969), *Summun Bukmun Umyun* (1970), *Thembi* (1971), *Black Unity* (1971), *Live at the East* (1972), *Village of the Pharoahs* (1973), and *Elevation* (1974). He explored Sufism and recorded *The Trance of Seven Colors* (Island Records, 1994) with Maleem Mahmoud Ghania, a Gnawa musician in Morocco. According to the album's liner notes,

> The Gnawa are the descendants of the black African Fulani, Peul and Bambara of Southern Mali and Guinee who originally came to Morocco as slaves beginning in the 16th century. . . . The central ritual of the Gnawa is the trance

music ceremony—with the purpose of healing or purification of the partic-ipants—an amalgam that incorporates both the Muslim panoply of saints and the original spirit system of their West African ancestors. The language used in the Moroccan ceremonies alternates between Arabic and Bambara.[8]

This volume has demonstrated that Islam played a more significant role in the lives of urban black people than was previously known, and that many black musicians converted to Islam or were influenced by the religion after World War II. The Muslim religion shaped the spiritual-ity, creativity, political values, social identities, and black masculinities and femininities embraced by jazz musicians in Boston, New York, and Philadelphia, and this book has offered a rich social history of black life in those cities from the 1940s to the 1960s. We have seen how southern migrants and Caribbean immigrants strategically positioned themselves in the northeastern cities and influenced resistance struggles, style, black Atlantic cool, and the emergence of bebop music in the jazz world. This book has demonstrated the dynamic role played by internationalism among the mid-twentieth-century jazz musicians who critiqued white supremacy in the United States and created the political synergy be-tween African American liberation movements, anticolonialism in the Third World, and the Cold War, a synergy that contributed to Islam's influence, visibility, and tone in black America.

By the late 1970s, a new generation of black fans celebrated the music of many of the artists discussed in this book. They attended jazz concerts in clubs, lofts, and college and university campuses in American cities; C. O. Simpkins published the first biography of John Coltrane in 1975. However, the market as well as "the audience for jazz . . . shrunk in the United States" during the post-Coltrane era, and hip hop, a new postindustrial musical form that emerged among black youth in New York City, began to fill the void with its own new sounds of rap, social protest, and Islamic messages.[9] Across black America, people acknowledged that the rap music of many of the early Islamic hip hop artists such as Poor Righteous Teachers, Mos Def, A Tribe Called Quest, Ice Cube, and Lupe Fiasco influenced the involve-ment of black youth with the Muslim religion in the twenty-first century.

Black youth in hip hop established countercultural crews including MCs (rappers), DJs (disc jockeys), graffiti artists, and break dancers whose artistic creativity, poetry, call-and-response forms, improvisation, dress, and style challenged and documented racial profiling, police brutality, drug addiction, gender relations, and the destruction of support systems, jobs, and affordable housing in African American urban communities during the Reagan-Bush era.[10] The rise of this powerful new black musical tradition and its global impact on popular culture intersected with the establishment of an American prison-industrial complex that went on to incarcerate almost one-third of young black men in the late twentieth century.[11] In this context, "rap music became the primary medium for . . . protesting the hardness of life for black youth in the hood."[12]

At the same time, Islam became more popular among African Americans, especially young black men, who were noteworthy for their conversion to the religion in prison, on college and university campuses, and in the hip hop community in the 1990s. *The Source: The Magazine of Hip-Hop Music, Culture & Politics* even predicted that if the trend continued "particularly in urban settings, the majority of young African American males will be Muslim" sometime during the first fifty years of the twenty-first century.[13] The conversion experiences of hip hop men and women to Islam had a lot to do with the rise of the Nation of Islam under Louis Farrakhan's leadership, the Million Man March in 1995, and the revival of Malcolm X's image in African American popular culture after Denzel Washington's Academy Award-nominated portrayal of the Muslim minister in Spike Lee's 1992 film *Malcolm X*.

The reworking of Malcolm's image took several forms in hip hop. Some black youth were attracted to his zoot suit and Nation of Islam identities and wore the hats and t-shirts that commodified his X and visual form. However, many MCs including Mos Def (Yasiin Bey) were inspired by Malcolm X's hajj and converted to Sunni Islam. Mos Def also made the pilgrimage to Mecca and dedicated his CD *Black on Both Sides* to the Black Panther Party leader Fred Hampton Jr.[14] He has led the way among the hip hop artists who have constructed religious, political, and musical identities that share connections between African American Islam, black radicalism, and the Third World.[15]

Finally, like many of the jazz artists in this book, Islam among hip hop musicians draws on the legacy of Malcolm X and the Black Power movement and serves as the basis for constructing new masculinities and femininities that speak profoundly to the themes of spirituality, cool dignity, and internationalism in the black struggles for social justice.

ACKNOWLEDGMENTS

It was a pleasure to work with my New York University Press editor Jennifer Hammer and editorial assistant Veronica Knutson on this book. Thank you to my colleagues Deborah Whaley, Zain Abdullah, and Edward E. Curtis IV for their support. Thanks as well to my cousin Hansen Foreman and Lindsey Reed for encouraging me during the research and writing for *Soundtrack to a Movement*. I am grateful for financial support from the American Council of Learned Societies and the University of Iowa's Arts and Humanities Initiative grants. Loving appreciation goes to my mother and father, Mavis and James Turner, for playing Duke Ellington's music in our Boston home.

NOTES

INTRODUCTION

1 Archie Shepp, *Fire Music* (Impulse!, 1965).

2 Quoted in Norman (Otis) Richmond, "Malcolm X and the Music," *San Francisco Bay View*, May 19, 2011, www.sfbayview.com.

3 Miles Davis with Quincy Troop, *Miles: The Autobiography* (New York: Simon and Schuster, 1989), 205–386.

4 Frank Kofsky, *John Coltrane and the Jazz Revolution of the 1960s* (New York: Pathfinder, 1998), 231.

5 Ashley Kahn, *The House That Trane Built: The Story of Impulse Records* (New York: Norton, 2006), 1.

6 Robert Farris Thompson, *Aesthetic of the Cool: Afro-Atlantic Art and Music* (Pittsburgh: Periscope, 2011), 16.

7 Robin D. G. Kelley, *Africa Speaks, America Answers: Modern Jazz in Revolutionary Times* (Cambridge: Harvard University Press, 2012), front flap.

8 Paul Gilroy, *The Black Atlantic: Modernity and Double Consciousness* (Cambridge: Harvard University Press, 1993), 74–75, 79.

9 Kelley, *Africa Speaks, America Answers*, 95–96.

10 Moustafa Bayoumi, "East of the Sun (West of the Moon): Islam, the Ahmadis, and African America," in *Black Routes to Islam*, ed. Manning Marable and Hishaam D. Aidi (New York: Palgrave Macmillan, 2009), 75.

11 Manning Marable, *Malcolm X: A Life of Reinvention* (New York: Viking, 2011), 303. Also see Manning Marable and Garret Felber, eds., *The Portable Malcolm X Reader* (New York: Penguin, 2013).

12 Etta James and David Ritz, *Rage to Survive: The Etta James Story* (New York: Villard, 1995), 112–13.

13 Yusef Lateef, *The Gentle Giant: The Autobiography of Yusef Lateef*, with Herb Boyd, (Irvington, NJ: Morton, 2006).

14 Diane M. Stewart and Tracey E. Hucks, "Africana Religious Studies: Toward a Transdisciplinary Agenda in an Emerging Field," *Journal of Africana Religions* 1, 1 (2013): 42.

15 Joseph Roach, *Cities of the Dead: Circum-Atlantic Performance* (New York: Columbia University Press, 1996); Mark Anthony Neal, *Looking for Leroy: Illegible Black Masculinities* (New York: New York University Press, 2013).

16 Gilroy, *The Black Atlantic. Soundtrack to a Movement* examines a shorter span of history and a richer variety of religious and musical forms than Gilroy. Also see

Allison Games, "Atlantic History: Definitions, Challenges, and Opportunities," *American Historical Review* 3, 3 (June 2006): 741–57; J. Lorand Matory, *Black Atlantic Religion: Tradition, Transnationalism, and Matriarchy in the Afro-Brazilian Candomblé* (Princeton: Princeton University Press, 2005); Kevin Yelvington, ed., *Afro-Atlantic Dialogues: Anthropology in the Diaspora* (Santa Fe: School of American Research Press, 2006); and Sohail Daulatzai, *Black Star, Crescent Moon: The Muslim International and Black Freedom beyond America* (Minneapolis: University of Minnesota Press, 2012).

17 Daulatzai, *Black Star, Crescent Moon*, back flap.

18 Kofsky, *John Coltrane and the Jazz Revolution of the 1960s*, 431.

CHAPTER 1. ISLAMIC AND CHRISTIAN INFLUENCES IN JAZZ

1 Stephan Thernstrom, *The Other Bostonians: Poverty and Progress in the American Metropolis, 1880–1970* (Cambridge: Harvard University Press, 1973), 179; Violet Showers Johnson, *The Other Black Bostonians: West Indians in Boston, 1900–1950* (Bloomington: Indiana University Press, 2006), 37; Mario Luis Small, *Villa Victoria: The Transformation of Social Capital in a Boston Barrio* (Chicago: University of Chicago Press, 2004), 27. Boston's population was 801,444 by 1950.

2 James F. Turner, interview by author, March 18, 2000, Boston; Nat Hentoff, *Boston Boy: Growing Up with Jazz and Other Rebellious Passions* (Philadelphia: Paul Dry Books, 2001), 5.

3 Johnson, *The Other Black Bostonians*, 1, 8, 26.

4 Mel King, *Chain of Change: Struggles for Black Community Development* (Boston: South End Press, 1981), 5.

5 Ibid.

6 Ibid., 60; Richard Brent Turner, *Islam in the African-American Experience*, 2nd ed. (Bloomington: Indiana University Press, 2003), 87; Colin Grant, *Negro with a Hat: The Rise and Fall of Marcus Garvey* (New York: Oxford University Press, 2008); Adam Ewing, *The Age of Garveyism: How a Jamaican Activist Created a Mass Movement and Changed Global Black Politics* (Princeton: Princeton University Press, 2014).

7 Johnson, *The Other Black Bostonians*, 88.

8 Ibid., 63.

9 Ibid., 62.

10 Ibid.

11 Ibid., 65.

12 Manuel Angelo, telephone interview by author, March 11, 2001, Washington, DC.

13 Johnson, *The Other Black Bostonians*, 127; US Census reports, 1910, 1920, 1930, in *Negroes in the United States, 1920–1932* (Washington, DC: US Government Printing Office, 1935), 74–75, 216–18; John Daniels, *In Freedom's Birthplace: A Study of Boston Negroes* (Boston: Houghton Mifflin, 1914).

14 Isabel Wilkerson, *The Warmth of Other Suns: The Epic Story of America's Great Migration* (New York: Vintage, 2010), 14; Stewart E. Tolnay, "The African American 'Great Migration' and Beyond," *Annual Review of Sociology* 29 (2003): 219.

15 Thernstrom, *The Other Bostonians*, 207.

16 Ibid., 201.

17 Johnson, *The Other Black Bostonians*, 35, 37.

18 Adelaide M. Cromwell, *The Other Brahmins: Boston's Black Upper Class, 1750–1950* (Fayetteville: University of Arkansas Press, 1994), 115–17; Manning Marable, *Malcolm X: A Life of Reinvention* (New York: Viking, 2011), 214.

19 Robert Farris Thompson, *Aesthetic of the Cool: Afro-Atlantic Art and Music* (Pittsburgh: Periscope, 2011), 16.

20 Robert C. Hayden, *Faith, Culture, and Leadership: A History of the Black Church in Boston* (Boston: Boston Branch of the NAACP, 1983), 3–11, 28–37; Lorraine Roses, "After Abolition: Church," BostonBlackHistory.org, www.wellesley.edu (accessed March 19, 2012).

21 Wallace D. Best, *Passionately Human, No Less Divine: Religion and Culture in Black Chicago, 1915–1952* (Princeton: Princeton University Press, 2005), 105–6.

22 Walter F. Pitts, *Old Ship of Zion: The Afro-Baptist Ritual in the African Diaspora* (New York: Oxford University Press, 1993), back flap; Sylviane A. Diouf, *Servants of Allah: African Muslims Enslaved in the Americas*, 15th anniversary ed. (New York: New York University Press, 2013), 274.

23 Hayden, *Faith, Culture, and Leadership*, 12–27; Roses, "After Abolition."

24 Johnson, *The Other Black Bostonians*, 56–57.

25 Karl Payne, telephone interview by author, March 2, 2001, Boston.

26 Johnson, *The Other Black Bostonians*, 56–57.

27 William C. Leonard, "A Parish for the Black Catholics of Boston," *Catholic Historical Review* 83, 1 (January 1997): 51.

28 George Lipsitz, *Time Passages: Collective Memory and American Popular Culture* (Minneapolis: University of Minnesota Press, 1990), 116–17; Hillel Levine and Lawrence Harmon, *The Death of an American Jewish Community: A Tragedy of Good Intentions* (New York: Free Press, 1992), 58.

29 Hentoff, *Boston Boy*, 6.

30 Thernstrom, *The Other Bostonians*, 197.

31 King, *Chain of Change*, 23.

32 Thomas J. Sugrue, *Sweet Land of Liberty: The Forgotten Struggle for Civil Rights in the North* (New York: Random House, 2008), back flap and xv.

33 Johnson, *The Other Black Bostonians*, 77; *Boston Chronicle*, July 21, 1934.

34 Johnson, *The Other Black Bostonians*, 78, 79; *Boston Chronicle*, August 27, 1935, May 4, 1935, April 26, 1947.

35 Johnson, *The Other Black Bostonians*, 77, 87, 89.

36 Ibid., 52.

37 Ingrid Monson, ed., *The African Diaspora: A Musical Perspective* (New York: Garland, 2000), 5.

38 Malcolm "Shorty" Jarvis, *The Other Malcolm—"Shorty" Jarvis: His Memoir*, with Paul D. Nichols (Jefferson, NC: McFarland, 1998), 25–26; Richard Vacca, *The*

Boston Jazz Chronicles: Faces, Places, and Nightlife, 1937–1962 (Belmont, MA: Troy Street, 2012), 137, 142, 143, 147.

39 Jarvis, *The Other Malcolm*, 30.

40 Kathy Peiss, *Zoot Suit: The Enigmatic Career of an Extreme Style* (Philadelphia: University of Pennsylvania Press, 2011), 27–28; *New York Times*, June 11, 1943; Luis Alvarez, *The Power of the Zoot: Youth Culture and Resistance during World War II* (Berkeley: University of California Press, 2008), 83–84.

41 Robin D. G. Kelley, *Race Rebels: Culture, Politics, and the Black Working Class* (New York: Free Press, 1996), 163.

42 Ibid., 165.

43 Travis A. Jackson, "Jazz Performance as Ritual: The Blues Aesthetic and the African Diaspora," in Monson, *The African Diaspora*, 25.

44 Quoted in Kelley, *Race Rebels*, 161; Ralph Ellison, "Editorial Comment," *Negro Quarterly*, Winter–Spring 1943, 301.

45 George Lipsitz, preface to Kelley, *Race Rebels*, xii.

46 Bruce Taylor, "Zoot Suit Culture and the Black Press," *Journal of American Culture* 17, 2 (June 1994): 27.

47 Ibid., 23.

48 Alvarez, *The Power of the Zoot*, 80.

49 Ibid., 155, 175–77. According to Catherine S. Ramirez, *The Woman in the Zoot: Gender, Nationalism, and the Cultural Politics of Memory* (Durham: Duke University Press, 2009), 1, the Zoot Suit Riots occurred from June 3 to 13, 1943.

50 Douglas Henry Daniels, "Los Angeles Zoot: Race, 'Riot,' the Pachuco, and Black Music Culture," *Journal of African American History* 87, 1 (Winter 2002): 202.

51 Alvarez, *The Power of the Zoot*, 195; "Mexicans and Negroes Victimized," *Amsterdam News*, June 19, 1943.

52 Peiss, *Zoot Suit*, 53, 107; Alvarez, *The Power of the Zoot*, 39.

53 Daniels, "Los Angeles Zoot," 202.

54 Peiss, *Zoot Suit*, 63; Manuel Delgado, Sleepy Defense Committee Records, Department of Special Records, Charles E. Young Research Library, UCLA; Alvarez, *The Power of the Zoot*, 45, 46; David J. Muhammad, "A Brief History of 'Latinos' in the Nation of Islam," *Final Call*, September 4, 2012.

55 Peiss, *Zoot Suit*, 94–95.

56 Kelley, *Race Rebels*, 180.

57 Dizzy Gillespie, *To Be, or Not . . . to Bop*, with Al Fraser (Minneapolis: University of Minnesota Press, 2009), 120.

58 Marable, *Malcolm X*, 44; Turner, *Islam in the African-American Experience*, 168.

59 Jacqui Malone, *Steppin' on the Blues: The Visible Rhythms of African American Dance* (Urbana: University of Illinois Press, 1996), 101.

60 Thompson, *Aesthetic of the Cool*, 29.

61 Alex Haley, *The Autobiography of Malcolm X* (New York: Ballantine, 1992), 77.

62 Kelley, *Race Rebels*, 169.

63 Guthrie P. Ramsey Jr., *Race Music: From Bebop to Hip-Hop* (Berkeley: University of California Press and Columbia College Chicago: Center for Black Music Research, 2003), front flap, 4.

64 Ibid., 27, 32, and front flap.

65 Katrina Hazzard-Donald, "Dancing under the Lash: Sociocultural Disruption, Continuity, and Synthesis," in *African Dance: An Artistic, Historical, and Philosophical Inquiry*, ed. Karaimu Welsh Asante (Trenton, NJ: Africa Third World Press, 1997), 107.

66 John Storm Roberts, *Black Music of Two Worlds: African, Caribbean, Latin, and African-American Traditions*, 2nd rev. ed. (New York: Schirmer, 1998), 228.

67 Jackson, "Jazz Performance as Ritual," 23.

68 Ibid., 66.

69 Roberts, *Black Music of Two Worlds*, 228; Jackson, "Jazz Performance as Ritual," 66.

70 Jackson, "Jazz Performance as Ritual," 66.

71 Ibid.

72 Ibid., 58–59.

73 Malone, *Steppin' on the Blues*, 29, 105.

74 Katrina Hazzard-Donald, "Dancing to Rebalance the Universe: African-American Secular Dance," *JOPERD*, February 1991, 36, 37.

75 Jackson, "Jazz Performance as Ritual," 69.

76 Karen Leonard, "Transnational and Cosmopolitan Forms of Islam in the West," *Harvard Middle Eastern and Islamic Review* 8 (2009): 177.

77 Graham Locke, *Blutopia: Visions of the Future and Revisions of the Past in the Work of Sun Ra, Duke Ellington, and Anthony Braxton* (Durham: Duke University Press, 1999), 83.

78 Harry G. Cohen, *Duke Ellington's America* (Chicago: University of Chicago Press, 2010), 56–57.

79 Locke, *Blutopia*, 78; Duke Ellington, "The Duke Steps Out," *Rhythm*, March 1931.

80 Duke Ellington, *Duke Ellington's Liberian Suite* (Columbia, 1948).

81 Duke Ellington, *The Far East Suite* (RCA Victor, 1967).

82 Duke Ellington, *Music Is My Mistress* (New York: Da Capo, 1973), 108.

83 Ibid., 108–9.

84 Christopher W. Chase, "Prophetics in the Key of Allah: Towards an Understanding of Islam in Jazz," *Jazz Perspectives* 4, 2 (August 2010): 158–59.

85 Ellington, *Music Is My Mistress*, 87.

86 Hisham Aidi, "Latino Muslims Are Part of US Religious Landscape," *Al Jazeera*, February 3, 2016, www.aljazeera.com.

87 Piri Thomas, *Down These Mean Streets* (New York: Knopf, 1967), 296, 297.

88 John Storm Roberts, *Latin Jazz: The First of the Fusions, 1880s to Today* (New York: Schirmer, 1999), 59.

89 Alvarez, *The Power of the Zoot*, 94, 149; Ramirez, *The Woman in the Zoot Suit*.

90 Kelley, *Race Rebels*, 166, 176.

91 Ibid., 175.

92 Ibid.

93 Nina G. Jablonski, *Living Color: The Biological and Social Meaning of Skin Color* (Berkeley: University of California Press, 2012), 172.

94 Ibid., 173–74.

95 Zain Abdullah, "Narrating Muslim Masculinities: The Fruit of Islam and the Quest for Black Redemption," *Spectrum* 1, 1 (Autumn 2012): 150.

96 Thelma Golden, ed., *Black Male: Representations of Masculinity in Contemporary American Art* (New York: Whitney Museum of American Art, 1994), 19.

97 Abdullah, "Narrating Muslim Masculinities," 153.

98 Charles Johnson, "A Phenomenology of the Black Body," in *Traps: African American Men on Gender and Sexuality*, ed. Rudolph P. Byrd and Beverly Guy-Sheftall (Bloomington: Indiana University Press, 2001), 234.

99 Paul Gilroy, *The Black Atlantic: Modernity and Double Consciousness* (Cambridge: Harvard University Press, 1993), 74–76.

100 Ramsey, *Race Music*, 98.

101 Gilroy, *The Black Atlantic*, 74–75.

102 Guthrie P. Ramsey Jr., *The Amazing Bud Powell: Black Genius, Jazz History, and the Challenge of Bebop* (Berkeley: University of California Press and Columbia College Chicago: Center for Black Music Research, 2013), 31.

103 Best, *Passionately Human, No Less Divine*, 104.

104 Vacca, *The Boston Jazz Chronicles*, 134, 136, 137.

105 A. H. Lawrence, *Duke Ellington and His World* (New York: Routledge, 2001), 301–2.

106 Ellington, *Music Is My Mistress*, 216.

107 Haley, *The Autobiography of Malcolm X*, 89.

108 Farah Jasmine Griffin, *Harlem Nocturne: Women Artists and Progressive Politics during World War II* (New York: Basic Civitas, 2013), ix, x.

109 Haley, *The Autobiography of Malcolm X*, chap. 5.

110 Amy Kate Bailey and Stewart Tolnay, *Lynched: The Victims of Southern Mob Violence* (Chapel Hill: University of North Carolina Press, 2015), 5; James Allen, ed., *Without Sanctuary: Lynching Photography in America* (San Francisco: Twin Palms, 2000), 13.

111 Carol Anderson, *Eyes Off the Prize: The United Nations and the African American Struggle for Human Rights, 1944–1955* (New York: Cambridge University Press, 2003), 13.

112 Abel Meeropol wrote "Strange Fruit" and Billie Holiday recorded the song in 1939. See David Margolick, *Strange Fruit: The Biography of a Song* (New York: Ecco, 2001), back flap; and John Szwed, *Billie Holiday: The Musician and the Myth* (New York: Penguin, 2016), 157.

113 Angela Y. Davis, *Blues Legacies and Black Feminism: Gertrude Ma Rainey, Bessie Smith, and Billie Holiday* (New York: Vintage, 1998), 186.

114 Ibid., 183, 184.

115 Ibid., 181.

116 Ibid., 184.

117 Ibid.

118 Ibid., xi, 184.

119 Patricia Hill Collins, *Black Sexual Politics: African Americans, Gender, and the New Racism* (New York: Routledge, 2004), 71, 72.

120 Davis, *Blues Legacies and Black Feminism*, 185–87.

121 Ibid., 187.

122 Collins, *Black Sexual Politics*, 69, 70.

123 Kendra Unruh, "From Kitchen Mechanics to 'Jubilant Spirits of Freedom': Black Working-Class Women Dancing the Lindy Hop," *Journal of Pan African Studies* 4, 6 (September 2011): 213, 215.

124 Johann Hari, "The Hunting of Billie Holiday: How Lady Day Found Herself in the Middle of the Federal Bureau of Narcotics' Early Fight for Survival," *Politico*, January 2015, www.politico.com; Hari, *Chasing the Scream: The First and Last Days of the War on Drugs* (New York: Bloomsbury, 2015). Farah Jasmine Griffin discusses Holiday's arrests in *If You Can't Be Free, Be a Mystery: In Search of Billie Holliday* (New York: Free Press, 2001), 37–45, 75–78.

125 Samuel A. Floyd Jr., *The Power of Black Music: Interpreting Its History from Africa to the United States* (New York: Oxford University Press, 1995), 138, 141; Ramsey, *The Amazing Bud Powell*.

126 Eric Porter, *What Is This Thing Called Jazz? African American Musicians as Artists, Critics, and Activists* (Berkeley: University of California Press, 2002), 59.

127 Ibid., 61.

128 Ibid., 57, 67, 68; Gary Giddins, *Celebrating Bird: The Triumph of Charlie Parker* (Minneapolis: University of Minnesota Press, 2013), 72; Griffin, *Harlem Nocturne*, 148.

129 Ramsey, *The Amazing Bud Powell*, 128.

130 Giddins, *Celebrating Bird*, 72.

131 Haley, *The Autobiography of Malcolm X*, 129.

132 Gillespie, *To Be, or Not . . . to Bop*, 48, 121, 122.

133 Sohail Daulatzai, *Black Star, Crescent Moon: The Muslim International and Black Freedom beyond America* (Minneapolis: University of Minnesota Press, 2012), back flap.

134 Guthrie, *Race Music*, 98.

135 Gillespie, *To Be, or Not . . . to Bop*, 291.

136 Ibid., 5, 92.

137 Charlie Parker and Dizzy Gillespie, *Diz 'n Bird at Carnegie Hall* (Roost, 1997).

138 Carl Woideck, *Charlie Parker: His Music and Life* (Ann Arbor: University of Michigan Press, 1998), 48.

139 Alvarez, *The Power of the Zoot*, 123.

140 Marable, *Malcolm X*, 57.

141 Eddie S. Meadows, *Bebop to Cool: Context, Ideology, and Musical Identity* (Westport, CT: Praeger, 2003), 5. There were also large black communities in Brooklyn, Bronx, and Queens in the 1940s.

142 Alvarez, *The Power of the Zoot*, 123.

143 Ibid., 123, 125; "Mixed Dancing Closed Savoy Ballroom," *Amsterdam News*, May 1, 1943.

144 Marable, *Malcolm X*, 52.

145 Erik S. McDuffie and Komozi Woodard, "'If You're in a Country That's Progressive, the Woman Is Progressive': Black Women Radicals and the Making of the Politics and Legacy of Malcolm X," *Biography* 36, 3 (Summer 2013): 507.

146 Ted Gioia, *The History of Jazz*, 2nd ed. (New York: Oxford University Press, 2011), 190.

147 Griffin, *Harlem Nocturne*, 5, 6.

148 Ibid., 6, 7.

149 Haley, *The Autobiography of Malcolm X*, 121.

150 Gerald Horne, *Facing the Rising Sun: African Americans, Japan, and the Rise of Afro-Asian Solidarity* (New York: New York University Press, 2018), 95–97.

151 Ibid., 97.

152 Turner, *Islam in the African-American Experience*, 101, 103.

153 Meadows, *Bebop to Cool*, 37.

154 Haley, *The Autobiography of Malcolm X*, 131.

155 Alvarez, *The Power of the Zoot*, 220, 221; "Harlem Riot Damages Hit $5,000,000 Mark," *Amsterdam News*, August 7, 1943; "Rumors of Soldier's Killing Caused Frenzied Mob to Riot," *Amsterdam News*, August 7, 1943; "Nothing Solved but Much Needed (An Editorial)," *Amsterdam News*, August 7, 1943.

156 Alvarez, *The Power of the Zoot*, 220, 221.

157 Ibid., 205; George Lipsitz, *Rainbow at Midnight: Labor Culture in the 1940s* (Urbana: University of Illinois Press, 1994), 82.

158 Kenneth B. Clarke and James Baker, "The Zoot Effect in Personality: A Race Riot Participant," *Journal of Abnormal and Social Psychology* 40, 1 (January 1945): 143.

159 Ibid., 148.

160 Turner, *Islam in the African-American Experience*, 110–13; Yohanan Friedmann, *Prophecy Continuous: Aspects of Ahmadi Religious Thought and Its Medieval Background* (Berkeley: University of California Press, 1989), 2–10.

161 Turner, *Islam in the African-American Experience*, 112; Friedmann, *Prophecy Continuous*, 49–82.

162 Caesar F. Farah, *Islam* (New York: Barrons, 1987), 104–50.

163 Turner, *Islam in the African-American Experience*, 114; Spencer Lavan, *The Ahmadiyya Movement: A History and Perspective* (Delhi: Monohar Book Service, 1974), 93, 95, 110–14.

164 Haley, *The Autobiography of Malcolm X*, 45–46.

165 Rodnell P. Collins, *Seventh Child: A Family Memoir of Malcolm X*, with Peter Bailey (Secaucus, NJ: Birch Lane, 1998), 39.

166 Marable, *Malcolm X*, 95; Hayden, *Faith, Culture, and Leadership*, 40.

167 Haley, *The Autobiography of Malcolm X*, 46.

168 Ibid., 9; Louis A. DeCaro Jr., *On the Side of My People: A Religious Life of Malcolm X* (New York: New York University Press, 1996), 40.

169 Jan Carew, *Ghost in Our Blood: With Malcolm X in Africa, England, and the Caribbean* (Chicago: Lawrence Hill, 1994), 117; Wilfred Little Shabazz, interview, August 15, 1992, quoted in DeCaro, *On the Side of My People*, 43.

170 Jarvis, *The Other Malcolm*, 31.

171 Ibid., 35, 36.

172 Marable, *Malcolm X*, 46.

173 Haley, *The Autobiography of Malcolm X*, 77–78.

174 Ibid., 59.

175 Ibid., 67.

176 Collins, *Seventh Child*, 38–39.

177 Ibid., 53.

178 Ibid., 61.

179 Ibid., 40; Marable, *Malcolm X*, 39.

180 Marable, *Malcolm X*, 46; Collins, *Seventh Child*, 40.

181 Haley, *The Autobiography of Malcolm X*, 122.

182 Thompson, *Aesthetic of the Cool*, 28.

183 Haley, *The Autobiography of Malcolm X*, 124.

184 Marable, *Malcolm X*, 48–51.

185 Haley, *The Autobiography of Malcolm X*, 119, 127.

186 Marable, *Malcolm X*, 63.

187 Haley, *The Autobiography of Malcolm X*, 154.

188 Ibid., 157.

189 Jarvis, *The Other Malcolm*, 55.

190 Ibid.

191 Ibid.

192 Ibid.

193 Ibid.

194 Ibid.

195 Ibid., 56, 57.

196 Ibid., 58.

197 Marable, *Malcolm X*, 67, 68; Massachusetts State Prison Commitment and Booking Data: Malcolm Little, 2-27-46, Massachusetts Department of Correction file of Malcolm Little, date of birth 5/19/1925, Commonwealth of Massachusetts Executive Office of Public Safety and Security Department of Correction MCI Concord, Central Records Unit.

198 Jarvis, *The Other Malcolm*, 128, 129.

CHAPTER 2. "TURN TO ALLAH, PRAY TO THE EAST"

1   Guthrie P. Ramsey Jr., *The Amazing Bud Powell: Black Genius, Jazz History, and the Challenge of Bebop* (Berkeley: University of California Press and Columbia College Chicago: Center for Black Music Research, 2013), 123.

2   Ibid., 138.

3   Ingrid Monson, *Freedom Sounds: Civil Rights Call Out to Jazz and Africa* (New York: Oxford University Press, 2007), 20.

4   Rashad Shabazz, "So High You Can't Get over It, So Low You Can't Get under It: Carceral Spatiality and Black Masculinities in the United States and South Africa," *Souls* 11, 3 (2009): 277.

5   Ibid., 276, 286.

6   Ibid., 289; Don Sabo, Terry A. Kupers, and Willie James London, eds., *Prison Masculinities* (Philadelphia: Temple University Press, 2001), 65.

7   Sabo, Kupers, and London, *Prison Masculinities*, 3; Sanyika Shakur, a.k.a. Monster Kody Scott, *Monster: The Story of an L.A. Gang Member* (New York: Grove, 1993); Piri Thomas, *Down These Mean Streets* (New York: Knopf, 1967).

8   Zain Abdullah, "Narrating Muslim Masculinities: The Fruit of Islam and the Quest for Black Redemption," *Spectrum* 1, 1 (Autumn 2012): 144, 145.

9   Ibid.; Edward E. Curtis IV, *Black Muslim Religion in the Nation of Islam, 1960–1975* (Chapel Hill: University of North Carolina Press, 2006), 9.

10   David Ake, *Jazz Cultures* (Berkeley: University of California Press, 2002), 67.

11   Ibid., 7.

12   Abdullah, "Narrating Muslim Masculinities," 150.

13   Ibid., 143.

14   Lillie A. Thomas-Burgess, "The Dynamics of Conversion from Christianity to Islam among Incarcerated African American Men," Ph.D. dissertation, Union Institute and University, 2010, 121.

15   Ibid., 122.

16   Robert Farris Thompson, *Aesthetic of the Cool: Afro-Atlantic Art and Music* (Pittsburgh: Periscope, 2011), 29.

17   Curtis, *Black Muslim Religion in the Nation of Islam*, 98.

18   Ibid., 7.

19   Eddie S. Meadows, *Bebop to Cool: Context, Ideology, and Musical Identity* (Westport, CT: Praeger, 2003), 37.

20   Ibid, 36.

21   Michael O. West and William G. Martin, "Contours of the Black International: From Toussaint to Tupac," in *From Toussaint to Tupac: The Black International since the Age of Revolution*, ed. Michael O. West and William G. Martin (Chapel Hill: University of North Carolina Press, 2009), 13.

22   Meadows, *Bebop to Cool*, 47.

23   Fatima Fanusie, "Fard Muhammad in Historical Context: An Islamic Thread in the American Religious and Cultural Quilt," Ph.D. dissertation, Howard Uni-

versity, 2008; Dawn-Marie Gibson and Jamillah Karim, *Women of the Nation: Between Black Protest and Sunni Islam* (New York: New York University Press, 2014), 3.

24 Z. I. Ansari, "Aspects of Black Muslim Theology," *Studia Islamica* 53 (1981); Ansari, "Religious Doctrines of the Black Muslims of America, 1930–1980," *Journal of Islamic Social Sciences* 9 (1987): 200; Muhammad Abdullah, interview by author, October 16, 1989, Hayward, CA; Richard Brent Turner, *Islam in the African-American Experience*, 2nd ed. (Bloomington: Indiana University Press, 2003), 165–66 for a summary of the FBI files on W. D. Fard.

25 Edward E. Curtis, "Islamism and Its African American Muslim Critics: Black Muslims in the Era of the Arab Cold War," *American Quarterly* 59, 3 (September 2007): 686.

26 Su'ad Abdul Khabeer, "Africa as Tradition in U.S. African American Muslim Identity," *Journal of Africana Religions* 5, 1 (2017): 30.

27 Keisha N. Blain, "'Confraternity among All Dark Races': Minnie Maud Lena Gordon and the Practice of Black (Inter)nationalism, 1932–1942," *Palimpsest: A Journal on Women, Gender, and the Black International* 5, 2 (2016): 152.

28 Erdmann D. Benyon, "The Voodoo Cult among Negro Migrants in Detroit," *American Journal of Sociology* 43 (July 1937–May 1938): 896; from an interview with Sister Carrie Mohammed.

29 "Nation of Islam Deserted," *African Mirror*, August–September 1979, 37.

30 Benyon, "The Voodoo Cult among Negro Migrants," 900–901.

31 Ibid., 901.

32 Gibson and Karim, *Women of the Nation*, 12; Elijah Muhammad, *Message to the Blackman in America* (Chicago: Muhammad Mosque of Islam, No. 2, 1965), 60. Fard taught the story of Yacub, the Nation of Islam mythology about "the origin of the races and the nature of black divinity and white wickedness and . . . the coming apocalyptic change that would reverse the status quo." See Zain Abdullah, "Malcolm X, Islam, and the Black Self," in *Malcolm X's Michigan Worldview: An Exemplar for Contemporary Black Studies*, ed. Rita Kiki and Curtis Stokes (East Lansing: Michigan State University Press, 2015), 207, 213.

33 Gibson and Karim, *Women of the Nation*, 6, 47.

34 Abdullah, "Narrating Muslim Masculinities," 146.

35 Claude Andrew Clegg III, "Rebuilding the Nation: The Life and Work of Elijah Muhammad, 1946–1954," *Black Scholar* 26, 3–4 (Fall 1996/Winter 1997): 49.

36 Benyon, "The Voodoo Cult among Negro Migrants," 907.

37 Ibid., 900; Herbert Berg, *Elijah Muhammad and Islam* (New York: New York University Press, 2009), 34.

38 Benyon, "The Voodoo Cult among Negro Migrants," 897.

39 Ibid., 896; Berg, *Elijah Muhammad and Islam*, 26, 27.

40 Berg, *Elijah Muhammad and Islam*, 36, 37.

41 Ibid., 38.

42 Turner, *Islam in the African-American Experience*, 168; Ernest Allen Jr., "When Japan Was Champion of the Darker Races: Satokata Takahashi and the Development of Our Own, 1933–1942," *Black Scholar* 24 (Winter 1994): 23–46.
43 Turner, *Islam in the African-American Experience*, 168.
44 Ibid., 168, 169.
45 Clegg, "Rebuilding the Nation," 49.
46 Meadows, *Bebop to Cool*, 45.
47 Ibid.
48 Ibid.; Clegg, "Rebuilding the Nation," 51.
49 Clegg, "Rebuilding the Nation," 50.
50 Meadows, *Bebop to Cool*, 45.
51 Clegg, "Rebuilding the Nation," 50.
52 Ibid.
53 Thomas-Burgess, "The Dynamics of Conversion," 4.
54 Ibid.
55 Ibid.
56 Manning Marable, *Malcolm X: A Life of Reinvention* (New York: Viking, 2011), 67.
57 Massachusetts Department of Correction file of Malcolm Little, Commonwealth of Massachusetts Executive Office of Public Safety and Security Department of Correction MCI Concord, Central Records Unit.
58 Ibid.
59 Ibid.
60 Alex Haley, *The Autobiography of Malcolm X* (New York: Ballantine, 1992), 177.
61 Peter Kihss, "Racist Falls under Harlem Fusillade: Malcolm X Is Slain, Police Arrest Negro Gunman," *Boston Herald*, February 22, 1965, 1.
62 Marable, *Malcolm X*, 73.
63 Haley, *The Autobiography of Malcolm X*, 178.
64 Ibid.
65 Marable, *Malcolm X*, 74,
66 Haley, *The Autobiography of Malcolm X*, 179; "Malcolm X Letter Discussing Boston's Jazz Scene Goes to Auction" (Letter by Malcolm X to a Nation of Islam member, March 9, 1950), *Fine Books and Collections*, January 14, 2015, www.finebooksmagazine.com.
67 Haley, *The Autobiography of Malcolm X*, 180.
68 Ibid., 181.
69 Malcolm "Shorty" Jarvis, *The Other Malcolm—"Shorty" Jarvis: His Memoir*, with Paul D. Nichols (Jefferson, NC: McFarland, 1998), 98.
70 Ibid.
71 Ibid., 70, 71.
72 Ibid., 84; Massachusetts Department of Correction file of Malcolm Little.
73 Jarvis, *The Other Malcolm*, 83. Malcolm pointed out that Shorty named one of his compositions "The Bastille Concerto." Haley, *The Autobiography of Malcolm X*, 220.

74 Jarvis, *The Other Malcolm*, 72.

75 Ibid., 108.

76 Ibid., 107.

77 Ibid.

78 Haley, *The Autobiography of Malcolm* X, 182.

79 Rodnell P. Collins, *Seventh Child: A Family Memoir of Malcolm X*, with Peter Bailey (Secaucus, NJ: Birch Lane, 1998), 77.

80 Ibid.

81 Ibid.

82 Ibid., 78, 79.

83 Haley, *The Autobiography of Malcolm X*, 186.

84 Ibid., 189.

85 Ibid., 190.

86 Ibid.

87 Ibid., 193.

88 Robin D. G. Kelley, *Africa Speaks, America Answers: Modern Jazz in Revolutionary Times*, 7.

89 Haley, *The Autobiography of Malcolm X*, 196.

90 Ibid., 197.

91 Ibid.

92 Ibid., 196.

93 Jarvis, *The Other Malcolm*, 125.

94 Ibid., 126.

95 Ibid., 127.

96 Ibid., 127, 128.

97 Ramsey, *The Amazing Bud Powell*, 121.

98 Ibid., 133.

99 Meadows, *Bebop to Cool*, 44.

100 Ibid., 45.

101 Ramsey, *The Amazing Bud Powell*, 130.

102 Thompson, *Aesthetic of the Cool*, 27, 28.

103 Malcolm to Philbert Little, November 28, 1948, Malcolm X Collection, Schomburg Center for Research in Black Culture, box 3, folder 1.

104 Thomas-Burgess, "The Dynamics of Conversion," 132.

105 Malcolm to Philbert Little, August 9, 1949, Malcolm X Collection, box 3, folder 1.

106 Malcolm X to Philbert Little, December 12, 1949, Malcolm X Collection, box 3, folder 1.

107 Malcolm to Philbert Little, December 18, 1949, Malcolm X Collection, box 3, folder 1.

108 Malcolm X. Little to Henrietta Little, March 25, 1951, Malcolm X Collection, box 3, folder 1.

109 Turner, *Islam in the African-American Experience*, 188.

110 Malcolm to Philbert Little, August 9, 1949, Malcolm X Collection, box 3, folder 1.

111 "Malcolm X Letter Discussing Boston's Jazz Scene."

112 Ibid.

113 Malcolm X. Little to Henrietta Little, March 25, 1951, Malcolm X Collection, box 3, folder 1.

114 Malcolm X. Little to Philbert Little, January 15, 1952, Malcolm X Collection, box 3, folder 1.

115 Ibid.

116 Massachusetts Department of Correction file of Malcolm Little.

117 Ibid.

118 Malcolm X to Philbert Little, March 26, 1950, Malcolm X Collection, box 3, folder 1.

119 Jarvis, *The Other Malcolm*, 129.

120 Ibid., 43, 129, 130.

121 Irene Zempi and Imran Awan, *Islamophobia: Lived Experiences of Online and Offline Victimisation* (Bristol, UK: Policy Press, 2016), 2.

122 Ibid., 5; Erik Love, *Islamophobia and Racism in America* (New York: New York University Press, 2017).

123 Sylvester A. Johnson, *African American Religions, 1500–2000: Colonialism, Democracy, and Freedom* (New York: Cambridge University Press, 2015), 1.

124 Ibid., 395.

125 Ibid.

126 Ibid., 377.

127 Ibid., 378.

128 "Local Criminals, in Prison, Claim Moslem Faith Now," *Springfield (MA) Union*, April 21, 1950; "Four Convicts Turn Moslems, Get Cells Looking to Mecca," *Boston Herald*, April 20, 1950, 3.

129 Jarvis, *The Other Malcolm*, 97. Jarvis also mentioned Charles O'Neil and Leroy Ferguson as potential converts to Islam.

130 "Local Criminals, in Prison, Claim Moslem Faith Now."

131 Karl Evanzz, *The Judas Factor: The Plot to Kill Malcolm X* (New York: Thunder's Mouth, 1992), 11, 12.

132 Marable, *Malcolm X*, 98.

133 Edward E. Curtis IV, *Muslim American Politics and the Future of US Democracy* (New York: New York University Press, 2019), 43.

134 Massachusetts Department of Correction file of Malcolm Little.

135 Godfrey G. Agrriesti to Gus Harrison, February 14, 1953, Out-State Progress Report, State of Michigan Division of Pardons, Paroles, and Probation, Lansing, in *The Portable Malcolm X Reader*, ed. Manning Marable and Garrett Felber (New York: Penguin, 2013), 47.

136 Ibid., 48, 49.

137 Haley, *The Autobiography of Malcolm X*, 231, 243.

138 Marable, *Malcolm X*, 104.

139 Haley, *The Autobiography of Malcolm X*, 228.

140 Ibid., 229.

141 Ibid., 229, 232.

142 Ibid., 244; Marable, *Malcolm X*, 104; Fatimah Fanusie, "Ahmadi, Beboppers, Veterans, and Migrants: African-American Islam in Boston, 1948–1963," in *The African Diaspora and the Study of Religion*, ed. Theodore Louis Trost (New York: Palgrave Macmillan, 2007), 51.

143 Jarvis, *The Other Malcolm*, 132.

144 Haley, *The Autobiography of Malcolm X*, 229.

145 Ibid., 244; Fanusie, "Ahmadi, Beboppers, Veterans, and Migrants," 58.

146 Bill Cunningham and Daniel Golden, "Malcolm X: The Boston Years: Retracing the Emergence of a Black Leader," *Boston Globe Magazine*, February 16, 1992, 35.

147 Ibid.

148 Quoted in ibid.

149 Ibid.; Fanusie, "Ahmadi, Beboppers, Veterans, and Migrants," 56, 57.

150 Ibid., 50, 51.

151 Ibid., 54.

152 Ibid., 54, 55, 59.

153 Ibid., 55; Jarvis, *The Other Malcolm*, 97.

154 Jarvis, *The Other Malcolm*, 97.

155 Fanusie, "Ahmadi, Beboppers, Veterans, and Migrants," 55, 56, 58.

156 "Local Criminals, in Prison, Claim Moslem Faith Now."

157 Fanusie, "Ahmadi, Beboppers, Veterans, and Migrants," 55.

158 Ibid., 56.

159 Ibid.

160 Ibid., 56, 62; Marable, *Malcolm X*, 113.

161 Fanusie, "Ahmadi, Beboppers, Veterans, and Migrants," 56.

162 Ibid.

163 Ibid.

164 Ibid., 58.

165 Ibid.; Marable, *Malcolm X*, 105.

166 Fanusie, "Ahmadi, Beboppers, Veterans, and Migrants," 58, 59.

167 Ibid., 58.

168 Ibid., 57.

169 Ibid., 59, 60.

170 Ibid., 57.

171 Ibid.

172 Ibid.

173 Sakia Mangum, "New Exhibit Examines History of Local African American Muslims," *Atlantic City Weekly*, March 31, 2015, https://atlanticcityweekly.com/archive/.

174 Fanusie, "Ahmadi, Beboppers, Veterans, and Migrants," 58.

175 Haley, *The Autobiography of Malcolm X*, 247.

176 Ibid.

177 Fanusie, "Ahmadi, Beboppers, Veterans, and Migrants," 60; Masjid Al-Qur'aan, "About Us," www.masjidalquran.org (accessed April 25, 2017).

178 Fanusie, "Ahmadi, Beboppers, Veterans, and Migrants," 50.

179 Abdullah, "Narrating Muslim Masculinities," 153, 155.

180 Ibid., 155.

181 Ibid., 155, 156. The Nation of Islam's communal masculinity still resonated with aspects of black patriarchy.

CHAPTER 3. THE FAITH OF UNIVERSAL BROTHERHOOD

1 Malcolm X, letter to a Nation of Islam member, March 9, 1950.

2 Mufti Muhammad Sadiq, *Moslem Sunrise* 1 (April 1922): 1.

3 Mufti Muhammad Sadiq, "One Year's Missionary Work in America," *Moslem Sunrise* 1 (July 1921): 12.

4 Richard Brent Turner, *Islam in the African-American Experience*, 2nd ed. (Bloomington: Indiana University Press, 2003), 117.

5 Ibid., 114–21; Sher Ali, "America's Intolerance," *Review of Religions* 19 (April–May 1920): 158–60; "Ahmadiyya Mission News," *Review of Religions* 19 (July 1920): 24; Sadiq, "One Year's Missionary Work in America"; Sadiq, "No Polygamy," *Moslem Sunrise* 1 (July 1921): 9.

6 "The Only Solution to Color Prejudice," *Moslem Sunrise* 2 (October 1921): 41.

7 "Ahmadiyya Mission News"; "Brief Report of the Work in America," *Moslem Sunrise* 2 (June 1923): 166.

8 Roger Didier, "Those Who're Missionaries to Christians," *Moslem Sunrise* 1 (October 1922): 139, 140.

9 Quoted in Turner, *Islam in the African-American Experience*, 129.

10 *Moslem Sunrise* 1 (July 1922): 119.

11 *Moslem World*, April–July 1923, 270.

12 *Moslem Sunrise* 2 (January 1923): 175, 191.

13 Sylvia Chan-Malik, *Being Muslim: A Cultural History of Women of Color in American Islam* (New York: New York University Press, 2018), 42.

14 Moustafa Bayoumi, *This Muslim American Life: Dispatches from the War on Terror* (New York: New York University Press, 2015), 47.

15 Turner, *Islam in the African-American Experience*, 126–30.

16 John H. Hanson, *The Ahmadiyya in the Gold Coast: Muslim Cosmopolitans in the British Empire* (Bloomington: Indiana University Press, 2017), 123.

17 Turner, *Islam in the African-American Experience*, 83.

18 Hanson, *The Ahmadiyya in the Gold Coast*, 126.

19 Ibid., 129.

20 Turner, *Islam in the African-American Experience*, 129; *Moslem Sunrise* 2 (April 1923): 263.

21 Turner, *Islam in the African-American Experience*, 133.

22 Ibid., 132; *Moslem Sunrise* 3 (July 1930): 11.

23 Turner, *Islam in the African-American Experience*, 136; Omar Cleveland, "The Democracy in Islam," *Moslem Sunrise* 4 (April–July 1931): 17.

24 Quoted in Turner, *Islam in the African-American Experience*, 135.

25 "Blot on the Good Name of America," *Moslem Sunrise* 15 (3rd quarter 1943): 26.

26 Turner, *Islam in the African-American Experience*, 136, 137.

27 Carol Anderson, *Eyes Off the Prize: The United Nations and the African American Struggle for Human Rights, 1944–1955* (New York: Cambridge University Press, 2003), 58, 59.

28 Ibid., 36, 37, 46, 47.

29 Robin D. G. Kelley, *Africa Speaks, America Answers: Modern Jazz in Revolutionary Times* (Cambridge: Harvard University Press, 2012), 99.

30 Edward E. Curtis IV, "'My Heart Is in Cairo': Malcolm X, the Arab Cold War, and the Making of Islamic Liberation Ethics," *Journal of American History* 102, 3 (December 2015): 776; Gamal Abdul Nasser, *Egypt's Liberation: The Philosophy of the Revolution* (Washington: Public Affairs Press, 1955).

31 Kelley, *Africa Speaks, America Answers*, 99.

32 Ibid.

33 Aminah Beverly McCloud, *African American Islam* (New York: Routledge, 1995), 20–21.

34 Yusef Lateef, *The Gentle Giant: The Autobiography of Yusef Lateef*, with Herb Boyd, (Irvington, NJ: Morton, 2006), 58; Richard Vacca, *The Boston Jazz Chronicles: Faces, Places, and Nightlife, 1937–1962* (Belmont, MA: Troy Street, 2012), 64.

35 Richard S. Ginell, "Sahib Shihab Biography," *AllMusic*, www.allmusic.com (accessed July 3, 2018).

36 "Moslem Musicians," *Ebony*, April 1953, 108.

37 Bobby Hancock, "Sahib Shihab: Seeds and Sentiments," *All About Jazz*, March 10, 2004, www.allaboutjazz.com.

38 Gladstone Scott Official Website, http://brenstudios.com (accessed April 4, 2018).

39 Fatimah Fanusie, "Ahmadi, Beboppers, Veterans, and Migrants: African American Islam in Boston, 1948–1963," in *The African Diaspora and the Study of Religion*, ed. Theodore Louis Trost (New York: Palgrave Macmillan, 2007), 52.

40 Ibid.

41 Ibid., 66.

42 Ibid., 53.

43 Ibid.

44 Ibid., 53, 54.

45 Kelley, *Africa Speaks, America Answers*, 94.

46 Ibid., 94, 97.

47 Ibid., 91, 92, 95, 103, 201.

48 Ibid., 104, 108; *Jazz Sahara: Ahmed Abdul-Malik's Middle Eastern Music* (Riverside, 1959); and *East Meets West: The Musique of Ahmed Abdul-Malik* (RCA Victor, 1960).

49 Kelley, *Africa Speaks, America Answers*, 108, 109.

50 Dizzy Gillespie, *To Be, or Not . . . to Bop*, with Al Fraser (Minneapolis: University of Minnesota Press, 2009), 287.

51 Ibid., 291.

52 Ibid., 293.

53 Ibid., 292.

54 Ibid., 293.

55 Tylor Stovall, *Paris Noir: African Americans in the City of Light* (Boston: Houghton Mifflin, 1996), 178.

56 Rashida K. Braggs, *Jazz Diasporas: Race, Music, and Migration in Post–World War II Paris* (Berkeley: University of California Press, 2016), 164.

57 Ibid., 183, 186.

58 Quoted in ibid., 165.

59 Maneer Hamid, telephone interview by author, December 12, 1994, Philadelphia.

60 Robert Dannin, *Black Pilgrimage to Islam* (New York: Oxford University Press, 2002), 58, 60, 61.

61 Ibid., 61, 62.

62 Ibid., 61.

63 "Muslim Leader Calls Moslem Leader 'Phony,'" *New York Amsterdam News*, October 3, 1959, 11.

64 Chan-Malik, *Being Muslim*, 140, 141.

65 Ibid., 111.

66 Ibid., 137; "Why Singer Believes in Four Wives," *Jet*, April 19, 1962.

67 Chan-Malik, *Being Muslim*, 150.

68 Ibid., 112.

69 "Dakota Staton, Hubby File Suit against Mr. Muhammad," *Pittsburgh Courier*, June 9, 1962, 1.

70 Ibid., 21.

71 Chan-Malik, *Being Muslim*, 143.

72 Louis A. DeCaro Jr., *On the Side of My People: A Religious Life of Malcolm X* (New York: New York University Press, 1996), 148.

73 Chan-Malik, *Being Muslim*, 146.

74 DeCaro, *On the Side of My People*, 149, 150.

75 Chan-Malik, *Being Muslim*, 149.

76 Ibid., 112, 113.

77 Dannin, *Black Pilgrimage to Islam*, 58; Lateef, *The Gentle Giant*, 56.

78 Lateef, *The Gentle Giant*, 56.

79 Ibid., 57.

80 Ibid.

81 Ibid., 58, 59.

82 Ibid., 36.

83 Leonard L. Brown, ed., *John Coltrane and Black America's Quest for Freedom: Spirituality and the Music* (New York: Oxford University Press, 2010), 198.

84 Muzaffar Ahmad Zafr, telephone interview by author, December 7, 1994, Dayton, OH; Rashid Ahmed, telephone interview by author, December 11, 1994, Milwaukee.

85 Lateef, *The Gentle Giant*, 75.

86 Yusef Lateef, *Other Sounds* (New Jazz, 1959).

87 Yusef Lateef, *Jazz for the Thinker* (New York: Savoy, 1957).

88 Lateef, *The Gentle Giant*, 77, 78.

89 Ibid., 88.

90 Leslie Gourse, *Art Blakey: Jazz Messenger* (New York: Schirmer, 2002), 14; Robin D. G. Kelley, *Thelonius Monk: The Life and Times of an American Original* (New York: Free Press, 2009), 126.

91 Gourse, *Art Blakey*, 14.

92 Lateef, *The Gentle Giant*, 57; Kelley, *Thelonius Monk*, 127.

93 Quoted in "Moslem Musicians," 108.

94 Ingrid Monson, *Freedom Sounds: Civil Rights Call Out to Jazz and Africa* (New York: Oxford University Press, 2007), 135, 136.

95 Samuel A. Floyd Jr., *The Power of Black Music: Interpreting Its History from Africa to the United States* (New York: Oxford University Press, 1995), 180.

96 Monson, *Freedom Sounds*, 99.

97 Kelley, *Thelonius Monk*, 489, n. 27.

98 Kenny Washington, liner notes for Art Blakey and the Jazz Messengers, *Drum Suite* (Sony BMG Music Entertainment, 2005), originally recorded 1956 and 1957. The band for *Drum Suite* included Bill Hardman (trumpet), Jackie McClean (alto saxophone), Sam Dockery (piano), Spankey DeBreast (bass), and Blakey (drums); along with the Art Blakey Percussion Ensemble: Oscar Pettiford (bass, cello), Ray Bryant (piano), Specs Wright (tympani, gong, drums, vocals), Jo Jones and Blakey (drums), Cándido Camero (bass, vocals, percussion, congas), and Sabu Martinez (vocals, bongos, congas, percussion).

99 Ibid.

100 Ibid.

101 Quoted in Monson, *Freedom Sounds*, 135.

102 Ibid., 147.

103 Ibid., 195.

CHAPTER 4. HARD BOP, FREE JAZZ, AND ISLAM

1 Patrick Denis Bowman, "The African-American Islamic Renaissance and the Rise of the Nation of Islam," Ph.D. dissertation, University of Denver and Iliff School of Theology, 2013.

2 Daoud A. Haroon, "A Tribute to Shaikh Daoud Faisal," pt. 1, https//sites.google.com/site/mancebomosaic/ (accessed October 10, 2018).

3 Ibid.

4 Sheikh Daoud Faisal, *Al-Islam, the Religion of Humanity* (Brooklyn: Islamic Mission of America, 1950); and Faisal, *Islam: The True Faith, the Religion of Humanity* (Brooklyn: Islamic Mission of America, 1965).

5   Robert Dannin, *Black Pilgrimage to Islam* (New York: Oxford University Press, 2002), 64.

6   Ibid., 33.

7   M. Naeem Nash and Edward E. Curtis IV, "Addeynu Allahe Universal Arabic Association," in *Encyclopedia of Muslim-American History*, vol. 1, ed. Edward E. Curtis IV (New York: Facts on File, 2010), 10, 11.

8   Edward E. Curtis IV, "Akram, Wali," in Curtis, *Encyclopedia of Muslim-American History*, vol. 1, 37.

9   Dannin, *Black Pilgrimage to Islam*, 98–102.

10 Ibid., 103.

11 Ibid., 104.

12 Ibid., 47–55.

13 Ibid., 112, 113.

14 Ingrid Monson, *Freedom Sounds: Civil Rights Call Out to Jazz and Africa* (New York: Oxford University Press, 2007), 111.

15 Cemil Aydin, *The Idea of the Muslim World: A Global Intellectual History* (Cambridge: Harvard University Press, 2017), 179.

16 Ibid., 178.

17 Penny M. Von Eschen, *Satchmo Blows Up the World: Jazz Ambassadors Play the Cold War* (Cambridge: Harvard University Press, 2004), 26.

18 Kenneth W. Heger, "Race Relations in the United States and American Cultural and Informational Programs in Ghana, 1957–1966," *National Archives* 31, 4 (Winter 1999), www.archives.gov.

19 Monson, *Freedom Sounds*, 113; Dizzy Gillespie, *To Be, or Not . . . to Bop*, with Al Fraser (Minneapolis: University of Minnesota Press, 2009), 413.

20 Gillespie, *To Be, or Not . . . to Bop*, 414.

21 Thomas J. Sugrue, *Sweet Land of Liberty: The Forgotten Struggle for Civil Rights in the North* (New York: Random House, 2008), xv.

22 Ibid.; Matthew J. Countryman, *Up South: Civil Rights and Black Power in Philadelphia* (Philadelphia: University of Pennsylvania Press, 2006), 3.

23 Gillespie, *To Be, or Not . . . to Bop*, 417.

24 Sohail Daulatzai, *Black Star, Crescent Moon: The Muslim International and Black Freedom beyond America* (Minneapolis: University of Minnesota Press, 2012), xxiii.

25 Gillespie, *To Be, or Not . . . to Bop*, photographs between 338 and 339.

26 Ibid., 419.

27 Ibid., 421.

28 Ibid., 421–22.

29 Ibid., 420.

30 Ibid., 421.

31 Quoted in ibid., 416.

32 Ibid., 415.

33 Randy Weston, "Melba Liston," *African Rhythms*, www.randyweston.info (accessed January 1, 2020); Erica Kaplan, "Melba Liston: It's All from My Soul," *Antioch Review* 57, 3 (Summer 1999): 420.

34 Gillespie, *To Be, or Not . . . to Bop*, 416.

35 Quincy Jones, *Q: The Autobiography of Quincy Jones* (New York: Doubleday, 2001); Von Eschen, *Satchmo Blows Up the World*, 37.

36 Samuel A. Floyd Jr., *The Power of Black Music: Interpreting Its History from Africa to the United States* (New York: Oxford University Press, 1995), 180.

37 Countryman, *Up South*, 46, 51.

38 Ibid., 1, 51.

39 Ibid., 6.

40 Brian L. Coleman, "Post-Conversion Experiences of African-American Male Sunni Muslims: Community Integration and Masculinity in Twenty-First Century Philadelphia," Ph.D. dissertation, University of Pennsylvania, 2009, 150, http://repository.upenn.edu.

41 "Moslem Musicians," *Ebony*, April 1953.

42 Ibid., 109.

43 Barbara Jean Hope, "With His Tears, a Lesson Shared," *Philadelphia Inquirer*, June 17, 2005, E5.

44 Ibid.

45 Barbara Jean Hope, "There's No Escape from the Battleground," *Philadelphia Inquirer*, March 4, 2001, E5.

46 Hope, "With His Tears, a Lesson Shared."

47 "Moslem Musicians," 107.

48 Ibid., 108.

49 Ibid., 109; "Lynn Hope—Fully Dressed," *Crown Propeller's Blog: Jump, Jazz, Jive, Vintage R' n 'B*, September 17, 2011, https://crownpropeller.wordpress.com.

50 Lewis Porter, *John Coltrane: His Life and Music* (Ann Arbor: University of Michigan Press, 1999), 96.

51 Burgin Mathews, "Blow, Lynn, Blow (The Lynn Hope Story)," November 1, 2018, https://burginmathews.com.

52 Hope, "With His Tears, a Lesson Shared."

53 Aydin, *The Idea of the Muslim World*, 186.

54 Ibid.

55 Maneer Hamid, telephone interview by author, December 12, 1994, Philadelphia.

56 McCoy Tyner official website, www.mccoytyner.com (accessed May 16, 2019).

57 C. O. Simpkins, *Coltrane: A Biography* (Baltimore: Black Classics Press, 1989), 115.

58 Ibid.

59 Richard Turner, "John Coltrane: A Biographical Sketch," *Black Perspective in Music* 3, 1 (Spring 1975): 3; Porter, *John Coltrane*, 38, 39; Bjorn Fremer, "The John Coltrane Story," in *Coltrane on Coltrane: The John Coltrane Interviews*, ed. Chris DeVito (Chicago: Chicago Review Press, 2010), 61, 62; John Coltrane House website, www.johncoltranehouse.org (accessed May 23, 2019).

60 Benny Golson and Jim Merod, *Whisper Not: The Autobiography of Benny Golson* (Philadelphia: Temple University Press, 2016), 13, 16, 20, 25, 26, 28; Fremer, "The John Coltrane Story," 63; John Coltrane and Don DeMichael, "Coltrane on Coltrane," in DeVito, *Coltrane on Coltrane*, 66, 68.

61 Quoted in Tom Perchard, *Lee Morgan: His Life, Music, and Culture* (London: Equinox, 2006), 39.

62 Ibid., 36, 42, 43.

63 Golson and Merod, *Whisper Not*, 20.

64 John Coltrane, *My Favorite Things* (Atlantic, 1961); Porter, *John Coltrane*, 92.

65 John Coltrane, *Giant Steps* (Atlantic, 1960).

66 Golson and Merod, *Whisper Not*, 12; Porter, *John Coltrane*, 88; *The Max Roach Trio Featuring the Legendary Hasaan* (Atlantic, 1965); Ben Ratliff, "The Jazz Musician Who Made One Masterpiece and Disappeared," *Vinyl Me Please*, July 11, 2018, www.vinylmeplease.com.

67 Bill Cole, *John Coltrane* (New York: Da Capo, 1993), 84; Porter, *John Coltrane*, 140; John Coltrane Quartet, *The Complete Africa/Brass Sessions* (MCA Records, 1995).

68 Clifford Allen, "Muhammad Ali: From a Family of Percussionists," *All About Jazz*, July 7, 2010, www.allaboutjazz.com; "Rashied Ali: Innovative Drummer Credited with Steering John Coltrane towards Free Jazz in the 1960s," *Guardian*, August 19, 2009, www.theguardian.com; "Ali, Rashied (Robert Patterson Jr.)," in *Encyclopedia of Jazz Musicians*, https://archive.vn/w630 (accessed May 25, 2019); Howard Mandel, "Rashied Ali (1935–2009), Multi-Directional Drummer, Speaks," *Jazz beyond Jazz: An Arts Journal Blog*, August 13, 2009, www.artsjournal.com.

69 Simpkins, *Coltrane*, 39, 40.

70 August Blume, "Interview with John Coltrane," in DeVito, *Coltrane on Coltrane*, 12.

71 "John Coltrane Memorial Week: Life and Legacy of John Coltrane," *Avenue of the Arts*, www.avenueofthearts.org (accessed May 24, 2019).

72 Porter, *John Coltrane*, 96, 97.

73 Quoted in Leonard L. Brown, ed., *John Coltrane and Black America's Quest for Freedom: Spirituality and the Music* (New York: Oxford University Press, 2010), 192.

74 Ibid., 193, 194.

75 John L. Esposito, *Islam: The Straight Path* (New York: Oxford University Press, 1992), 90.

76 Kristina Nelson, *The Art of Reciting the Qur'an* (Cairo: American University in Cairo Press, 1985), 14.

77 Porter, *John Coltrane*, 133.

78 Quoted in Brown, *John Coltrane and Black America's Quest for Freedom*, 193.

79 George Avakian, liner notes for Miles Davis, *'Round about Midnight* (Columbia, 1957).

80 Farah Jasmine Griffin and Salim Washington, *Clawing at the Limits of Cool: Miles Davis, John Coltrane and the Greatest Jazz Collaboration Ever* (New York: St. Martin's, 2008), 144.

81 See John Tynan, "Hope for the Addicted: The Story of the Synanon Foundation," *Down Beat* 28, 4 (February 2, 1961): 15–19; and Charles Winick, "The Use of Drugs by Jazz Musicians," *Social Problems* 7, 3 (Winter 1959–1960): 240–53.

82 William H. James and Stephen L. Johnson, *Doin' Drugs: Patterns of African American Addiction* (Austin: University of Texas Press, 1996), 148.

83 Bill Coss, "Shafi Hadi," *Down Beat* 30, 9 (April 11, 1963): 15.

84 Perchard, *Lee Morgan*, 84–85; Eric Nisenson, *Open Sky: Sonny Rollins and His World of Improvisation* (New York: Da Capo, 2000), 68; Ashley Kahn, *Kind of Blue* (New York: Da Capo, 2000), 199.

85 Nisenson, *Open Sky*, 40, 67, 68.

86 Porter, *John Coltrane*, 97, 98, 105.

87 John Coltrane, liner notes for *A Love Supreme* (Impulse!, 1965).

88 Fred M. Donner, *Muhammad and the Believers: At the Origins of Islam* (Cambridge: Belknap Press of Harvard University, 2010), 61.

89 "John Coltrane Memorial Week."

90 Donner, *Muhammad and the Believers*, 63.

91 Porter, *John Coltrane*, 107.

92 Ibid., 253, 254.

93 Ibid., 107–10.

94 John Coltrane, liner notes for *Thelonious Monk with John Coltrane* (Jazzland, 1998).

95 Ibid.

96 Coltrane and DeMichael, "Coltrane on Coltrane," 68, 69.

97 Ted Gioia, *The History of Jazz*, 2nd ed. (New York: Oxford University Press, 2011), 273.

98 Quoted in Arthur Taylor, *Notes and Tones: Musician-to-Musician Interviews* (New York: Coward, McCann, and Geoghan, 1982), 106.

99 Marc Crawford, "The Drummer Most Likely to Succeed," *Down Beat*, March 30, 1961, 21.

100 Ibid.

101 Monson, *Freedom Sounds*, 161.

102 Ibid., 154.

103 Peniel E. Joseph, *Dark Days, Bright Nights: From Black Power to Barack Obama* (New York: Basic Civitas, 2010), 12.

104 Ibid., 3.

105 Quoted in Monson, *Freedom Sounds*, 245.

106 Steve Kemple, "Say It Loud: The Black Power Revolution in Music," *Cuepoint*, February 26, 2016, medium.com/cuepoint.

107 Peniel E. Joseph, *Waiting 'Til the Midnight Hour: A Narrative History of Black Power in America* (New York: Owl Books, 2007), 43.

108 Babatunde Olatunji, *The Beat of My Drum: An Autobiography*, with Robert Atkinson (Philadelphia: Temple University Press, 2005), 174.

109 Ibid., 6.

110 Ibid., 78, 79.

111 Ibid., 33.

112 Ibid., 5; Robin D. G. Kelley, *Africa Speaks, America Answers: Modern Jazz in Revolutionary Times* (Cambridge: Harvard University Press, 2012), 2, 3.

113 "African Drummer Entertains Washington Mosque," *Muhammad Speaks*, July 19, 1963, 14; "Of Drums and Drummers," *Muhammad Speaks*, September 15, 1962, 4; Olatunji, *The Beat of My Drum*, 177, 196, 197.

114 Olatunji, *The Beat of My Drum*, 180.

115 "The Muslims Present an Evening with Max Roach and Abbey Lincoln," *Muhammad Speaks*, August 28, 1964, 14.

116 "Racial Prejudice in Jazz," pt. 1, *Down Beat* 29 (March 15, 1962): 20–26.

117 "Racial Prejudice in Jazz," pt. 2, *Down Beat* 29 (March 29, 1962): 22–25; "The Need for Racial Unity in Jazz," *Down Beat* 30 (April 11, 1963): 16–21.

118 Frank Kofsky, "Abbey Lincoln," *Radio Free Jazz*, February 1977, 11, 14.

119 Eric Porter, *What Is This Thing Called Jazz? African American Musicians as Artists, Critics, and Activists* (Berkeley: University of California Press, 2002), 150, 151; "Abbey Lincoln: Metamorphosis," *Down Beat*, September 14, 1961, 19; "The Girl in the Marilyn Monroe Dress," *Ebony*, June 1957, 7–31.

120 Quoted in Gary G. Vercelli, "Profile: Aminata Moseka/Abbey Lincoln," *Down Beat*, September 1, 1979, 42, 43.

121 Ibid., 43.

122 Kofsky, "Abbey Lincoln," 14.

123 Alice Walker, "In Search of Our Mothers' Gardens: Womanist Prose," in *Crossing the Danger Water: Three Hundred Years of African-American Writing*, ed. Deidre Mullane (New York: Anchor, 1993), 722; Patricia Hill Collins, *Black Sexual Politics: African Americans, Gender, and the New Racism* (New York: Routledge, 2004); Kimberlé Crenshaw, "Demarginalizing the Intersection of Race and Sex: A Black Feminist Critique of Antidiscrimination Doctrine, Feminist Theory and Antiracist Politics," *University of Chicago Legal Forum* 1, article 8 (1989).

124 Abbey Lincoln, "A Ringing Challenge: Who Will Revere the Black Woman?," *Negro Digest*, September 1966, 16.

125 Quoted in George T. Simon, "Singer Proud to Be Different," *New York Herald Tribune*, July 8, 1962.

126 Max Roach, "Max Roach on the Future of Jazz: Says Racial Self-Help Is Cure for Whites' Control of Music Negroes Created," *Muhammad Speaks*, December 30, 1962, 20.

127 Monson, *Freedom Sounds*, 188.

128 Max Roach, "Max Roach on Jazz: How Whites Made $Billions from Negro Art Form," *Muhammad Speaks*, December 15, 1962, 20, 21; and Roach, "Max Roach on the Future of Jazz," 20, 22.

129 Quoted in Bob Rusch, "Max Roach: Interview," *Cadence*, June 1979, 7.

130 Edward E. Curtis IV, *Black Muslim Religion in the Nation of Islam, 1960–1975* (Chapel Hill: University of North Carolina Press, 2006), 3, 4.

131 Muneer Nasser, telephone interview by author, December 10, 2018.

132 Abdul Basit Naeem, "Cites October 19th Benefit Concert as Example of New Outlook on Music," *Muhammad Speaks*, October 20, 1967, 10.

133 Ula Yvette Taylor, *The Promise of Patriarchy: Women and the Nation of Islam* (Chapel Hill: University of North Carolina Press, 2017), back flap.

134 Sharony Andrews Green, *Grant Green: Rediscovering the Forgotten Genius of Jazz Guitar* (San Francisco: Miller Freeman, 1999), 65, 66.

135 Quoted in ibid., 68.

136 Ibid., 65.

137 Quoted in ibid., 67.

138 Ibid., 76.

139 Ibid., 83, 97.

140 Ibid., 121.

141 Ibid., 119, 120, 167.

142 Ibid., 112.

143 Ibid., 123.

144 Quoted in ibid., 129, 130.

145 Ibid., 139–42.

146 Quoted in ibid., 149.

147 Ibid.

148 Quoted in ibid.

149 Quoted in Randy Roberts and Johnny Smith, *Blood Brothers: The Fatal Friendship between Muhammad Ali and Malcolm X* (New York: Basic Books, 2016), 306.

150 Quoted in Green, *Grant Green*, 185.

151 Quoted in ibid., 186.

152 Sylvester A. Johnson, *African American Religions, 1500–2000: Colonialism, Democracy, and Freedom* (New York: Cambridge University Press, 2015), 378, 379.

153 Ibid., 198–200.

154 Curtis, *Black Muslim Religion in the Nation of Islam*, 173.

155 Ibid., 169.

156 "Buffet Honoring Muhammad Underscores Black Unity," *Muhammad Speaks*, November 4, 1966, 16; "Chicago Muslim Takes Black Jazz to Ethiopian Television," *Muhammad Speaks*, June 2, 1967, 27.

157 "Special: Notice from the Messenger," *Muhammad Speaks*, May 12, 1968, 3.

158 Joe Walker, "Muslim Unity Bazaar Like 'Marketplace in Mid-East,'" *Muhammad Speaks*, December 20, 1968, 38.

159 "Buffalo Bazaar Highlights Messenger's Program," *Muhammad Speaks*, October 28, 1966.

160 "African Bazaar" ad, *Muhammad Speaks*, June 21, 1963, 18; "African Asian Bazaar" ad, *Muhammad Speaks*, July 19, 1963, 14; "Another Great African Asian Bazaar"

ad, *Muhammad Speaks*, April 24, 1964, 17; "Unity Bazaar" ad, *Muhammad Speaks*, May 8, 1964, 15; "African Asian Unity Bazaar" ad, *Muhammad Speaks*, June 5, 1964, 20; "Unity Bazaar," *Muhammad Speaks*, April 30, 1965, 20; "Benefit Show and Dinner," *Muhammad Speaks*, October 22, 1965, 4; "The Muslims Present a Gigantic Unity Bazaar" ad, *Muhammad Speaks*, October 15, 1965, 6; "Unity Bazaar" ad, *Muhammad Speaks*, November 11, 1966, 18; "Record Unity Bazaar Throng Treated to Outstanding Musical Entertainment," *Muhammad Speaks*, April 21, 1967, 18; Monson, *Freedom Sounds*, 228, 229; "Evening with F.O.I. Key Event Even in Washington DC," *Muhammad Speaks*, April 14, 1967, 26; Thomas Sharrieff, "Miami Mosque Entertains Top Black Professionals," *Muhammad Speaks*, December 16, 1966, 16; Curtis, *Black Muslim Religion in the Nation of Islam*, 170–73; Walker, "Muslim Unity Bazaar Like 'Marketplace in Mid-East,'" 38; "Muhammad's Mosque No. 27 Presents an Afternoon of Entertainment" ad, *Muhammad Speaks*, January 3, 1969, 37.

161 "Musical Men," photo, *Muhammad Speaks*, March 10, 1967, 27.

162 "St. Louis Musicians," photo, *Muhammad Speaks*, September 2, 1966, 27; "N.Y. Mosque's Annual Unity Bazaar to Feature Top Talent, Unique Displays," *Muhammad Speaks*, March 31, 1967, 24.

163 Quoted in Darryl Cowherd, "Muslim Musicians Reveal Trials of Black Artists," *Muhammad Speaks*, April 7, 1967, 12.

164 Ibid., 19.

165 Perchard, *Lee Morgan*, 50.

166 Ibid., 51, 52, 56, 57.

167 Ibid., 74.

168 Ibid., 84, 85.

169 Ibid., 123, 124.

170 Ibid., 138.

171 Ibid., 126.

172 Ibid., 136.

173 "Lee Morgan," *Blue Note Records*, www.bluenote.com (accessed August 2, 2019).

174 Perchard, *Lee Morgan*, 149.

175 Ibid., 149, 150.

176 Ibid., 149.

177 Ibid., 150.

178 Ibid.

179 Ibid., 186.

180 Quoted in ibid., 185.

181 Ibid.

182 Ibid.

183 Etta James and David Ritz, *Rage to Survive: The Etta James Story* (New York: Villard, 1995), 19, 34, 37.

184 Ibid., 49.

185 Ibid., 52.

186 Ibid., 56–90.

187 Ibid., 101.

188 Ibid., 108.

189 Ibid., 111.

190 Ibid.

191 Ibid., 112.

192 Ibid.

193 Taylor, *The Promise of Patriarchy*, 105.

194 James and Ritz, *Rage to Survive*, 112.

195 Ibid., 112, 113; Manning Marable, *Malcolm X: A Life of Reinvention* (New York: Viking, 2011), 172.

196 James and Ritz, *Rage to Survive*, 112.

197 Ibid., 113.

198 Ibid.

199 Ibid., 112; Dawn-Marie Gibson and Jamillah Karim, *Women of the Nation: Between Black Protest and Sunni Islam* (New York: New York University Press, 2014), 41.

200 Gibson and Karim, *Women of the Nation*, 32.

201 James and Ritz, *Rage to Survive*, 112.

202 Michael Paul Mackey, "From Pittsburgh to Pershing: Orchestration, Interaction, and Influence in the Early Work of Ahmad Jamal," Ph.D. dissertation, University of Pittsburgh, 2017, 58.

203 Quoted in ibid., 69, 70.

204 Ibid., 70, 71.

205 Moorish Science Temple, "The Prophet Noble Drew Ali and Marcus Garvey Connection," https://moorishamericannationalrepublic.com (accessed September 11, 2019).

206 Jamal's trio recorded the following albums on the Argo label from 1958 to 1961: *Ahmad Jamal Trio, Vol. 4* (1958), *Ahmad Jamal at the Penthouse* (1960), *Happy Moods* (1960), and *All of You* (1961).

207 Mackey, "From Pittsburgh to Pershing," 86.

208 Quoted in George E. Pitts, "Ahmad Jamal's a Man with a Purpose," *Pittsburgh Courier*, November 29, 1958, 17.

209 "Ahmad's Way of Life," *Down Beat*, March 19, 1959, 17.

210 "College Age Devotees for Jamal Music," *Newport News (VA) Press*, May 24, 1959.

211 Jay Walz, "Pianist-Investor Is a Hit in Cairo: Jazz Musician Ahmad Jamal Finds Moslem Faith Aids Him on African Visit," *New York Times*, November 20, 1959.

212 Ibid.

213 Maytha Alhassen, "*Islam in America* by Mahmoud Yousef Shawarbi," *Comparative American Studies* 13, 4 (December 2015): 255; Mahmoud Yousef Shawarbi, *Islam in America* (Cairo: Lajnat al-Bayan al-'Arabi, 1960).

214 Alhassen, "*Islam in America* by Mahmoud Yousef Shawarbi," 261.

215 Ibid., 262.

216 Ibid., 260.

217 Quoted in "Cairo Educator Says: 'All Muslims Are Brothers,'" *Courier*, November 12, 1960, 2.

218 Quoted in Marc Crawford, "Ahmad Jamal: Musician and Businessman," *Down Beat*, March 16, 1961, 19.

219 Ibid.

220 "Ahmad Jamal's Alhambra Supper Club Is New Concept in Nightspots," *Ebony*, October 1961, 58.

221 Ibid., 56.

222 Ibid., 54, 55.

223 Matt Collar, "Ahmad Jamal Biography," *AllMusic*, www.allmusic.com (accessed October 15, 2019).

224 Quoted in Jeff Sewald, "Ahmad Jamal, Jazz Master: A Life's Recounting in the Subject's Own Words," *Pittsburgh Quarterly*, Fall 2017, https://pittsburghquarterly.com.

225 Muneer Nasser, *Upright Bass: The Musical Life and Legacy of Jamil Nasser: A Jazz Memoir* (Gaithersburg: Vertical Visions Media Group, 2017), 2, 8, 10, 12, 13, 18, 211, 212.

226 Ibid., 42, 43.

227 Ibid., xvi.

228 Ibid., 42.

229 Ibid., 43.

230 Quoted in ibid., 195.

231 Ibid., 44.

232 Ibid., 62.

233 Ibid., 58, 59.

234 Ibid., 61.

235 Ibid., 61, 62.

236 Ibid., 62.

237 Ibid., 62, 63.

238 Ibid., 64.

239 Ibid., 64–68.

240 Ibid., 69.

241 Ibid., 70, 71.

242 Ibid., 71.

243 Ibid., 71–74.

244 Ibid., 126.

245 Daoud A. Haroon, "Flow of Baraka," https//sites.google.com/site/mancebomosaic/ (accessed November 2, 2019).

246 Frank Stasio and Anita Rao, "From Shoe Shiner to Ethnomusicologist, Meet Daoud Haroon," *The State of Things*, program, WUNC 91.5 North Carolina Public Radio, Chapel Hill, December 15, 2014, www.wunc.org.

247 Haroon, "A Tribute to Shaikh Daoud Faisal," pt. 1.

248 Ibid.

249 Daoud A. Haroon, "Hajj 1967," http://mancebomosaic.com/ (accessed April 5, 2013).

250 Stasio and Rao, "From Shoe Shiner to Ethnomusicologist."

251 Ibid.

252 Ibid.

253 Ibid.

254 Rasul Miller, "Profile of Bilal Abdurahman," *Sapelo*, February 23, 2016, https://sapelosquare.com.

255 "Bio—Jesse Hameen II," Jessehameenii.com (accessed January 10, 2020).

256 Idris Muhammad, *Inside the Music: The Life of Idris Muhammad* (Xlibris, 2012), 175–77.

257 Moustafa Bayoumi, *This Muslim American Life: Dispatches from the War on Terror* (New York: New York University Press, 2015), 45.

258 Ibid., 47.

259 Scott Saul, *Freedom Is, Freedom Ain't: Jazz and the Making of the Sixties* (Cambridge: Harvard University Press, 2003), 209, 212.

260 Franya J. Berkman, *Monument Eternal: The Music of Alice Coltrane* (Middletown, CT: Wesleyan University Press, 2010), 53.

261 Porter, *John Coltrane*, 145.

262 Quoted in Berkman, *Monument Eternal*, 52.

263 Carl Clements, "John Coltrane and the Integration of Indian Concepts in Jazz Improvisation," *Jazz Research Journal* 2, 2 (2008): 156; Porter, *John Coltrane*, 210.

264 Ravi Shankar, "On Appreciation of Indian Classical Music," Ravi Shankar Foundation, www.ravishankar.org (accessed November 18, 2019).

265 Regula Burkhardt Qureshi, *Sufi Music of India and Pakistan: Sound, Context, and Meaning in Qawwali* (Chicago: University of Chicago Press, 1995), xiii.

266 Brown, *John Coltrane and Black America's Quest for Freedom*, 203; Inayat Hazrat Khan, *The Music of Life* (Santa Fe: Omega, 1983), 53.

267 Porter, *John Coltrane*, 202; Yusef Lateef, *The Gentle Giant: The Autobiography of Yusef Lateef*, with Herb Boyd (Irvington, NJ: Morton, 2006), 95.

268 Ben Ratliff, *Coltrane: The Story of a Sound* (New York: Farrar, Straus and Giroux, 2007), xi.

269 Eric Nisenson, *Ascension: John Coltrane and His Quest* (New York: St. Martin's, 1993), 94.

270 Randy Weston and Willard Jenkins, *African Rhythms: The Autobiography of Randy Weston* (Durham: Duke University Press, 2010), 60.

271 Ibid., 40.

272 See the following albums by Randy Weston: *Little Niles* (United Artists, 1959); *New Faces at Newport* (Metro Jazz, 1958); *The Modern Art of Jazz by Randy Weston* (Dawn, 1957); *Trio and Solo* (Riverside, 1957); *Jazz a La Bohemia* (Riverside, 1956); *With These Hands* (Riverside, 1956); *Get Happy with the Randy Weston Trio* (Riverside, 1956); and *The Randy Weston Trio* (Riverside, 1955).

273 Weston and Jenkins, *African Rhythms*, 82.

274 Kelley, *Africa Speaks, America Answers*, 53.

275 Weston and Jenkins, *African Rhythms*, 92.

276 Randy Weston African Rhythms website, www.randyweston.info (accessed November 23, 2019).

277 Monson, *Freedom Sounds*, 147.

278 Weston and Jenkins, *African Rhythms*, 139.

279 Ashley Kahn, *The House That Trane Built: The Story of Impulse Records* (New York: Norton, 2006), 52.

280 Quoted in ibid.

281 Dom Cerulli, liner notes for John Coltrane Quartet, *The Complete Africa/Brass Sessions* (Impulse!, 1995).

282 Monson, *Freedom Sounds*, 125.

283 "USIS Program in Lebanon" (November 1961): Briefing books, Box 301, Series 2, File 17 Tours: State Department materials, Middle East tour, Smithsonian Institution National Museum of American History, Archives Center; Duke Ellington Collection, Series 7, Photographs Collection 301: Box 9 no. F 23, Box 10 no. 022170, and Box 12 no. 320, Smithsonian Institution National Museum of American History, Archives Center; Duke Ellington, *Music Is My Mistress* (New York: Da Capo, 1973), 303.

284 Ellington, *Music Is My Mistress*, 301, 302.

285 Duke Ellington Collection, Middle East Tour, September 9, 1963, Collection 301: Box 2, File 1, Smithsonian Institution National Museum of American History, Archives Center.

286 Ebongue Soelle, "A Trumpet That Breaks Social Barriers from Triumph to Triumph Duke Ellington," *Dakar-Matin*, April 6, 1966, Duke Ellington Collection, Collection 301, Box 3, Series 2: Performances and Programs 1933–1973, Folder 3: Report First World Festival of Negro Arts Dakar, Senegal, Africa, Smithsonian National Museum of American History, Archives Center.

287 Ellington, *Music Is My Mistress*, 337.

288 Saul, *Freedom Is, Freedom Ain't*, 239, 234.

289 Quoted in DeVito, *Coltrane on Coltrane*, 334.

290 Quoted in Kahn, *The House That Trane Built*, 131.

291 Monson, *Freedom Sounds*, 300.

292 Quoted in Kahn, *The House That Trane Built*, 197.

293 Shoichi Yui, Kiyoshi Koyama, Kazuaki Tsujimoto, et al., "Interviews with John Coltrane," in DeVito, *Coltrane on Coltrane*, 272.

294 Saul, *Freedom Is, Freedom Ain't*, 267.

295 Richard Brent Turner, *Islam in the African-American Experience*, 2nd ed. (Bloomington: Indiana University Press, 2003), 215.

296 Edward E. Curtis IV, *Muslim American Politics and the Future of US Democracy* (New York: New York University Press, 2019), 78.

297 William W. Sales Jr., *From Civil Rights to Black Liberation: Malcolm X and the Organization of Afro-American Unity* (Boston: South End Press, 1994), 107, 108.

298 Quoted in Curtis, *Muslim American Politics*, 74.

299 A. B. Spellman, "Revolution in Sound: Black Genius Creates New Music in Western World," *Ebony*, August 1969, 84, 88.

300 Saul, *Freedom Is, Freedom Ain't*, 257.

301 Bayoumi, *This Muslim American Life*, 46.

302 Ibid., 46, 47.

303 Quoted in Ashley Kahn, *A Love Supreme: The Story of John Coltrane's Signature Album* (New York: Viking, 2002), 144.

304 Quoted in Brown, *John Coltrane and Black America's Quest for Freedom*, 194.

305 Quoted in Kahn, *A Love Supreme*, 159, 160.

306 Ibid., 160.

307 Iain Anderson, *This Is Our Music: Free Jazz, the Sixties, and American Culture* (Philadelphia: University of Pennsylvania Press, 2007), 93.

308 Ibid., 94.

309 Ibid., 109.

310 Ibid.

311 Ibid.

312 George E. Lewis, *A Power Stronger Than Itself: The AACM and American Experimental Music* (Chicago: University of Chicago Press, 2008), 42.

313 Anderson, *This Is Our Music*, 115.

314 Quoted in Val Wilmer, *As Serious as Your Life: Black Music and the Free Jazz Revolution, 1957–1977* (London: Serpent's Tail, 2018), 51.

315 Quoted in Kahn, *The House That Trane Built*, 131, 132.

316 Spellman, "Revolution in Sound," 88.

317 Ibid.

318 Quoted in Porter, *John Coltrane*, 266.

319 John Scheinfeld, *Chasing Trane: The John Coltrane Documentary* (Universal Music Enterprises, 2017).

320 Quoted in ibid.

321 Spellman, "Revolution in Sound," 87.

322 Ibid., 86.

323 Ibid., 84, 89.

324 Quoted in Brown, *John Coltrane and Black America's Quest for Freedom*, 195, 196.

CONCLUSION

1 Ingrid Monson, *Freedom Sounds: Civil Rights Call Out to Jazz and Africa* (New York: Oxford University Press, 2007), 4, 5.

2 "Death of John Coltrane," *Muhammad Speaks*, July 28, 1967, 21.

3 Edward E. Curtis IV, *Muslim American Politics and the Future of US Democracy* (New York: New York University Press, 2019), 87.

4 Ibid.

5 Ibid., 86.

6 Alice Coltrane, *Monastic Trio* (Impulse!, 1968).

7 Franya J. Berkman, *Monument Eternal: The Music of Alice Coltrane* (Middletown, CT: Wesleyan University Press, 2010), 49, 7.

8 Eric Rosenzvieg and Peter Wetherbee, liner notes for Maleem Mahmoud Ghania with Pharoah Sanders, *The Trance of Seven Colors* (Island Records, 1994).

9 Monson, *Freedom Sounds*, 319.

10 Richard Brent Turner, *Islam in the African-American Experience*, 2nd ed. (Bloomington: Indiana University Press, 2003), xxvi.

11 Ibid.

12 Ibid.

13 Brett Johnson and Malik Russell, "Time to Build," *The Source: The Magazine of Hip-Hop Music, Culture & Politics* 158 (November 2002): 120.

14 Turner, *Islam in the African-American Experience*, xviii; Mos Def, *Black on Both Sides* (Rawkus, 1999).

15 Sohail Daulatzai, *Black Star, Crescent Moon: The Muslim International and Black Freedom beyond America* (Minneapolis: University of Minnesota Press, 2012).

INDEX

AAUA. *See* Addeynu Allahe Universal Arabic Association

Abdullah, Muhammad, 77. *See also* Muhammad, Wallace D. Fard

Abdullah, Zain, 42

Abdul-Malik, Ahmed Hussein (Jonathan Tim, Jr.), 111–12, 179

Abdurahman, Bilal, 178–79

"Acknowledgement," 191

activism, 122, 167; antiracist, 48, 152; political, 53, 194

activists, jazz musicians as, 122–23

Addeynu Allahe Universal Arabic Association (AAUA), 127, 128, 138

Adeyola, Sabu, 179–80

Affair, 155

Africa, 171–73; African American Islam in, 130–37

Africa/Brass, 184, 186

African American ancestral wisdom, 36

African American Islam, 1–2, 5, 27, 150–57; in Africa, 130–37; black masculinity in, 42–43; colorism in, 42; dance and, 35; Puerto Ricans and, 39; Sunni Islam and, 126–30. *See also* golden age, of African American Islam

African American religious internationalism, 2, 5–6, 15, 53–54, 71–72, 200; Gillespie and, 52; Islam and, 56; Malcolm X and, 63–69; Roach, M., and, 150; Sunni Islam and, 127

African diaspora, 10; in Boston, 19–20; dance and, 34

African drumming, 153

African Methodist churches, in Boston, 23

African music, 185–86

African Quarter, 179

African Times and Orient Review (newspaper), 103–4

Afro-American Unity, Organization of, 59, 189

Afro-Caribbean Immigrants, in Boston, 17–27

Ahmad, Bashir, 110

Ahmad, Hazarat Mirza Ghulam, 57, 99, 106

Ahmad, Nasir, 4

Ahmadiyya Muslim Community, 5, 8, 16, 106–7, 113–14; bebop and, 99, 109–19; in Boston, 56–58; in India, 56–58; James, E., and, 169–70; jazz influenced by, 100–105; jazz musicians and, 58, 119–23, 140–41, 170–81; Nation of Islam contrasted with, 108, 110

Ahmadiyya Muslim missionaries, 4, 57–58, 104, 107, 128–29

Akram, Wali (Walter Gregg), 128–29, 138

"Alabama," 188

Algeria, 176

AlHambra, 173

Ali, Duse Mohamed, 103–4

Ali, Muhammad (Cassius Clay), 7, 161

Ali, Rashied, 143

almsgiving (zakat), 147

Alvarez, Luis, 30

American Federation of Musicians recording ban (1942–1944), 51

ancestral wisdom, African American, 36

antiracist activism, 152

anti-war, Nation of Islam as, 32

appropriation, of jazz, 77

Arabic, study of, 112

Arabic names, 108, 168, 170; symbolism of "X," 89

Arab instruments, 118

Armstrong, Louis, 12, 27

arrests: Jarvis, 68–69; of Malcolm X, 68–69, 81

Asians, racism toward, 100–101

Asiatic identity, 75–76

assassination, of Malcolm X, 59, 193

Atlantic City Temple No. 10, 96–97

At Last!, 168

Austin, Juanita Naima, 7, 144–45, 146–47, 148

The Autobiography of Malcolm X (Malcolm X), 62, 66, 81, 193

Bandung conference (1955), 131

Baptist churches, 22, 23

Baraka, Amiri, 193–94

BARTS. *See* Black Arts Repertory Theater/School

Basheer, Ahmed, 52

ABOUT THE AUTHOR

RICHARD BRENT TURNER is Professor in the Department of Religious Studies and the African American Studies Program at the University of Iowa. He is the author of *Jazz Religion, the Second Line, and Black New Orleans: After Hurricane Katrina* and *Islam in the African-American Experience.*